Right-Brain
Project Management
A Complementary Approach

Right-Brain
Project Management
A Complementary Approach

B. Michael Aucoin

MANAGEMENTCONCEPTS

𝆏𝆏𝆏
MANAGEMENTCONCEPTS
8230 Leesburg Pike, Suite 800
Vienna, VA 22182
(703) 790-9595
Fax: (703) 790-1371
www.managementconcepts.com

Printed in the United States of America

Library of Congress Cataloging-in-Publication Data

Aucoin, B. Michael.
   Right-brain project management : a complementary approach / B. Michael Aucoin.
      p. cm.
      ISBN 978-1-56726-206-3
   1. Project management.. I. Title.
HD69.P75A93 2007
658.4'04—dc22

2007007901

10   9   8   7   6   5   4   3   2   1

About the Author

B. Michael Aucoin is the President of Leading Edge Management, LLC, and Electrical Expert, Inc., located in College Station, Texas. He provides corporate training in project management and engineering management, drawing upon his extensive experience in the management of diverse technology projects and his skill in training. He also provides forensic consulting and litigation support in electrical engineering, including expert witness consulting.

Dr. Aucoin has experience in electric power, energy management, energy strategy, project management, and engineering management. He has worked for large and small technology companies, and has been a university researcher and lecturer. Projects he has worked on have been recognized with the R&D 100 Award from *R&D Magazine* and the Outstanding Engineering Achievement Award from the National Society of Professional Engineers. Dr. Aucoin is also a recipient of a Third Millennium Medal from the Institute of Electrical and Electronics Engineers as well as an IEEE Working Group Award as co-editor of an electric power tutorial course. He is the author of *From Engineer to Manager: Mastering the Transition* (Artech House, 2002).

Dr. Aucoin received a Bachelor of Science in Engineering Science from the University of New Orleans, a Master of Engineering in Electrical Engineering from Texas A&M University, and a Doctor of Engineering from Texas A&M. He is a Registered Professional Engineer in Texas and has earned the Project Management Professional (PMP®) certification from the Project Management Institute.

■ Contents

■ Foreword

Pick a project you are currently working on. Answer this: Is it in a good mood or a bad mood? Now ask yourself: What kind of a mood am I in right now?

Notice that the answers popped up instantaneously. That's because they came from your right brain. If it were in charge, your left brain would have appointed a committee and embarked on an extensive fact-finding mission followed by a detailed analysis. If logic, linear thinking, and deterministic approaches are the domain of the left brain, then emotion and intuition are the province and providence of the right brain.

A project that spends its life in a bad mood because the team, customers, and other stakeholders are unhappy is a project in trouble—one that is running on empty when it comes to motivation, innovation, trust, and confidence. These emotion-driven qualities are rooted in our right brain and serve as the lifeblood for succeeding on what Mike Aucoin refers to as "contemporary projects."

■ Today's Projects

Contemporary projects are aggressive. They feature speed, complexity, and ambiguity. For these volatile ventures, not only does the desired result evolve as you go along, but the path to get there is often circuitous if not unknown. Think of a heat-seeking missile in pursuit of a fast-moving target.

Prior to the widespread adoption of agile project management practices in recent years, the field of project management was dominated by approaches that were heavily rooted in left-brain thinking. These conventional approaches put the emphasis on the use of tools, rules, templates, and procedures rather than on people and interactions. Moreover, they tend to insist on following the plan (aka staying the course) rather than responding to change.

Unfortunately, well-intended conventional approaches have often been applied inappropriately. The result has been methodologies that try to torture contemporary projects into submission while stifling innovation and making project managers and their teams slaves to rules and tools.

■ Dancing at the Edge of Chaos

Mike Aucoin gives us a wealth of essential practices and techniques that allow our right brain to kick in. This book is a veritable toolkit for unleashing the vast and creative resources of this underutilized, and perhaps even underrespected, part of our head. Inside his toolkit you will find a set of seven principles, along with supporting practices, that enable project leaders and teams to thrive on complexity and ambiguity while keeping these jazz-like performances in control.

Although adamant about the benefits of right-brain project management, Mike recognizes the value of conventional project management approaches. That is, most aggressive projects are a blend of the known and the unknown, although heavily weighted toward the latter. To make sense out of today's volatile ventures, the successful project manager must become a whole-brain project manager, one who judiciously enlists resources from both the right and the left sides. This is precisely what it takes to achieve mastery over the paradoxical nature of today's projects, where opposites find themselves dancing in partnership: structure dances with freedom, the head dances with the heart, and reason dances with intuition.

■ Maturing in Project Management

My own experience tells me that many of today's managers of contemporary projects lead lives that vacillate between frantic and quiet desperation. Following Mike's advice will help you become even more than an excellent project manager. You will become a whole person, one who is able to master the most important and often the most neglected project of all: your own self-growth. This can mean the difference between a life of self-mastery and a life of self-misery. Using Jane Loevinger's nine stages of ego development, Mike notes that the maturing project manager progresses from impulsive behavior to becoming an autonomous and integrated person who can tolerate ambiguity, foster emotional interdependence, and transcend conflict.

Nearly 300,000 project managers have earned their PMP® (Project Management Professional) designation, the certification bestowed by the Project Management Institute. For a growing number of PMPs, along with the coveted acronym comes the realization that projects mean people. And for those who are making the transition to applying both left- and right-brain approaches, this book provides the vehicle.

▮ Partnering with Yourself

If the corpus collosum is the link that connects the resources of the left and the right brains, then this book is the missing handshake that joins both sides in partnership to deliver projects that bring value to the customer *and* also leave a legacy.

Mike's work is not only a harbinger of where project management is rapidly heading, but it is a keen exposé of the often forgotten side of project management: people. In the words of Jim Lewis, author of numerous project management books, "Projects are people." This book gives us the mood music and the dance steps.

This is both a revelatory and a revolutionary book. It is destined to become for project management what Viktor Frankl's book, *Man's Search for Meaning*, has become for modern psychology and self-fulfillment, Margaret Wheatley's book, *Leadership and the New Science*, has meant for leading today's organizations, and Stephen Covey's book, *The Seven Habits of Highly Effective People*, has meant for personal and spiritual development.

Doug DeCarlo

Doug DeCarlo is the author of eXtreme Project Management: Using Leadership, Principles and Tools to Deliver Value in the Face of Volatility *(San Francisco: Jossey-Bass, 2004).*

■ REFERENCES

Stephen R. Covey, *The Seven Habits of Highly Effective People* (New York: Simon & Schuster, 1989).

Viktor Frankl, *Man's Search for Meaning* (New York: Touchstone, 1984).

Jane Loevinger, *Ego Development* (San Francisco: Jossey-Bass, 1976).

Margaret J. Wheatley, *Leadership and the New Science* (San Francisco: Barrett-Koehler, 1992).

■ Preface

If I had more sense, I would have realized much earlier that writing this book would be a right-brain project. But before coming to this realization, I had to hit a brick wall.

I planned and wrote the first draft of the book in a very left-brain fashion. It was logical and rational, and the content covered all the major stereotypes we have come to associate with the right brain. And when I read through the draft, I could readily tell that it was awful.

Let me cut to Chapter 18 with a sneak preview. There Colin Funk offers a perspective on the "project challenge," a place where we experience a formidable obstacle to progress on the project. So many of us have hit such a brick wall on our projects. The interesting thing about the project challenge is that it is as much an internal challenge as an external one. It is a personal challenge to change—perhaps attitude or perspective. The internal shift and the external one go hand in hand: meeting the internal challenge enables us to overcome the external one.

My brick wall, my project challenge, was to make something worthwhile out of the awful draft of the book—to somewhere find lemonade among the lemons. It was obvious that cosmetic changes would not do. The project needed an overhaul.

My internal challenge was for me to see this project from a new perspective.

Many authors will tell you that writing a book is a journey, and I am here to tell you that writing this book was all that and more. The true journey started when I came face to face with the brick wall. The trip over the wall to the other side started with a change in mindset and a change in management approach. And that is what right-brain project management is all about.

Once I began to approach this book as a right-brain project, I turned away from my preconceived notions and took steps to make sense of how the right brain operates in project management. I pulled on the exposed threads of this topic, and in following them, found some fascinating and completely unexpected ingredients of what it means to do right-brain work on a project.

At first glance, these threads seemingly have nothing to do with projects; upon further examination, though, it becomes clear that they have everything to do with projects! And so in this book we will travel through philosophy, emotion, intuition, the Project Management Institute's *A Guide to the Project Management Body of Knowledge (PMBOK® Guide)*, complexity, personal development, morality, spiritual survival, trust, and what it means to be a hero. Oh, and we will rub elbows with a few folks like Paul McCartney, Jack Nicholson, and Marge Gunderson from *Fargo*. We will go to a couple of sporting events and a few movies along the way. Did you know that movies like *Napoleon Dynamite* and *Pretty Woman* offer useful insights to the project manager?

It is important to me that whatever this book offers be grounded in real-world knowledge and experience—straight from the project street. I will provide extensive references to research and the experiences of project managers who use these right-brain approaches successfully on a regular basis in their work. Several professionals will offer their creative insights for managing projects. We will study several projects that performed phenomenally because they made heavy use of right-brain ingredients. The book also highlights some great techniques for accessing powerful right-brain capabilities with our right-brain toolkit features.

This book begins with an exploration of the current landscape for project management, highlighting contemporary projects that are complex and aggressive. Effective management of contemporary projects is as much about personal development as it is about Gantt charts. With this in mind, we will shift into topics that address how people grow and develop patterns of thinking and attitudes that have a profound effect on the management of projects. We will talk about what truly motivates people to get out of bed and right to their projects—to overcome whatever stands in the way of their objectives. We will talk about the profound changes that take place on projects and how to navigate those changes well.

Our journey then takes us through the seven principles of right-brain project management. These principles are founded on the powerful and rich processing capabilities of the right brain, and they map well into the unique and demanding needs of complex and aggressive projects.

Right-brain project management is not a recipe or prescription. Compared with conventional project management, it represents a shift in attitude and a shift in perspective. It is not a replacement for conventional project management; the two are complementary and very powerful together.

Ultimately, contemporary projects need an integration of left- and right-brain approaches. Because contemporary project management is overwhelmingly left brain, I have chosen to focus on right-brain perspectives. However, it is critical to understand that an appropriate balance of left- and right-brain techniques works best.

Finally, the book concludes with the personal, internal challenge of the contemporary project. The formidable challenges of today's projects call us to grow in character, each in our own ways. The project is a story, and we are the characters.

Let us begin.

Mike Aucoin
College Station, Texas
maucoin@leadingedgemgmt.com
www.leadingedgemgmt.com

■ What's Wrong with Project Management?

■
■
■

If you want to make God laugh, have a definite plan.

ANONYMOUS ■

S am, the project manager, had a "deer in the headlights" look as she prepared to address the stakeholder meeting and deliver more bad news.

Her project, like many of her peers' projects, was late and over budget. Finishing the project would likely require that some features be abandoned or deferred. Sam felt bad about how things had gone astray and feared that the stakeholders would decide to terminate her project.

She began to speak. "Let us start with the status of the project and then talk about where to go from here."

In this book, we will do just that: we will talk about the status of the project (and, by extension, project management) and where to go from here.

For too many projects and too many project managers, Sam's story is familiar. As someone who provides training in project management, it is a story that I sadly hear all too often.

■ But, First ... What's *Right* with Project Management

To begin talking about what is wrong with project management, let us first say that a lot is *right* with project management.

Every year, numerous projects are completed to the satisfaction of stakeholders and team members. These projects often proceed to conclusion without trauma; many other projects hit close to the mark with relatively little trouble.

Some projects even surpass all expectations and accomplish the truly remarkable. Such efforts deserve close study to discover the source of their energy, and we will spotlight examples of these projects in this book.

Clearly, effective management of projects, while elusive, is attainable.

There is much reason to celebrate these project management successes. If one gives any deference to either Murphy's Law (whatever can go wrong, will go wrong) or Newton's Second Law of Thermodynamics (the universe tends toward disorder), then any effort that overcomes these laws to accomplish something of value is a testament to human ingenuity, will, and industry.

▨ Unmet Expectations

Notwithstanding the project management successes, we all know that *lots* of projects are train wrecks. Of course, in any statistical population of performances, there will be those that underperform the mean. Nevertheless, this situation should not be acceptable to those who invest their time or money in troubled projects. While we cannot realistically expect every project to be phenomenal, it is reasonable to expect that every project will at least meet agreed-upon goals.

The prevalence of troubled projects suggests to many that if project management cannot produce success more reliably, then something is wrong with project management. "It is no exaggeration to claim that project management as a discipline is in crisis ...."[1]

Let us say simply that the overall impression of projects and project management is that they are disappointing. There is typically a mismatch between what is expected of projects, project managers, and project management, and what they actually deliver. This mismatch can be viewed from three perspectives:

- Expectations are unreasonable.
- Performance is not sufficient.
- Both expectations and performance are out of line.

Many who manage or execute projects in today's Church of Real World Projects will eagerly stand and shout "Amen" to the proposition that expectations on projects are unreasonable. Project teams are expected to work miracles with unproven technologies on a blazingly fast schedule with the barest of resources, not to mention with team members who have never met because they are scattered around the globe.

This approach might work if a successful outcome were somehow guaranteed. However, with increasing expectations comes increasing uncertainty that the outcome will meet those expectations. These expectations also reduce the likelihood that the project will finish at all.

Depending on one's perspective, a case can be made either way about the reasonableness of expectations on projects. Although it is appropriate to be realistic about what can be achieved, the topic eventually leads to a dead end for a simple reason: it is ultimately a moot point.

It is certainly possible, and perhaps likely, that expectations are unreasonable. It is also unlikely, however, that individuals with the power to make decisions will lower their expectations.

Humans have an innate and endearing preoccupation with greener grass. Someone, possibly the folks in the marketing department, will salivate over the opportunity to promise something faster, better, or cheaper—or better yet, all three. Project sponsors, customers, and upper management are typically willing partners in the quest for the impossible or merely unlikely.

If there is little that can be done to push back on expectations, project managers and teams have two options.

The first option is to say *no*. Perhaps a widespread project worker strike would convince those with unrealistic expectations to back off, but such a strike is not likely to happen. Individual project workers may say *enough!*—but it will likely be to the detriment of their careers. Faced with such negative consequences, the second choice, and the one taken by the vast majority of people, is to grit your teeth and soldier on.

■ Mediocre Performance

While it may be tempting to assign all the blame for substandard project performance to excessive expectations, we must also conclude that the way project management is practiced leaves something to be desired. Consider the following statistics.

In its 2004 survey of 10,640 projects, PriceWaterhouseCoopers found that only 2.5 percent of companies achieve budget, scope, and schedule targets on all projects.[2]

The 2004 Standish Group survey of information technology (IT) projects indicated that only 34 percent of such projects succeed while 15 percent fail completely and 51 percent are challenged with budget overruns, late delivery, or reduced benefits.[3] Nevertheless, this performance is a considerable improvement over previous experience for the ten years that Standish has conducted the survey.

It is reasonable to conclude that mediocre performance has come to be expected as the experience of project management in organizations.

Perhaps there is an interaction between unrealistic expectations and mediocre performance. I once had a supervisor who stated that he took any project schedule estimates given by a subordinate and automatically cut them in half. His rationale was that engineers and software specialists were always purposely pessimistic in their estimates to avoid having to stretch their limits. I was glad we had that little conversation, because from that time forward, I automatically doubled or tripled any estimate I gave him.

The consequences of project failures and disappointments are significant. In a revealing analysis, Oak Associates applied the results of the Standish survey to financial performance.[4] The impact of typical survey performance as compared with completing all projects successfully is an astonishing 58 percent reduction in sales and a 92 percent reduction in profit!

To restate, if performance on the failed and underperforming projects were improved so that all projects performed as expected, the gain in sales would be 136 percent and the improvement in profit would be an unbelievable 1135 percent!

It is amazing that companies can stay in business with mediocre project performance. It is also no wonder that organizations have a sense of disappointment in project management.

As shocking as these numbers are, perhaps the greatest effect of poor performance reaches beyond the business bottom line. When projects fail to meet financial and performance targets, morale suffers collateral damage. The most common intangible impacts are staff cynicism and negative cultural effects.[5] Considerable stress is associated with projects that go poorly, and the effects can become additive. These consequences have a profound impact on the company environment and a detrimental effect on subsequent project work.

Companies that experience project failures also report that their relationships with customers suffer through decreased customer satisfaction or loss of competitive advantage.

■ Rules ... and More Rules

What is being done about project performance?

The majority of suggestions and recommendations in the project management community aimed at improving performance involve implementing better standard project management processes. This approach focuses on improving the maturity of project processes used in planning and executing the project.

Without a doubt, maturation of project processes is valuable and worthwhile, and it has been proven to increase the effectiveness of project performance. The downside of this approach is that it takes time and effort to make these improvements. Consider a widely used measure of maturity, the Capability Maturity Model developed by the Software Engineering Institute at Carnegie Mellon University. Using this measure, the median maturity level across industries is level two,[6] with level five being the highest level. The survey that determined this median concluded that there is "… a relatively low degree of project management maturity across industries."[7] For an organization to improve by one level in the maturity progression requires "a very concerted effort"[8] and may take a year or more.

Insights abound about the problems and limitations of project management as it is practiced in organizations today. Fundamentally, it may be helpful to think about rewriting the rules.

Before we consider rewriting the rules, however, it is useful to take a look at some different perspectives on what is troubling project management. Why do so many people perceive that project management is failing to meet the mark? Four observations can shed some light.

■ Where Are the "Jump Out of Bed" Projects?

One of the primary reasons for high expectations on projects is that "… projects are important vehicles for implementing corporate strategy and effecting change."[9] While this explains the expectations, something else is at work here.

Observation 1: Most projects lack a compelling motivation.

Projects, and organizations, often fail to work on what is really important.

If you ask project stakeholders for the justification for their project, they will likely refer to customer requirements or financial benefits. There is nothing wrong with such reasons, and they are absolutely necessary.

But, as the timeless song says, "Is that all there is?"

Would projects be more successful if teams felt that what they were doing was *critical* to someone? Would teams be more motivated if they felt some strong emotional push to achieve the end results?

The motivation we're talking about here is not just the rational "I know this is in my best interest" type of reasoning. The motivation we seek is the impetus to get out of bed in the morning and get into the office because the project is *that* important.

It may come as a bit of a shock that organizations often do not work on what is really important. This is not to trivialize the projects that are done and the products they produce. It is simply an observation that project management, strategic management, and portfolio management do an inadequate job of establishing a *compelling* reason for the projects selected.

What do we mean by a compelling reason for the project? This justification is far more than the benefits to the customer and the financial benefits to the organization. The key issues are: What is it about a project that makes us eager to work on it? What will make us want to drop everything to work on this project? What will provide a satisfying reward for everyone at the end of the project?

Projects are often executed distantly removed from the "soul" of the organization (if the organization can be said to have a soul). This is largely a result of the misperception that project management is simply a method for executing a company's operations.[10]

If the overall company strategy can be considered the soul of the company, project managers and their projects are often considered cogs in the machine, not prime movers. This perspective is illustrated in the PriceWaterhouseCoopers survey: organizational considerations caused 59 percent of project failures.[11] If projects are important, why do organizations fail to support them well?

If we take as a predicate that a company's values are embodied in its strategy, then any disconnect between strategy and project execution is serious indeed.

■ Make Sense ... and Make Success

Organizations do an inadequate job of establishing a common understanding in project teams and stakeholders of where the project is going. In project management circles, this is frequently cited as poor communication. Good communication and common understanding are critical to project success, and poor communication is a pervasive problem.

While many reasons contribute to the difficulty encountered in reaching a common understanding of project goals, it seems that what is commonly called poor communication is better approached as difficulty in making sense of the project.

> *Observation 2: Projects and organizations have a hard time making sense of the project.*

While communication processes and techniques are important, in reality the difficulty in communication comes largely from two sources. First, poor communication is really a symptom of the lack of compelling motivation. Second, project stakeholders pay far too little attention to the *processes* of communication on a project.

The distinction between communication and sense-making is important and valuable. A focus on communication implies that early in the project there exists a definite and reliable embodiment of what everyone is working on, presumably what is described in the customer requirements or specifications. While this may be true for some projects, it is often a fallacious assumption.

In reality, many projects are commissioned with an *evolving* understanding of the end point. There is nothing intrinsically wrong with this approach, but it becomes a huge problem if everyone involved doesn't understand this reality. The project processes must be consciously designed and executed to accommodate this evolving understanding.

Improvement in communication focuses on technique; sense-making focuses on collectively developing and understanding the end point. Conventional communication remedies are predominantly aimed one way: to enhance the team's knowledge of the documented end point. This is the perspective illustrated in the famous line by the prison "captain" in the movie *Cool Hand Luke*, "What we've got here is a failure to communicate."

Sense-making assumes that everyone on the team has a valuable perspective to bring to the table. It is this network of the team in conjunction with the customer, sponsor, and stakeholders that together identifies and then creates the solution.

> *Observation 3: Project teams struggle with complexity and ambiguity, as well as with pressures to resolve these issues quickly.*

Contemporary projects are affected to a significant degree by complex and ambiguous issues. Many projects attempt to incorporate unproven technologies. Other projects commit to specific results with only a rudimentary definition of what is to be accomplished. Virtual teams are assembled with no history of experience together. Overlaid on these complexities is usually a tight schedule and a paucity of resources.

These issues of complexity, ambiguity, and time pressure greatly exacerbate problems of making sense. It is no wonder that most teams vacillate between two approaches: running hard and hoping to figure it out, and being frozen by the incomprehension of it all.

Project managers are typically taught to take steps to lower project risks. Accordingly, a common approach is to attempt to eliminate complexity and ambiguity. However, this approach is not compatible with the real world.

None of us is clairvoyant. Even the most thoughtful, enlightened planning process will not eliminate the unknown or unforeseen. To believe that we can "control" the future through planning is folly. We are better off accepting this reality and adapting accordingly.

If the environment at the start of a project is uncertain, the appropriate approach is to accept—and adapt to—the complexity and ambiguity. Adaptation requires agility. Unfortunately, however, many processes in an organization work against agility.

To a large extent, conventional project management is the application of rules (and to an increasing extent bureaucracy) with the aim of establishing predictability. In many cases, this approach is important and necessary, but it stifles the ability of teams to be quick and creative.

Organizations generally do not fully take advantage of the creativity and agility of their teams. This creativity is essential to dealing with complexity, ambiguity, and time pressure. Clearly, project teams need tools to access creative skills successfully and to use them effectively for project success.

In conventional project management, much attention is directed to the uncertainties and risks that are inherent to the product of the project, and relatively little to the interpersonal uncertainties. In many cases, little can be done up front about the former. But by directly and deliberately addressing the interpersonal uncertainties, the team develops the ability to greatly improve its handling of the product uncertainties.

■ Limitations of Standard Approaches

As with just about any human activity, improvements can be made in project performance. The relevant question is, "Which methods will provide the benefits we seek with a reasonable effort?"

Peruse a project management bookshelf and you will find all sorts of prescriptions for improving management performance. Numerous courses are available to improve various aspects of project performance. The options available are dizzying.

The vast majority of these methods are founded on a common theme: improvement in the execution of the rules that embody project management processes. This approach is entirely valid and beneficial, and it has been proven time and again to be helpful in project performance.

Yet many in the project management community express the sense that these methods don't quite scratch the itch. What is needed is not just another rule-based approach. What is needed is an entirely new approach that does not discount, but instead takes advantage of, all the benefits of existing rule-based project management methods.

■ What Is Missing?

What is it that separates the wildly successful projects from those that fail, or those that are merely mediocre? Is it mature project processes? Good documentation? A skillful and charismatic project manager?

While these ingredients can be helpful, they still may not be sufficient.

The fundamental problem with project management is what is missing, and what is missing is life, what is missing is people.

We need to breathe life into projects. Life animates—an individual, a team, a project, or a company. Giving life to a project involves making it more human.

When was the last time you described a project as being full of life?

Most projects in organizations are approached robotically, based solely on financial projections, specifications, and earned value. These ingredients are absolutely necessary to satisfy the business requirements of any project. But is that all there is? "When a Boeing engineer talks about launching an exciting and revolutionary new aircraft, she does not say, 'I put my heart and soul into this project because it would add 37 cents to our earnings per share.'"[12]

These elements, of themselves, do not animate people, projects, or organizations. Something else is needed.

> *Observation 4: Project management has enough domain tools. What is needed now for project success are maturity, social skills, and passion.*

The significant issues on projects involve people. These issues either give life to the project or drain life from it. "[T]echnical project management tools and methods are so well developed and widely used that it is time to turn the focus on developing leadership skills."[13]

Here is where this book comes in.

Where does life come from on a project? Where do we find the tools for mastery of the complex project? The answer to these questions is the right brain.

The inherent objective of any project is to bring smiles to the faces and pride to the hearts of all those associated with the project. The key to achieving this objective is the right brain.

The right brain provides access to the compelling motivation that projects need for success. We connect and communicate most effectively with other team members and stakeholders through the right brain, which is the way we tap creativity. The right brain has an amazing capability to handle complex, ambiguous problems and to make decisions quickly on incomplete, "intuitive" information using its impressive processing power.

The right brain is the vehicle for making the transition from existing rules that are limited in their effectiveness for contemporary projects, to discovering and applying new approaches that are more suited for the world as it is. In essence, the right brain holds the key for moving from conventional project management approaches to a more effective, complementary project management style.

Our abilities to work collaboratively with others depends to a large extent on right-brain processing, not the least of which is how we process information and situations that have a moral component. The ability to act according to the welfare of others guides effective teamwork and leadership, which are crucial to projects in organizations.

But more than all this, the right brain is the door through which we embark upon and fulfill the personal development needed to overcome the formidable challenges of today's projects. In short, the right brain is uniquely equipped to tackle all the challenging issues faced by contemporary project management.

Unfortunately, the right brain is commonly not understood, and is therefore treated with skepticism; its capabilities are ignored or avoided. The irony is that we all use the right side of our brains, knowingly or not.

This is not to say that project management should rely entirely on the right brain. Not only is that not possible, but it is not desirable: left-brain approaches are equally valuable and needed.

Those who integrate right- and left-brain approaches to project management will realize many benefits on an individual level; research and experience demonstrate that an integrated approach also offers valuable business benefits. To practice right-brain project management, you won't need extensive training. In fact, you learned long ago how to put your right brain to work. ▪

■ ENDNOTES

1 Lauri Koskela and Gregory Howell, "The Underlying Theory of Project Management Is Obsolete," Project Management Institute, http://www.pmi.org. Accessed May 2006.

2 "Boosting Business Performance through Programme and Project Management," PriceWaterhouseCoopers, 2004, http://www.pwc.com. Accessed June 2006.

3 "Standish: Project Success Rates Improved Over 10 Years," http://www.softwaremag.com. Accessed June 2006.

4 John M. Nevinson, "The Business Benefits of Better Projects," Oak Associates, Inc., 2005, http://www.oakinc.com. Accessed October 2005.

5 "Global IT Project Management Survey," KPMG, 2005, http://www.pmi
.org. Accessed June 2006.

6 Kevin P. Grant and James S. Pennypacker, "Project Management Maturity:
An Assessment of Project Management Capabilities Among and Between
Selected Industries," *IEEE Transactions on Engineering Management,*
Vol. 53, No. 1, February 2006, pp. 59–68.

7 Ibid., p. 66.

8 Ibid.

9 Peter Morris and Ashley Jamieson, *Translating Corporate Strategy into
Project Strategy* (Newtown Square, PA: Project Management Institute,
2004), p. viii.

10 Ibid., p. 3.

11 "Boosting Business Performance through Programme and Project
Management," PriceWaterhouseCoopers, 2004, http://www.pwc.com.
Accessed June 2006.

12 James C. Collins and Jerry I. Porras, "Building Your Company's Vision,"
Harvard Business Review, September–October 1996, pp. 65–77.

13 Irja Hyvari, "Project Management Effectiveness in Project-Oriented Business Organizations," *International Journal of Project Management,* Vol.
24, 2006, pp. 216–225.

CHAPTER 2

■ Child's Play ... and Maturity

All children are artists. The problem is how to remain an artist once he grows up.

PABLO PICASSO ■

D o you remember your first project? Or the first time you managed a project?

The obvious initial answer is to think of your first project with your first employer. But I'd like you to go back further ... much further.

Go past all the projects you completed in college, past your science fair project, past your projects from school and kindergarten. Go past even those craft projects from preschool.

■ Toddling through Projects

This line of questioning is a trick—it would be very surprising if you really did remember your first project. If you're like most people, you probably managed your first project before you were out of diapers.

That's right. While taking a break from their project management training, tomorrow's project managers are singing along with The Wiggles right now.

On your first project, you defined the scope, subdivided the work into smaller parts, and even executed scope changes. You gained practice for your workplace projects by throwing a tantrum when you didn't get all the resources you wanted. You may have "negotiated" (by force, perhaps) some key resources from a sibling.

If you were lucky, your project sponsor praised you for the completed project, say, erecting a tower made of blocks. Without intending to do so, you took a project from concept to completion. How in the world did you learn project management at such a tender age?

Far more than mere "child's play," we learned and practiced a number of critical project management concepts while coloring the masterpiece our parents proudly hung on the refrigerator door. We learned and practiced project management without knowing the concepts or even knowing that we were using them.

To understand and consider the current state of project management, and to develop approaches to mastering the challenges of contemporary projects, it is helpful to study how we develop as human beings and how we think. Thinking about how we think will give us insights into what will work best for those project management issues that cause us grief.

■ An Instinct for Projects

It was a project like many others. The team members had been thrown together having never previously worked as a team. They organized a project so challenging, it had little chance of success. With inadequate tools and resources, the team encountered one critical problem after another.

What's more, the project had to be performed surreptitiously; if the project became known, the team members would be severely punished.

While this scenario (minus the punishment) would describe many projects, the one I have in mind is "The Great Escape," the true story of prisoners of war during World War II, which was cast into one of the favorite movies of all time. This team self-organized a project to orchestrate a mass escape from a maximum security German prisoner of war camp. On the night of the escape, 76 prisoners left the camp.

How is it possible that such a group can use primitive resources under significant duress, without project management skills, and accomplish such an astonishing feat?

We are constantly surrounded by and immersed in projects, consciously or not, and deliberately or not. Billions of people in the world plan and execute projects on a regular basis. Yet, they have never taken a project management course or read a book about project management, nor could they even give you the definition of project management. How is it possible for so many to execute projects successfully with no training?

Project management is an "intuitive" or even "instinctive" capability of human beings. It is something that comes naturally; it is hardwired into us, much like breathing, speaking, crawling, and walking.

Projects are often used to accomplish or obtain what we want, and to a large degree they are the vehicles for how we learn. Projects are the means we use to initiate change. Because we have an innate and endearing preoccupation with greener grass, we are always pursuing projects.

If the management and execution of projects is instinctive or intuitive, then there is much to be gained by leveraging the natural capabilities of people in the performance of projects. Before we expand on this thought, let us return to our toddler to examine what we learn about projects at an early age.

■ Building Blocks of Project Management

While engaging in the child's play of building blocks, we are laying the foundation for valuable principles that will be critical throughout our lives, including our careers.

Let's take a look at the types of thinking we develop in our childhood years that form the building blocks for project management.

▪▪▪ CAUSE AND EFFECT, OR DETERMINISM

At the root of our training in project management is our learning the principle of cause and effect. I seek an effect, and I can take steps to cause it. This is a major development in the life of a toddler, and it is the underlying principle that animates projects, whether they are as simple as organizing a closet or as complicated as a putting a man on the moon. Through cause and effect, we are able to plan an outcome and believe that the outcome will happen. If we were unable to rely on the principle of cause and effect, our lives would be far more chaotic—and far more frightening.

▪▪▪ INDETERMINISM

We soon encounter another important principle, the opposite of determinism, and it drives us crazy. While cause and effect works much of the time, in many situations it does not. These become sources of great frustration, and therefore opportunities for more of those tantrums. Perhaps there is no path from cause to effect, no matter how hard we wish for one. Perhaps there is a path, but it is not yet known to us. When stymied, we make a different attempt at finding the link between cause and effect.

▪▪▪ EXPERIMENTATION

At this age, the obvious approach to learning is trial and error to determine the right pattern that will create the path from cause to effect. Sometimes we succeed and other times we don't. Through experimentation, we discover three critical principles:

- Some outcomes are not predictable.
- Experimentation often leads to valuable knowledge.
- Through persistence, we can often achieve our objectives, even when we meet with obstacles.

▪▪▪ ADAPTATION

A corollary to experimentation is adaptation. We learn to change strategies when we perceive that what we are doing is not working.

An important ingredient of adaptation is the ability to recognize and choose appropriate times to change strategies.

▪▪▪ ABSTRACTION

Now here's a big one. Somewhere between the ages of six and twelve, a child formulates the ability to represent objects and ideas through concepts. This developmental stage is known as *abstraction*. The capability to think abstractly is crucial to planning as well as to seeing relationships between the big picture *(holism)* and the details *(reductionism)*.

▪▪▪ ANALYSIS AND SYNTHESIS

When objects or concepts are disassembled into parts, we practice analysis. In contrast, synthesis is the combination of two or more elements to create a new system. Analysis is necessary for understanding issues and for solving problems that are rule-based. Synthesis is an essential component of creativity and solving problems that are novel and unfamiliar.

▪▪▪ EMOTIONAL KNOWLEDGE

While we no doubt experience emotion in some form even as newborns, an important developmental milestone occurs when we become conscious of our own and others' emotions.

▪▪▪ EMOTIONAL SOCIALIZATION

Once we are knowledgeable about emotions, a subsequent milestone occurs through understanding the social context of emotions. We act in certain ways to elicit or avoid emotions in others, as well as the resultant emotions we experience. For example, the conditions of embarrassment, dishonor, or shame are powerful forces in project work and form an important foundation for how humans make decisions.

••• META-COGNITION

Meta-cognition is the ability to reflect, or to "think about thinking." It is the ability to examine our thoughts and actions and to evaluate areas for change, development, or improvement.

■ Increasing Sophistication

This list is by no means exhaustive of the types of thought processes we learn, but highlights those that are important to project management. While these developmental building blocks and capabilities grow in maturity and sophistication with age, the fundamental elements are all in place by the school-age years.

Understandably, the management skills required to carry out the school science fair project are limited compared with the skills required to manage a project portfolio at a Fortune 500 company. Clearly, our projects and the requisite skills mature over the years.

As toddlers, we execute projects because we want to, with little or no planning. Necessarily, our early projects are primitive; they are designed for immediate gratification and the explicit benefits they will bring.

As we grow older, our projects become more formal and collaborative, such as projects done at school. Other projects are performed for "barter"—the project is done not for its intrinsic value to us but because it provides some other benefit. I may choose to clean my room, for example, not because I like a clean room, but to avoid losing a privilege. These experiences help develop skills in negotiation that we will need eventually to navigate workplace politics.

Over time, school projects grow in complexity. No doubt by the end of college, every student has encountered group projects in which people issues are significant. When my kids worked on group projects, their common complaints were not about the content of the work, but rather about the "difficult" project team members. Inevitably, some kids wouldn't work at all, or only wanted the "plum" tasks.

Nowhere in the syllabus did we ever see a learning objective to the effect of "Encounter and gain skill with interpersonal issues on projects." Nevertheless, this became the most important part of school projects, as well it should have. This is exactly what it will be like for these students when they become adults in the workplace. School and extracurricular projects introduce children and teens to the many nuances of leadership and teamwork issues that pervade project work.

After leaving school and entering the workplace, we encounter fully the pressures exerted on our projects by the marketplace. To accommodate these forces, many individuals and their organizations seek training and expertise in good project management practices. As Peter Senge, author of *The Fifth Discipline*, states: "Organizations learn only through individuals who learn. Individual learning does not guarantee organizational learning. But without it no organizational learning occurs."[1]

The techniques commonly learned and practiced in the discipline of project management lead us back to our opening question, "What's wrong with project management?" The present condition of project management came about to a large extent because of how we think and how we believe the world works. To understand the limitations of project management practices, we must examine the concepts and assumptions that support them. It's time to get philosophical.

■ What's Your Worldview?

What in the world does philosophy have to do with project management? Well ... everything!

To understand where we are in project management, we need to pull on the thread that led us here. Our struggle with the management of projects takes us back to philosophers who did a lot of mental heavy lifting centuries ago and had a profound influence on how we perceive the workings of the world. By studying what they had to say, we can see the way more clearly to handle our contemporary project problems.

Pulling on the thread of project management philosophy to seek its origin leads us back to René Descartes and Isaac Newton. Our views of the world and the current practice of project management are overwhelmingly affected by these two giants of philosophy.

Descartes, a 17th century French philosopher, is considered the founder of modern philosophy. Incredibly gifted, he was responsible for the development of algebra and geometry. (The Cartesian coordinate plane is named in his honor.) Isaac Newton, one of the greatest scientists in history, followed Descartes, and both were instrumental in the Scientific Revolution. It is largely through Newton that we came to understand the fundamental physical laws that have led to the many technological benefits we enjoy today.

The legacies of Descartes and Newton can be capsulized in four characteristics, which describe their view of how the world operates:

- The natural world functions like a machine; the world is *mechanistic*.
- We can observe and rely on predictable cause-and-effect relationships; the world is *deterministic*.
- We gain knowledge through thought and reason; the world is *rationalistic* (as opposed to an empirical approach in which knowledge is gained through experience).
- Anything that is complex can be dissected into smaller parts and understood; the world is *reductionistic* (that is, the whole is equal to the sum of its parts).

The fantastic and amazing developments of civilization since the Enlightenment occurred largely because of the profound benefits of applying this worldview and exercising these methods of thought.

Think about how this worldview is applied to project management. With determinism, we develop the project plan and know that executing it will bring about the end product. What is a work breakdown structure but the product of reductionistic thinking? Rational thought enables us to deduce the steps that lead to milestones.

In short, Descartes would see the project and the team as a machine whose components use inputs to produce a desired output. As long as the process is familiar, and we stay within the capabilities of the machine, we can rely predictably on its function. Project management in such an environment is a valuable and efficient way to achieve the objectives; it is rational.

But what if the project is complex or uncertain? And what if we are working on the project with other human beings who are sometimes complex and unpredictable? If we are schooled in Descartes and Newton, the temptation is to apply their philosophies more emphatically.

This is where much of the project management community finds itself today. To a large extent, the tools of conventional project management began with Descartes and Newton. They brilliantly serve the familiar, predictable project, but they struggle with what is indeterminate, what is unpredictable, and what is not yet known.

For a revised view of how the world operates, let us get familiar with another mental heavy lifter, Immanuel Kant.

■ Synthesis: Greater than the Sum of Parts

Immanuel Kant was an 18th century German philosopher who addressed the subject of cause and effect a bit differently. What he had to say offers a perspective on the operation of the world that is much more appropriate for today's complex projects.[2]

If Descartes, Newton, and Kant were sitting around a table discussing philosophy over beer, all three would pretty much agree about the natural, non-living world. But when the discussion turned to the living world of organized beings (or organisms), Kant would differ sharply.

Kant would say that for organisms, the whole is not the sum of its parts. Each constituent part is both cause and effect. For example, the leaves on a tree both give to and receive from the roots, and each is changed because of the other.

Cause-and-effect relationships may not be explicit for an organism. The reaction of the organized being to an external action is to a certain extent unpredictable. This is absolutely the case with humans who, in addition to being very diverse in nature, can think, feel, adapt, and learn.

Therefore, when dealing with organized beings, we cannot rely on the mechanistic/deterministic/rationalistic/reductionistic approach to produce expected results. A machine cannot synthesize, but an organism can.

As Kant would say, for an organism, the whole is *greater than* the sum of its parts.

Another important element to the Kantian worldview is self-organization. Because components of an organism are both cause and effect to one another, the components do not need an external organizing force. The actions of one component can influence and change another, and vice versa; changes accumulate and can converge. This understanding is key in the management of complex projects where agility is crucial.

■ Immanuel Kant, Project Manager

How might Kant's thinking apply to a human organization such as a project team? Kant would say that a project team—like any human organization—behaves like an organism.

As an organism, the project team is capable of growing in capability and complexity. Think about Bill Hewlett and Dave Packard the first day in their garage, then think about the corporate giant HP 50 years later, and you get the picture. A "machine" could not do what they did; Descartes and Newton could not sufficiently explain it.

This is not to say that we should discard the Descartes/Newton worldview when working on projects. To the contrary, we absolutely need it. But we also need to understand its limitations.

Kant would say that human beings, and all of nature for that matter, behave paradoxically—as both machine and organism. It is the appreciation of this paradox that makes the right brain/left brain partnership work.

We need to apply "worldviews" appropriately so that we can use what works best according to the situation. Projects behave like machines in many instances. Projects also behave like organisms in many instances. When it comes to the "people" aspects of projects, because projects are planned and executed by human beings, we can be certain that stakeholders and project teams will behave like Kant's organisms.

■ Causation and Uncertainty

Before leaving these philosophical subjects, let's consider three more recent concepts.

The first is *probabilistic causation*. Simply put, the cause-and-effect relationship does not apply in all cases. For example, it has been shown that a high-fat diet is correlated to an increase in heart attacks. But we also know that many people who eat a high-fat diet never have a heart attack while some unfortunate people die of a heart attack even though they have never consumed a high-fat meal in their lives.

The other two concepts, which are related, are often credited to Werner Karl Heisenberg, the influential 20th century German physicist. His *uncertainty principle* and *observer effect* arose from his work in quantum physics, but they have also been seen at play in human social and organizational systems.

The uncertainty principle posits that when we observe a system, we are uncertain that what we are observing is the reality of the system. The observer effect means that the very act of observing a system changes the behavior of the system.

These last three principles serve as a caution for project managers in thinking about the conclusions we draw from the project environment. The worldviews of Kant and Heisenberg suggest that while we may not be able to rationally understand and plan the project completely, we can know that the team will be capable of adapting in a beneficial way over the course of the project.

By the way, Heisenberg has one of the great epitaph lines of all time. The grave of the founder of the uncertainty principle marks his presence with, "He lies somewhere here."

If you are handicapping the project management race, while the Descartes/Newton team has a significant lead, when it comes to complex projects, expect the Kant/Heisenberg team to come on strong.

■ Tensions in Project Management Models

These building blocks of thought and the associated worldviews incorporate important elements of project management skills. These elements can come into conflict depending on the needs and perspectives of the various actors on a project. When we consider how the actors come to an issue with different perspectives, we will be better able to manage and resolve the conflicts that can arise.

▪▪▪ DETERMINISM VERSUS INDETERMINISM

This is one of the key areas of tension in all of management, not just in project management. For a manager, it is very tempting to implement steps that will have a predictable outcome. Shareholders, stakeholders, superiors, and customers often seek, if not demand, a predictable outcome to projects. Yet, contemporary projects inevitably encounter complexity and ambiguity, hence the outcome becomes more indeterministic. The result is considerable stress for the project manager trying to make sense of it all.

▪▪▪ EXPERIMENTATION VERSUS FOLLOWING THE PLAN

An excellent strategy for addressing the ambiguous is to experiment and adapt. Much can be gained when stakeholders accept ambiguity and the need to experiment. Because this approach runs counter to staying with a plan in the pursuit of a predictable outcome, one of a project manager's primary objectives becomes to lead stakeholders toward tolerating temporary experimentation.

▪▪▪ ANALYSIS AND SYNTHESIS

Conventional project management approaches use both skills, but synthesis is generally used in a more controlled manner. Contemporary projects demand advanced synthesis skills, which will lead us heavily into right-brain territory and into conflict with the rationalistic personality of most organizations.

▪▪▪ RATIONALITY AND EMOTIONAL KNOWLEDGE

The emotional and social components of project work are typically ignored or glossed over as being irrational. Workplaces avoid even a healthy consideration of emotion on projects. Nonetheless, emotion plays a major role in the planning and execution of projects and has a primary function in decision-making. Emotional knowledge is a subject that deserves considerable attention in project management.

■ Development into Maturity

Personal development into maturity is perhaps the most critical element in the ability to manage contemporary projects in the workplace.

Developmental psychologist Jane Loevinger formulated a theory of personal development that describes the stages of human maturation according to how we make decisions and how we interact with other people and with the world. In other words, her theory is a representation of how we mature in our view of the world, of people, and of life. Loevinger's theory consists of nine stages of the development of the *ego*, a term that describes personal development without the negative connotation of the word in common use.

Particularly relevant for projects is that the Loevinger system is a good indicator of a person's individual and social maturity. Therefore, as a concept, it is useful for understanding the types of skills that are valuable for project management and leadership. Table 2-1 provides a summary of Loevinger's social maturation stages.[3]

A key point to understand in the Loevinger system, and indeed with most considerations related to personal development, is that moving into each new stage represents a fundamental shift in how a person perceives the world. This maturation in perspective has a profound effect on how we interpret our own actions and the actions of those around us, as well as the things to which we pay attention.

In terms of projects, personal development is not related to age or intelligence. Of course, a certain level of intelligence and

▪ Table 2-1. Loevinger's Nine Stages of Ego Development

Stage	Characteristics
Infancy	Pre-social stage; no ego; not differentiated from the rest of the world
Impulsive	Characterized by restraints, rewards, and punishments; centered in the present; physical cause and effect
Self-Protective	Beginning of self-control; anticipates rewards and punishments
Conformist	Security comes from belonging; conforms to rules and norms of group; judges only behavior of others, not intentions
Self-Aware	Distinguishes self from norms and expectations; first inner life
Conscientious	Has goals, ideals, and sense of responsibility; sees self apart from group and internalizes rules; sees self from other point of view; sees motives of others; guilt is from hurting another, not breaking rules
Individualistic	Can become distant from role identities; greater tolerance of self and others; recognizes that relationships bring dependency; psychological cause and effect; awareness of inner conflict
Autonomous	Tolerates ambiguity; concern for emotional interdependence; self-fulfillment; integrates ideas and identities
Integrated	Transcends conflicts; self-actualizing

the attainment of particular qualifications are required to be a project manager in a contemporary organization. But our capability to master the challenging contemporary project environment springs more from personal development.

Personal development evolves through our experiences of life and the choices we make when faced with challenges or opportunities for growth. The key issues are character and how we learn to see and interact with the world around us.

Several of the Loevinger stages in the higher areas of maturity are most relevant for project management. These stages—self-aware, conscientious, individualistic, and autonomous—are those most likely to be encountered among adults in the workplace.[4] The transitions involved in these stages are particularly relevant to project management.

The self-aware stage is a transitional stage in which we begin to see issues from different perspectives. Such a development is critical for work as a project manager, but this is only the beginning.

In making the transition to the conscientious stage, an individual becomes more self-reflective. He or she can perceive relationships according to emotions and motives rather than simply by actions. The conscientious stage is also marked by the development of a personal morality. In this context, "morality" refers to the norms of interaction with others, and would include, for example, fairness and tolerance of differences.

Development into the individualistic stage is characterized by seeing greater value in relationships. Another significant development is that an individual begins to tolerate paradox. This development continues more fully into the autonomous stage, in which an individual becomes comfortable with inner conflict. This development is critical to enable a person to make choices and commitments while experiencing internal conflict and ambiguity. An individual in the autonomous stage can proceed effectively in the face of ambiguity and inner conflict, while someone in a lower stage will likely experience considerable distress or may even get stuck. A more mature individual will have the important skills needed to apply to ambiguity on projects.

Maturation through these developmental states brings with it a growing ability to tolerate and master the significant issues associated with contemporary projects. Many of the issues that cause trouble on contemporary projects require a corresponding personal maturity in the individualistic and autonomous stages. We expect a high level of skill in the project manager, and ego stage maturity should clearly be on the list.

But let's not place the need for maturity entirely on the shoulders of the project manager. When we have a team composed of individuals who have a high degree of ego development, the project can benefit tremendously.

Research backs up this linkage. The maturity level through the stages of personal development is directly linked to managerial abilities.[5] Individuals who have developed to the autonomous stage have been demonstrated to perform better as managers.

One study specifically examined the performance of organizational development (OD) consultants according to their stage of personal development.[6] An OD consultant is commonly engaged to lead an organization through change. We can use this performance as a valuable surrogate for project managers because these two groups have much in common in their work. Both OD consultants and project managers are agents of change, and both have assignments that are temporary. This research demonstrated a strong correlation between the stage of personal development and effective performance as an OD consultant.[7]

Here is the payoff to our exploration of personal development. By understanding the maturity and interpersonal milestones attained through developmental stages, we can better understand what is needed for success as a project manager.

■ The "Other" Intelligences

Descartes' influence also extended to the understanding of human intelligence. For decades the dominant emphasis on intelligence was the measure of cognitive intelligence, or IQ. Furthermore, the rational approach to human behavior was seen in cognitive psychology, which viewed the brain as a computer.

In the last two decades, this singular view of intelligence has given way to the belief that multiple intelligences reside in the brain. As stated by Dr. Paul Eslinger, Professor of Neurology at the Penn State University College of Medicine, "The human brain and potential is not just what we're able to think but what we're able to feel, and how we're able to integrate these two streams of experience and knowledge."[8]

With this growing understanding of the brain, two other constructs of intelligence become key: emotional intelligence (EI) and moral intelligence (MI).

■ Emotional Intelligence

One of the most significant issues on projects—and one that is typically discounted—is emotion. Most organizations suppress the consideration of emotion in the workplace. In terms of projects, we are not talking about gushing emotional sharing, but rather the typical emotional component of humans functioning in daily life.

The degree or stage of an individual's emotional intelligence is also a measure of maturity and as such is strongly related to the skills needed for project management. Table 2-2 presents the five elements of emotional intelligence.[9]

An individual's degree of emotional maturity is strongly related to managerial and leadership abilities—in other words, the ability to manage and execute projects. This linkage makes sense because so many of the issues involved in making a project a success involve the "soft" issues or "people" issues. Research has shown that higher levels of emotional intelligence in the project manager are linked to improved project performance.[10] Individuals with higher levels of emotional intelligence have also been shown to be more effective in the matrix organizations that many companies use to organize projects.[11]

- **Table 2-2. Goleman's Five Elements of Emotional Intelligence**

Knowing one's emotions	The ability to identify one's emotions; to understand links among emotions, thought, and actions
Managing emotions	The capacity to manage one's emotions; to control emotions or to shift undesirable emotions to more effective ones
Motivating oneself	The ability to enter into emotional states by choice; to summon emotions toward the attainment of goals
Recognizing emotions in others	The capability to empathize; to read, and be sensitive to, other people's emotions
Handling relationships	The ability to sustain satisfactory and beneficial relationships; to lead and influence the emotions of others

■ Moral Intelligence

Morality is a topic that has become increasingly difficult to discuss in the public arena. Although the topic is intertwined with religion, and religion certainly incorporates morality, the two subjects differ. We can address morality as distinct from religion or imposing certain values of right and wrong on others.

Let us focus on the meaning of morality as ethics: treating people with respect and dignity. Maturing in morality is growing in the ability to value oneself and others. In this light, morality is the capacity to perceive interests beyond our own and the ability to act with care, fairness, and even selflessness when interacting with others.

Moral intelligence is closely related to emotional intelligence; recent research has clearly demonstrated a strong link between moral reasoning and emotions. It is helpful to understand that a subset of emotions is moral emotions. These guide our decision-making when we face a situation with outcomes that may cause good or harm to ourselves and others.

■ Maturity in the Organization

Here is a compelling thought: not only do we need project managers and team members with mature emotional and moral intelligence, but we also need organizations that are similarly mature. We need organizations that value differing perspectives and tolerate ambiguity, and that have healthy systems for processing emotions.

Recent decades have seen outstanding developments in the project management profession toward systems of project management maturity; that is, organizational processes that progress in maturity. One example of these systems is the Capability Maturity Model and its successor, the Capability Maturity Model Integration (CMMI)[12] developed by the Software Engineering Institute at Carnegie Mellon University. The Project Management Institute (PMI) has adopted the Organizational Project Management Maturity Model (OPM3®) as the standard for its maturity model. CMMI and OPM3® provide guides for the process skills needed for increasing levels of maturity for project work.

Making the effort to grow in process maturity is an excellent way for an organization to improve project success. Yet, we now see that complex, contemporary projects also demand other kinds of maturity from both individuals and organizations: maturity in ego and maturity in emotional intelligence.

■ Maturity Makes for Better Projects

We have covered a lot of ground on how humans think, how we develop and mature, and how our outlook on the world affects the performance of projects. These insights offer significant benefits for improving success on contemporary projects. Through natural stages of human development into more advanced stages, and by applying an appropriate worldview, we can gain in mastery of the skills that promote effective project management.

The state of maturity we seek is not just for individuals but for the project organization as a whole. This state can be achieved to a significant degree through the group values, attitudes, and processes that an organization establishes.

A practical strategy is to screen for project managers who have reached the autonomous stage of development. As part of the job description, the organization can include the role of facilitating work and processes that incorporate the autonomous stage.

For example, the project manager can take the lead at the start of the project by presenting to the group the core belief that ambiguity is not only acceptable but inevitable in the early project stages. While various stakeholders and team members may initially feel uncomfortable with this concept, signaling this belief as a group norm offers a much better chance that it will become reality.

To a certain extent, humans progress in maturity when the external environment prompts and supports growth. This is why it is important for project organizations to value and support the Kantian worldview and the emotional life of a project.

Several important themes run through this worldview and the corresponding developmental milestones. When these milestones are achieved, they significantly further the mastery of contemporary project situations. These milestones are:

- *Ability to master emotions internally*—to respond effectively to the inevitable challenges of complex projects
- *Ability to effectively read and respond to the emotions of others*—to use emotional energy in a positive way, as a team
- *Ability to tolerate paradox, ambiguity, and anxiety*—to proceed confidently while the team converges toward resolution of these issues on the project
- *Ability to resolve issues creatively*—to apply new ways of thinking so that the project objectives can be achieved efficiently
- *Willingness to grow*—to accept the challenges of projects and see in them opportunities to develop in maturity.

These are all highly desirable traits in project managers and teams on contemporary projects. It is beneficial to have a project manager who is mature in these developmental areas, as well as for the project organization to value growth in these areas. This breakthrough thinking, energy, and teamwork are often sorely needed on projects with high expectations.

As important as it is to have effective tools and skills, the ability to perform well on contemporary projects includes an important "inner game" as well.

We began this chapter with the observation that project work is an intuitive and natural component of human existence. Likewise, progression through stages of maturity and the innate pull to grow are also instinctive parts of our human condition. We were born to perform projects and to manage projects, and we were born to master increasing complexity on projects.

These are the elements that form the foundation for the techniques of right-brain project management. To continue our exploration, let us now turn our attention to the ultimate project resource that makes it all possible: the brain. ▪

■ ENDNOTES

1 Peter M. Senge, *The Fifth Discipline* (New York: Currency Doubleday, 1990), p. 139.

2 Ralph D. Stacey, Douglas Griffin, and Patricia Shaw, *Complexity and Management* (London: Routledge, 2000), pp. 19–29.

3 Jane Loevinger, *Ego Development* (San Francisco: Josey-Bass, 1976).

4 Gervase R. Bushe and Barrie W. Gibbs, "Predicting Organization Development Consulting Competence from the Myers-Briggs Type Indicator and Stage of Ego Development," *The Journal of Applied Behavioral Science,* Vol. 26, No. 3, 1990, pp. 337–357.

5 K. Merron, D. Fisher, and W. R. Torbert, "Meaning Making and Management Action," *Group and Organization Studies,* Vol. 12, 1987, pp. 274–286.

6 Gervase R. Bushe and Barrie W. Gibbs, "Predicting Organization Development Consulting Competence from the Myers-Briggs Type Indicator and Stage of Ego Development," *The Journal of Applied Behavioral Science,* Vol. 26, No. 3, 1990, pp. 337–357.

7 Ibid.

8 David Pacchioli, "The Moral Brain," *Research Penn State Magazine,* Penn State University, October 2, 2006, http://www.rps.psu.edu/indepth/brainscans1.html. Accessed November 2006.

9 Daniel Goleman, *Emotional Intelligence* (New York: Bantam Books, 1994), pp. 43–44.

10 William Leban and Carol Zulauf, "Linking Emotional Intelligence Abilities and Transformational Leadership Styles," *Leadership and Organization Development Journal,* Vol. 25, No. 7, pp. 554–564.

11 Thomas Sy and Stéphane Côté, "Emotional Intelligence: A Key Ability to Succeed in the Matrix Organization," *Journal of Management Development,* Vol. 23, No. 5, 2004, pp. 437–455.

12 CMMI is a registered trademark of the Software Engineering Institute at Carnegie Mellon University.

CHAPTER 3

■ Two Brains Are Better than One

■
■
■

Perhaps it is good to have a beautiful mind, but an even greater gift is to discover a beautiful heart.

JOHN NASH ■

It is capable of recalling every state capital and can wrestle with weighty questions of consciousness, "self," and the meaning of life. It can establish the theory of relativity, or catch the nuance of a double entendre. It has invented the wheel and used it reliably in a million different applications. It shows off by spelling *antidisestablishmentarianism*—backwards—and is responsible for falling head over heels in love.

Welcome to the marvels of the human brain.

Between your ears is the most powerful force in the world, a processing juggernaut whose capabilities are believed to be almost limitless. The human brain is capable of so much more than any engineered computer in large part because of its multifunctional processing style and its capability to build exponentially upon what has been learned before.

The study of the human brain, its functions, and its capabilities is a relatively new and exciting field. A limited understanding of the brain was developed several decades ago, but only in the last ten years have we made extensive advances in our understanding of how it operates. It seems fair to say that our understanding of the brain is still very limited, and much more remains to be learned.

What we do know about the brain and how it processes information is relevant to the study of project management, particularly our focus on the complex, contemporary project.

■ Structure and Operation of the Brain

The mind and its astounding capabilities result largely from the incorporation of two complementary but significantly different processing styles. From an evolutionary standpoint, these capabilities have benefited humans enormously. While this incorporation offers the benefit of some redundancy, its primary purpose is to provide two different approaches to thinking, or two ways of looking at the world.

Having two processing styles is very valuable, if not necessary, for the functioning, survival, and growth of humans. We need to be able to follow rules and structure as well as to be able to adapt to unusual situations. Our brains have made it possible for us to explore new worlds and then to create permanent communities in those worlds. These complementary capabilities have enabled humanity to adapt to significantly varying environmental conditions and to complex and unprecedented threats, as well as to evolve in intellectual capability.

At the same time, humans have been able to capture and exploit the knowledge gained in each endeavor into rules that can be reliably communicated to peers and descendants to preserve and expand on knowledge. Indeed, this complementary architecture of thought makes it possible for us to live so well under conditions that range from pleasant California to the South Pole, to the sea floor, and to the surface of the moon.

One of the key structural features within the brain is the extensive interconnectedness of its components. This web of about one quadrillion connections enables very powerful parallel processing of information in ways that far exceed the capabilities of the most powerful computers.

The cerebral cortex is the structure that separates the human brain from the brains of other creatures. The cerebral cortex contains two symmetrical hemispheres: the right side and the left side. The left and right hemispheres are connected by a structure called the corpus callosum. With an interconnection of approximately 300 million nerve fibers, the corpus callosum enables the two sides of the brain to share information readily.

Research performed several decades ago developed the understanding that the two hemispheres function in different ways with significantly different programming styles. These two "brains" came to be known as the left brain and the right brain. This early research has been shown to be overly simplistic; the reality is a bit more complicated.

Later research confirmed that the brain has these two different processing styles, but found that they do not necessarily reside in separate hemispheres. Furthermore, the human brain has an incredible capacity to renew itself and develop alternate pathways to respond to injury. Functions previously resident in one area of the brain can be learned elsewhere if the need arises.

This is not a textbook on neuroscience, so we won't go further into the physiology of the brain. For our purposes, it does not matter where the functions are physically performed, only that the processing styles of "left brain" and "right brain" are incorporated within the brain. We will use these terms to refer to styles or functions of thinking and processing information, rather than the physical parts of the brain.

■ Early Research on Brain Specialization

The breakthrough in brain specialization originated from research conducted by Roger Sperry in the 1960s. For this work, Sperry received the Nobel Prize in 1981.

Sperry studied individuals who had suffered disease or injury that disabled part of the brain. In other cases, he studied individuals who had been treated for epilepsy; the treatment for these individuals at the time was to sever the corpus callosum, effectively stopping communication between the left and right sides of the cerebral cortex. Other, non-invasive studies were performed on healthy individuals using approaches that served to access one side of the brain at a time. His work led to fascinating findings.

Sperry discovered that when one removes or disables the right brain, verbal language is unimpaired but becomes more computer-like. The subjects he studied could not understand metaphors, inflections, and emotional tone. Individuals with no right-brain function also exhibited a flat personality and had limitations related to conceptual insights, imagination, and initiative. Simple spatial tasks became confusing.

Patients who lost their left-brain function lost the ability to talk but remained completely conscious and able to function in a non-verbal way. They were able to communicate with pictures, and they retained their personality and emotional processing.

Based on Sperry's research, we can summarize the functions of the two brains. The left brain processes information in words, it is responsible for speech, and it processes step-by-step logic in sequence. The left brain seeks to apply rules in its actions.

The right brain is non-verbal, it is more visual and emotional, and it attempts to create new patterns or to recognize patterns from disguised or fragmented pieces of information. The left brain is unable to process information in this way. The right brain also recognizes concepts that are not easily put into words and is comfortable with metaphors. These functions are critical aspects of creativity.

The left and right brains operate and communicate in different ways. The left brain processes the literal meaning of words. The right brain processes inferred meaning, tone, inflection, and body language. The left brain processes information for logical and factual content, while the right brain processes information for emotional and conceptual content.

The processing styles of the two brains are summarized in Table 3-1.

▪ **Table 3-1. Left-Brain and Right-Brain Processing Styles**

Left brain	Right brain
Verbal communication, uses words	Uses visual, spatial, tactile communication
Relies on logic	Processes emotions, offers intuition
Prefers to execute known rules	Seeks new associations, creative thought
Operates sequentially	Comfortable with disconnected information
Prefers predictable behavior	Comfortable with some ambiguity
Executes patterns	Learns patterns
Prefers what is explicit, concrete	Prefers abstract concepts, metaphor
Operates with complete information	Operates with incomplete information
Unable to make decisions independently	Critical to decision-making

■ Getting Emotional over Decisions

Although it seems counterintuitive, patients who lose right-brain function also lose the ability to make decisions. Shouldn't the ability to make decisions reside in the logical left brain? Don't people make decisions by gathering information and then considering the advantages and disadvantages of options?

Of course we analyze information in decision-making. Nonetheless, our ability to *make* a decision is ultimately based on emotion.

Decisions are made based on the relative positive and negative emotions associated with the available options. These emotions reside in memories associated with similar situations and outcomes from the past. Suppose I have bad news about a project that should be conveyed to my boss. What emotions did I feel the last time I broke bad news to him? While I may know logically the importance of being forthright, if my last experience was unpleasant, I may very well keep the information to myself.

Dr. Antonio Damasio is a professor of neuroscience at the University of Southern California, where he directs the Brain and Creativity Institute. As a researcher, Damasio has studied the role of emotion in thinking. He shares the fascinating story of a patient he studied, a successful attorney named Elliot who had radical surgery to remove a brain tumor.[1] The surgery required that parts of the brain be removed and connections be severed. These actions affected the part of the brain that processes emotions. The attorney recovered from surgery and returned to normal life with no loss in his intelligence or ability to speak; upon first encounter, there was no indication of any change in him.

When one spent more time with Elliot, however, it became clear that something was not right. He showed no range in emotion and apparently could not experience or understand emotion. Unfortunately, his relationships began to suffer and his marriage ended in divorce.

What also became clear was that Elliot lost the ability to make decisions; even the most trivial decision would stump him. He would get stuck on the simple task of scheduling an appointment. Simple, logical pros and cons meant nothing to him and offered him no help whatsoever. He had no emotional memory or frame of reference to *feel* the consequences of any decision.

As Robert Keith Leavitt is often quoted as saying, "People don't ask for facts in making up their minds. They would rather have one good, soul-satisfying emotion than a dozen facts."

The fact that decision-making is based on emotion has significant implications for individuals and groups working on projects. Consider the troubled project—one that is far over budget and far behind schedule, with no end in sight.

Very strong emotions are in play among the project actors in such a situation. One stakeholder has such a personal commitment that she would not even consider terminating the project. Another team member feels so frustrated over the stalled progress that he wishes management would put an end to the pain. The project manager, seeking to avoid the shame of failure, says publicly that a breakthrough is near while knowing privately that this is wishful thinking. It is strong emotion—and avoidance of addressing the emotion—that keeps many a troubled project going long after everyone knows it is doomed.

Organizations have trouble acknowledging this charged emotional environment. It is far easier to reach a decision on the project based on a logical analysis of the situation, and leave the individuals to handle the emotional fallout. However, the participants would experience far fewer traumas if the organization were to acknowledge and address the emotional aspects in a healthy manner, regardless of the decision made regarding the future of the project.

■ The Moral Brain

To delve further into how emotions affect our decisions and to consider the interplay with morality, let us go back to the year 1848 and meet Phineas Gage.

Gage was the foreman for construction of a railroad line near Cavendish, Vermont. In preparing an explosive charge to excavate rock, he packed the charge with a three-foot long tamping iron. Tamping created a spark that ignited the gunpowder and propelled the iron completely through his head. Remarkably, Gage regained consciousness within a few minutes and could speak. Despite this unfortunate accident and serious injury, Gage soon recovered and within a year returned to work. While his basic mental faculties remained intact, his personality had changed dramatically. Before the accident, Gage was considered an excellent foreman. After the accident, he showed little concern for others and was profane in the extreme. As described by friends and acquaintances, he was "no longer Gage." He lost his job and was eventually featured in a circus act.

The classic case of Phineas Gage provided the first insights into what makes humans social or antisocial, or what we have come to describe as *moral intelligence*. Our understanding of moral intelligence is evolving, but it has been enhanced significantly by intriguing findings in recent years from studies of the brain using functional magnetic resonance imaging (fMRI). Using fMRI, researchers can observe which parts of the brain are active when a person is subjected to a stimulus or situation that has a moral component.

For the fMRI tests, normal adults viewed images of emotionally charged scenes with and without moral content. While certain regions of the brain were active for both types of images, certain distinct areas fired only in response to the images with moral content. Of even greater interest, the activation of these regions occurred very quickly; it was an automatic response. When the same experiment was conducted with a group of individuals with diagnosed antisocial disorders, their moral circuitry did not activate reliably. These fMRI studies have led to the growing understanding that "everyday" morality is essentially an instinctual, gut response.

While humans also reason according to moral values, such as when trying to solve a dilemma, this processing is slower and is performed elsewhere in the brain. With such decision-making, rational and emotional elements of the brain work together in an integrated fashion.[2]

These findings lead us to the key issue of morality. It is one thing to articulate values of right and wrong, but it is another thing altogether to actually *do the right thing*. Anthropological studies have shown that values of morality and interpersonal behavior are surprisingly common across human societies and cultures. "Most of us know right from wrong .... The essential challenge of moral intelligence is not knowing right from wrong but doing versus knowing."[3]

How do we as individuals or organizations "walk the walk"? One way is to make moral decisions personal.

Researchers often use hypothetical moral dilemmas to understand human moral reasoning. These studies lead to the curious result that morality changes dramatically depending on our degree of closeness to others. We tend to be subjective in moral decisions involving people we know and objective with people we do not know.

A classic situation is the trolley dilemma. A runaway trolley is headed for five people who will be killed if no one intervenes. The only way to save them is to throw a switch that will guide the trolley to another track—where it will kill one person instead of five. The dilemma is posed to the subject of the study: kill one person or five? Most people say they would minimize the effects of the tragedy by throwing the switch.

Now the dilemma is changed ever so slightly. Again the trolley is headed for five people, but this time, the observer stands overhead on a footbridge with a bystander, a stranger, who is a larger person. The trolley can be stopped only by pushing the stranger to the track below in front of the trolley, but the stranger will die in the process. Again the dilemma is: kill one person or five?

While the moral mathematics remain the same, in this situation most people would not push the stranger to the track below, and instead would allow the five to be killed. What has changed?

In the first case, the action taken by the observer is impersonal. While human consequences will result, the action is taken on a mechanism. In the second case, the action is *personal*: the observer must force someone close at hand to their death. While strong emotions are involved in both dilemmas, the emotions are different and lead to different moral decisions.

This model has been confirmed by fMRI studies. Similar activity was observed in the brain for moral/impersonal decisions and non-moral decisions, while moral/personal decisions involved a unique area of the brain. In short, the brain demonstrates a highly regimented distinction between moral decisions that are "personal" and those that are "impersonal." We exhibit greater concern for the welfare of those who are close compared with those who are not close, and we are reluctant to cause direct harm to others.[4,5]

These findings suggest that we have brain networks that are specialized for the generation of moral emotions, and these networks are different from those involved in basic emotions. "Moral emotions differ from basic emotions in that they are intrinsically interpersonal."[6]

In their book, *Moral Intelligence*, Doug Lennick and Fred Kiel suggest the following four elements of moral intelligence, which are universal across cultures:[7]

- Integrity
- Responsibility
- Compassion
- Forgiveness.

While emotional intelligence and moral intelligence overlap considerably, there are important differences. Emotions are neutral with respect to values, while moral intelligence embodies beneficial human values. "Emotional skills can be used for good or evil. Moral skills, by definition, are directed toward doing good .... Without a moral anchor, leaders can be charismatic and influential in a profoundly destructive way."[8]

Morality is a significant element of trust. For contemporary projects to be successful, teams need a high level of trust. Team members must be able to access and invoke personal, moral emotions, and to use moral skills to make good decisions. While we are on the job, our neurons are firing with emotions and moral reactions. When we make a direct connection with other individuals on our project team, with stakeholders, and with customers, we are more likely to consider their needs and make project decisions that are beneficial to them.

■ Right Brain/Left Brain Partnership

If the human brain is the most powerful computer in the world, the architecture of the brain can be considered to consist of two coprocessors. For the most part, these coprocessors see the same input data, but they use different programming languages. They share information directly, but they have different processing algorithms. They output data in different languages, and they are both capable of functioning independently.

The left and the right brains have an excellent partnership—a working relationship that hands off tasks that are better suited to the other side. Part of the "programming" of the brain is to determine what type of processing is needed for a given task or situation. While both sides of the brain can be involved in the task at hand, the side that is more suited to the task will take control, and the other side will defer. For example, if the task is to recite the letters of the alphabet, the left brain will control. On the other hand, if the task is to navigate at sea, the right brain will likely control.

Many tasks involve some combination of right-brain and left-brain processing needs, for example, a task that includes both known patterns and ambiguous situations. The processing architecture and the extensive interconnectedness of the brain make it possible for us to simultaneously consider many pieces of information or constraints, each of which may be imperfectly specified and ambiguous.[9]

Consciousness

Consideration of left-brain and right-brain functions inevitably leads to questions about consciousness. It is commonly believed that consciousness resides in the left brain and that the right brain controls unconscious or subconscious thought. This view misses the mark about how these two hemispheres operate.

Generally, we are conscious of thought from one side of the brain at a time. This experience is a result of the brain architecture and its extensive network of interconnections.

Many of us spend the majority of our time involved in left-brain tasks. Therefore, it is reasonable to perceive that the left brain is controlling conscious thought most of the time. But this does not mean that the right brain is "unconscious." It simply means that the activities of the left brain are more immediately accessible.

Metabolic studies have shown that the right hemisphere consumes the same amount of energy as the left, implying that the hemispheres perform the same amount of work. This finding has been confirmed by measurements of the electrical activity on each side of the brain.

Part of what seems to be "unconscious" about the right brain is simply that although we know that it processes information and influences our behavior, we have difficulty verbally explaining its actions and its information. Thus, right-brain information can at times seem difficult to access and understand.

We can take steps to quiet the dominant left brain so we can hear what the right brain has to say. For example, traditional psychological tests such as a Rorschach test and word association are specifically designed to access right-brain processing.

Consider the analogy of an iceberg. The part of the iceberg that is visible above the surface of the water can be likened to what we perceive in conscious thought. The large part of the iceberg below the water surface can be considered unconscious thought. Although this thought is not perceived, it is nonetheless real and active.

■ Learning and Applying: The Two Brains at Work

The right brain excels at learning. By nature, learning new patterns or insights involves encountering information that is different from what is already known. The right brain is called into action to connect the new information to previously known patterns. The left brain can then apply the new knowledge in the form of patterns or rules. The right brain learns the patterns and the left brain applies them reliably.

Different types of knowledge are suited to each brain style. For example, studying the rules of professional golf regarding taking a penalty for a shot out of bounds would go directly to the left brain.

On the other hand, the right brain is much better with knowledge that is complex, visual, or kinesthetic. These types of skills are information-rich and holistic, and they are difficult to explain with words alone. Often the best way to learn such tasks is to watch someone who is skilled and attempt to copy his or her actions.

Learning to hit a golf ball is almost impossible for the left brain to handle, because it is difficult to dissect the complex motions into discrete steps and rules. It is not uncommon for duffers to take lessons from a golf pro and find that their swing actually deteriorates when they consciously think about particular steps using rules and left-brain processing. It is not possible for the step-by-step left-brain style to process all of the many muscle movements and perceptions that go into the rather simple task of hitting a golf ball. The style of learning needed is classically right brain.

■ Do You Use Your Right Brain?

Many believe that there are "right-brain people" and "left-brain people." This distinction is typically used to describe differences in skill, personality, and career preferences. It is true that some people tend to be more skilled in logical rule functions, such as computer programmers. Other people are more comfortable operating in a creative space. However, all people are capable of operating in both domains.

William "Ned" Hermann developed a helpful way to classify dominant brain processing styles. The Hermann Brain Dominance Instrument™ (HBDI™)[10] (see Table 3-2) is a model of the physiology of the brain and the thinking styles an individual prefers.[11] The four styles of brain dominance relate to the four quadrants created from the right and left hemispheres and the front and back halves of the brain. The front, or cerebral, half of the brain is the area where most conscious thought takes place. The back, or limbic, half of the brain controls emotional behavior. While most individuals gravitate to certain preferred or dominant modes of thinking, we generally operate to some extent in all four quadrants.

If you have a hard time thinking of yourself as a right-brain person, simply remember the last time you drove a car.

Assuming that you've been a driver for some time, chances are you don't think that much about driving. People do all sorts of things that occupy their attention while driving: talking on a cell phone, eating, and yelling at kids in the back seat. Some people do quite dangerous activities while driving, such as reading or even knitting. I've seen a photo of someone who was eating a meal with chopsticks while driving!

▪ Table 3-2. HBDI™ Four-Quadrant Model of Thinking Preferences

Cerebral mode	
Left	*Right*
Upper left	*Upper right*
(Rational)	*(Experimental)*
Logical	Visual
Analytical	Conceptual
Mathematical	Imaginative
Factual	Synthesizing
Lower left	*Lower right*
(Ordered)	*(Feeling)*
Controlled	Emotional
Organized	Interpersonal
Detailed	Empathetic
Sequential	Expressive
Left	*Right*
Limbic mode	

While neglecting for a moment whether anyone should do these things, how is it even possible to do anything else while driving? It's because of the right brain.

The right brain can process a huge amount of visual and physical information simultaneously and in real time, and can do so largely without involving the driver's attention. The next time you drive, be thankful for your right brain.

■ Intuition

As with conscious thought, the concept of intuition is rife with misunderstandings. Intuition is also called a "gut feeling" or "sixth sense," and it is definitely a right-brain activity.

While it may be hard to get a grasp on intuition, it is a real phenomenon. The right brain can analyze large amounts of data quickly and make connections among disparate and incomplete sets of information to reach a conclusion almost instantaneously. The whole process can seem somewhat mystical and difficult to understand, especially when considered in comparison to how the left brain works. Therefore, intuition is often discounted, especially in organizations.

This does not mean that intuition is always correct or always useful; it simply means that it can be a powerful tool for individuals and organizations to use.

■ Connection to Personality

Just as individuals may operate more comfortably on one side of the brain or the other, so too do we typically operate more comfortably with certain personality styles.

Personality can be considered a dominant or preferred style of thinking or method of processing information. While the concept of personality has been studied most extensively for individuals, organizations also exhibit personality styles, as explained in the book *Companies Are People Too*, by Sandra Fekete.[12]

One of the most widely recognized systems for classifying personality styles is the Myers-Briggs Type Indicator (MBTI®).[13] The MBTI® classifies personality types in four dimensions, with each dimension having two poles. A given individual may exhibit a style somewhere along the continuum of the two poles. The Myers-Briggs classification is provided in Table 3-3.[14]

To explore personality, let us consider the Myers-Briggs dimension Intuitive/Sensing. This dimension considers the types of information an individual prefers. A Sensing person prefers concrete and precise data, while an Intuitive person is most comfortable with general concepts. Both styles are valuable depending on the context.

Conflict can arise if people with opposite styles work together but fail to appreciate their differences. A Sensing individual will likely get frustrated trying to nail down the specifications for a product in a meeting with an Intuitive person who enjoys talking about

- **Table 3-3. MBTI® Personality Preferences**

Extraversion (E) and Introversion (I) Dimension: Preference for internal or external thought activity
We each have the world of thoughts and feelings inside ourselves and the world of interactions and experiences outside. When we interact with or gain energy from the world outside, we exhibit extraversion. When we reflect on our thoughts or gain energy from self-awareness, we are exhibit introversion.
Sensing (S) and Intuitive (N) Dimension: Preference for facts or concepts
We receive information through the five senses, but we can use the information in two different ways. A Sensing person prefers to process information in a concrete, factual manner, while an Intuitive person prefers to use information to create abstractions.
Thinking (T) and Feeling (F) Dimension: Decisions based on reason or values.
A Thinking person makes decisions based on logic and reason. A Feeling person makes decisions according to a value system, and often incorporates the values of others into the decisions.
Judging (J) and Perceiving (P) Dimension: Preference for planning or flexibility.
People who exhibit the Judging preference prefer order, through lists, schedules, and closure. Those who exhibit the Perceiving preference prefer flexibility and spontaneity.

new ways that the product can benefit a customer. When each person recognizes the value of the different styles and can move into the other style, the team can accomplish dramatic results.

It is fascinating to see that personality styles can be considered right-brain and left-brain styles. This observation applies to all the Myers-Briggs dimensions except the Extravert-Introvert classification, which is an internal versus external orientation. The remaining three dimensions exhibit right- and left-brain characteristics, as shown in Table 3-4. These classifications can give us insights into how we work as individuals as well as how we can work more effectively in groups, including our project teams.

▪ **Table 3-4. Left- and Right-Brain Personality Preferences**

Left Brain	Right Brain
Sensing	Intuitive
Thinking	Feeling
Judging	Perceiving

In considering personality styles, it is important to emphasize that there are no right or wrong styles. Each style has strengths and weaknesses that are situational. We are also not "programmed" like robots into a permanent way of thinking. People can deliberately choose to exercise a non-dominant style or to appreciate another person with a differing style. Such capabilities are crucial to success for project teams.

■ Application to Projects

Now that we understand the fundamentals of brain functioning and thinking and personality styles, what are the implications for project work?

Project work is performed by people, individually and in teams. We can benefit from understanding how people think and what styles lend themselves most readily to particular projects. Furthermore, there is much to be gained by using both sides of the brain as appropriate on project work.

Left-brain techniques are perfect for those projects that involve the application of known approaches with teams of people who are familiar with each other. But what if a project involves new technology, processes, or team members? Relying on a left-brain style here is somewhat like trying to force a square peg in a round hole: it can be done, but the results are not necessarily what everyone wants. It is much better to consider and apply techniques that are appropriate to the need.

The MBTI® Perceiving style is helpful for a project that has a significant component of ambiguity. While it is helpful to have individuals with Perceiving preferences on the team, it is also important to lead the team deliberately into acting more Perceiving. Having a Judging preference on a project that requires experimentation and adaptation will understandably frustrate the team.

Such an approach ties into maturity and emotional intelligence. When a person starts to act in his non-dominant personality type, he will likely feel anxious. If I am a Judging person trying to address ambiguity on a project, and I decide to act more Perceiving, it may very well feel uncomfortable. Here is a situation that calls for growth in maturity, in terms of both personal development and emotional intelligence.

To succeed, I must tolerate the ambiguity as well as see the world from a new perspective. I must be able to master my anxiety as I embark on new goals. I must also accept the inner conflict that may come with new ways of thinking that may challenge my long-held beliefs.

To continue with our exploration into right-brain project management, we need to go to the source of energy for projects and examine what makes people want to work on projects. We need to understand motivation. ▪

■ ENDNOTES

1 Antonio Damasio, *Descartes' Error* (New York: Putnam, 1994), pp. 34–43.

2 David Pacchioli, "The Moral Brain," *Research Penn State Magazine*, Penn State University, October 2, 2006, http://www.rps.psu.edu/indepth/brains-cans1.html. Accessed November 2006.

3 Richard E. Boyatzis, foreword to *Moral Intelligence*, by Doug Lennick and Fred Kiel (Upper Saddle River, NJ: Wharton School Publishing, 2005), pp. xxiii–xxiv.

4 Joshua D. Greene, R. Brian Sommerville, Leigh E. Nystrom, John M. Darley, and Jonathan D. Cohen, "An fMRI Investigation of Emotional Engagement in Moral Judgment," *Science,* Vol. 293, Issue 5537, September 14, 2001, pp. 2105–2108.

5 Joshua Greene and Jonathan Haidt, "How (and Where) Does Moral Judgment Work?" *TRENDS in Cognitive Sciences,* Vol. 6, No. 12, December 2002.

6 Jorge Moll, et al., "The Neural Correlates of Moral Sensitivity: A Functional Magnetic Resonance Imaging Investigation of Basic and Moral Emotions," *The Journal of Neuroscience,* Vol. 22, No. 7, April 1, 2002, pp. 2730–2736.

7 Doug Lennick and Fred Kiel, *Moral Intelligence* (Upper Saddle River, NJ: Wharton School Publishing, 2005), p. 7.

8 Ibid., pp. 9–10.

9 J. L. McClelland, D. E. Rumelhart, and G. E. Hinton, "The Appeal of Parallel Distributed Processing," *Parallel Distributed Processing, Vol. 1: Foundations,* James L. McClelland, David E. Rumelhart, and the PDP Research Group (Cambridge, MA: MIT Press, 1987), pp. 3–4.

10 Hermann Brain Dominance Instrument and HBDI are trademarks of Hermann International.

11 Ned Herrmann, *The Creative Brain* (Lake Lure, NC: Ned Herrmann Group, 1993), pp. 47, 220.

12 Sandra Fekete, *Companies Are People, Too* (Hoboken, NJ: John Wiley & Sons, 2003).

13 Myers-Briggs Type Indicator and MBTI® are registered trademarks of Consulting Psychologists Press, Inc.

14 Lenore Thomson, *Personality Type: An Owner's Manual* (Boston: Shambala Publishing, 1998), pp. 27–55.

CHAPTER 4

■ Motivation:
The Need to Act

■
■
■

A musician must make music, an artist must paint, a poet must write, if he is to be ultimately at peace with himself. What a man can be, he must be.

ABRAHAM MASLOW ■

She uncovered amazing secrets in tiny samples of matter. Her work made possible a form of imaging that enabled us to see what could not previously be seen.

Marie Curie was a pioneering scientist who made major advances in the study of radium and other radioactive materials. Her work with these materials helped form the foundation for imaging and the use of radiation to treat disease—discoveries that transformed diagnostics in medicine and other fields such as engineering. She became the first woman in France to earn a doctorate and the first person to be awarded Nobel Prizes in two different disciplines. These accomplishments are all the more impressive because they came at a time when women were considered a social underclass.

But we are not interested here in studying Marie Curie the scientist. Rather we will consider Marie Curie the human being and what motivated her discoveries.

Marie Curie was driven in her work. She worked long and tireless hours in a laboratory that was cold, dark, and dirty. She was driven to succeed, even using her own money to pursue research objectives. Dedicated to the widespread application of her findings, she did not seek patents on them so that everyone could freely benefit. When World War I broke out, she suspended her research to fund and staff mobile X-ray labs. In that bloody war, her efforts made it possible to avoid many battlefield amputations; for the first time, doctors could visualize internal injuries and bullets lodged in the wounded.

Marie Curie was driven. But she was driven not by money, by fame, or by the search for knowledge for its own sake.

Her compelling drive, and her life's work, was to ease suffering.

Yes, Marie Curie was one of history's great scientists. But she was something more—a great human being, with great empathy and desire to serve others—and this is what made her a great scientist. It was Marie Curie's motivation that animated her work and her greatness.

The subject of motivation is an important one for project management. What motivates people? How can projects become a significant source of motivation for individuals and teams?

■ Is That All There Is?

Do you sometimes struggle with motivation in your job? Do you perhaps feel frustrated with the lack of motivation of those who work for you? If so, you are not alone. Many people in organizations show up and do an adequate job just to receive a paycheck. Some even show an above-average level of commitment but still don't reach their capabilities. This creates a problem because many contemporary projects need a heightened level of personal investment to succeed. But more importantly, if our motivation and personal investment to work are merely adequate, it begs the question, "Is that all there is?"

We are not implying that most people are lazy or slackers. On the contrary, the majority of people are dedicated, hard workers.

A line from the movie *Fargo* captures the point of motivation. Police officer Marge Gunderson, played by Frances McDormand, has just apprehended one of the individuals involved in a bizarre web of crimes, all committed for money. With an almost motherly wisdom (and a priceless dialect), she cuts to the heart of the matter when she tells him, "There's more to life than a little money, ya know. Don'tcha know that?"

As with any group activity, a balance is struck in the workplace. Parties gather together to work, perhaps to engage in projects, largely through economic self-interest. Organizations need people to perform work, and individuals need the income that results from that work.

At least that's how most people view work: it may be a place to punch the clock or a place to do something enjoyable that pays the bills. Many have the attitude, "Give me a decent salary but don't expect too much of me. I'll put in my time, but not my heart."

This is an unfortunate, albeit understandable, arrangement. Workplace employment is a contractual commitment, not a vow of marriage.

But it seems that something is missing.

On the other hand, some people pour themselves into their work, much like Marie Curie. For them work is not a job, but a means of expression, an opportunity to contribute or do something worthwhile. In many cases, these people receive no compensation— it is "volunteer work," a labor of love.

What is the difference between these two scenarios? What is lacking in the first and abundant in the second? What is the source of motivation?

The answer is very important to project management. Where motivation is present, projects often proceed with incredible ease; where motivation is lacking, projects become a chore to be endured. When a group of people *really* wants to accomplish something, they will overcome every obstacle. But if the group is not enthusiastic about the result, any challenge will likely get the best of them.

The late management icon Peter Drucker described all knowledge workers as "volunteers." In our advanced industrial and information marketplace, knowledge workers have many opportunities for work; for the most part, they choose their employers. But Drucker's observation has a much more dramatic meaning.

When we're at work, we can be there in body and mind only, or we can be there in body, mind, and soul. The "soul" part is completely voluntary. We will pour ourselves into endeavors that engage our souls and merely keep time for those that do not.

The subject of motivation is fundamental to project success. To understand motivation, we need to understand people. To grasp where we are today, it is once again helpful to review history.

■ Cogs in the Machine

The Enlightenment and the Scientific Revolution had a profound influence on the organization of work; once again, guidance came from Descartes and Newton. If the natural world could be understood as a machine, its parts disassembled and analyzed, then so too could the workplace. This thinking made possible the establishment of factories and the innovation of the assembly line by Henry Ford.

The Scientific Revolution spread to the organization of work as "scientific management." In this belief system, work activities could be analyzed, rationalized, ordered, and made more efficient. While it is reasonable to approach machines with this attitude, unfortunately it was also applied, in extreme forms, to people.

Workers became cogs in the machine.

The most well-known proponent of scientific management in the early 20th century was Frederick Taylor. Taylor believed in the formal analysis of work directed toward efficiency. In his approach, work should be designed to require no thought on the part of workers—they become units of production. Organization and worker come together only for mutual monetary reward. "In this mechanistic view, organisational actors are not seen as thinking, feeling beings who have an element of choice in how they conduct their daily lives. Taylor's workers are not 'paid to think', they are expected to be reliable, efficient and, most of all predictable."[1]

Some of Taylor's contemporaries applied similar rationalistic and mechanistic styles to administrators and managers. These scientific management thinkers elevated the bureaucratic personality as the only one of value in the workplace. Emotions were not to interfere with organizational life. "Through the creation of rationally defined ways of organizing, expressed in the form of formal structures, hierarchies and rules, it was thought that the method had been found whereby all subjective interferences could be managed 'out' of working life."[2]

This view of work is cynical and ultimately inhuman. While explicit and extreme Taylorism is now gone from the workplace, its more subtle forms still exist. And to a large extent, its adherence to rationality and its avoidance of emotion still dominate.

■ Human Relations

A significant shift away from Taylorism began with an unexpected finding in the 1920s. Elton Mayo, from the University of Pennsylvania, was engaged to perform research funded to demonstrate that better factory illumination would lead to higher productivity. Mayo conducted his study at the Western Electric Hawthorne plant.

When illumination levels at the factory were raised, output increased as expected. Thankfully, Mayo knew how to conduct research, and he also planned controls. These controls led to puzzling results, however. When illumination was lowered, productivity stayed high. When illumination was kept constant, productivity still remained high. Whatever was done with illumination, within reason, productivity increased.

Mayo had stumbled onto two breakthrough findings. The first was the realization that workers became more productive when someone of importance took an interest in what they were doing. Second, in contradiction to the prevailing views of scientific management, workers were shown to be far more complex than mere cogs in the machine.

The Hawthorne studies initiated the human relations school of management, which led to a number of significant developments in the 20th century. By way of introduction to these developments, let us first talk about the needs that humans experience.

■ Maslow's Needs Hierarchy

The social scientist Abraham Maslow tackled a weighty question: what do we want in life?

The answers to this existential question cover the landscape, but they are largely contextual to the life of each individual. Maslow categorized the answers according to needs in hierarchical levels. Our needs, our interests, are based on what we already have. As we meet more basic needs, we develop new needs and desires that are as yet unsatisfied. Maslow's needs hierarchy (summarized in Figure 4-1) progresses from most basic to most advanced.

Maslow's characterization makes a lot of sense; it's hard to think about reaching your potential when you suffer from chronic hunger and poverty. On the other hand, once you have a job that pays well,

▪ Figure 4-1. Maslow's Needs Hierarchy

Self-transcendence; pursuit of knowledge, appreciation of aesthetics, morality; embracing reality

Self-actualization: achieving fulfillment

Esteem and recognition: from self and others

Love: relationships, friendships, community

Security: shelter, comfort, freedom from harm

Physiology: air, water, food

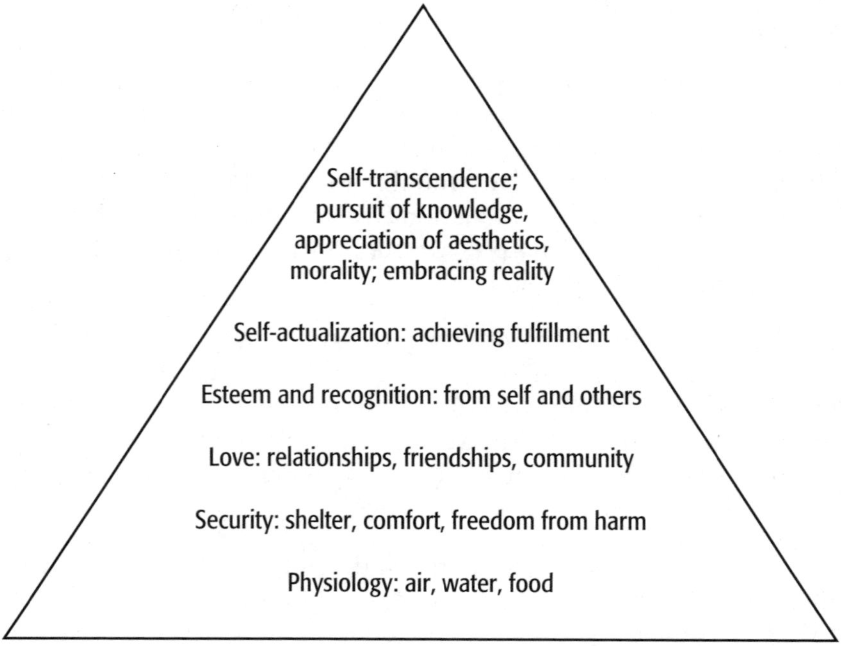

a nice home, and a healthy family, the mind necessarily turns to other interests.

The majority of people we encounter in industrialized countries have generally fulfilled the lower three levels of Maslow's hierarchy. While we may occasionally struggle with issues of security or love, we generally focus on fulfillment of the needs for recognition, esteem, self-actualization, knowledge, understanding, and aesthetics.

These needs levels are a natural if not instinctive part of the human experience. Maslow's hierarchy recognizes the natural progression of individuals, groups, and humanity from basic survival to bonding to creation and lasting contribution.

While needs in the lower two levels are easy to identify—"I'm thirsty" or "I'm exposed to the elements"—needs in the higher levels can seem a bit more elusive and ambiguous. An individual may experience an unspecified "itch" without really knowing where to scratch. Various attempts to find the right scratch can be helpful, downright destructive, or merely palliative.

■ Hidden Motivation

Maslow's hierarchy provides a helpful, high-level framework for human motivation, but there is more to be examined.

Studies by Richard Maddock and Richard Fulton have led to a model of motivation based on powerful silent motives. They categorize the mind into four areas (as shown in Table 4-1), according to thoughts that are apparent to others and those that are apparent only to ourselves. Maddock and Fulton suggest that the most powerful motivators are in emotions and passions that are not necessarily visible to others and may not even be readily accessible to ourselves.[3] These motivators within "The Silent Side" can serve as powerful, if not readily perceived, forces that animate our emotions, decisions, and actions. In other words, these motives reside in the right brain.

One of the strongest sources of motivation is what Maddock and Fulton call "spiritual survival." Rather than refer to a religion, "spir-

▪ **Table 4-1. Categorization of Thoughts–Hidden Motivators**

	Motivations You Can See	*Motivations You Can't See*
Motivations Others Can See	OPEN AREA Logic Explanations Shared Reality	BLIND AREA Rationalizations Excuses Justifications
Motivations Others Can't See	SECRET AREA Secrets	SILENT AREA Motives Emotions Passion

itual survival … denotes a striving for something beyond physical existence; values and beliefs that transcend the mortal world and live on after us. Spiritual survival is what people are passionate about!"[4]

Examples of spiritual survival motives cover the spectrum. Maddock and Fulton cite Paul Fleischman's ten elements of spiritual survival (see Table 4-2) as critical sources of passion for people.[5]

Passions can include faith, sports, world peace, a job, a hobby, or just about any human endeavor. These passions can be in control and healthy, or they can become out-of-control, unhealthy addictions.

One of the most accessible ways to see spiritual survival motives in action is to consider the plot and character development in any number of movies or books. The main character typically suffers some complication that tests her character and the response reveals what is important to her.

Literary artists understand that the specific events in plot and character development are metaphors for many larger issues that we encounter in life—good versus evil, for example—and these stories almost always involve some element of spiritual survival. *Star Wars* is not only about good conquering evil but also about the conquest of internal doubts. Project work can engage similar metaphorical stories, although perhaps not as dramatically.

These challenges in essence represent turning points that call on individuals to demonstrate true character. We must caution that

▪ **Table 4-2. Fleischman's Elements of Spiritual Survival**

Element	Description
Witness significance	Belief in a higher power that listens, sees, and understands
Order	Belief in the basic order of our world
Holism	Affirmation and acceptance of the person
Mission	A need for importance; to feel like one's life and work have purpose
Membership	To be part of a larger network that affirms and accepts a person and his or her beliefs
Release	Release of new power
Love	Love, bonding, and marriage, as well as patriotism
Sacrifice	The ability to give of oneself
Meaningful death	The goal of any spiritual program
Inner peace	Making the transition from self-centeredness and worry to peace

this type of motivation absolutely cannot be artificial and manipulative: it must concern a genuine and important need.

■ Theory X, Theory Y

In the management profession, the understanding of motivation, and its influence on management style, underwent profound changes with the advent of the human relations era. These changes are most easily appreciated through the work of Douglas MacGregor.

For the sake of argument, let's start with the premise that people don't really want to work; they'd rather be doing something else. If I am a manager, how do I accomplish organizational objectives with unmotivated workers? The traditional answer to this question is to coerce them, that is, to threaten punishment for failure to perform.

Let's face it: human beings can be unpredictable and difficult to motivate. As a manager, you may be sorely tempted to throw your weight around and start barking orders. The military has had success with this approach for thousands of years. The boot camp style of motivation works and is necessary because few people would willingly run onto the battlefield and dodge bullets.

A softer version of this approach is still in play in the workplace. Instead of coercion, bribery is used, in the form of commissions and bonuses. While there is nothing wrong with these tactics, again the implicit assumption is that people don't really want to work and must be "persuaded" to do so.

Management researcher Douglas MacGregor named this approach to management "Theory X." This theory is based on the belief that people do not want to work, and the way to motivate them is therefore through coercion or manipulation. You have no doubt seen many examples of Theory X at work in organizations.

In contrast, MacGregor identified "Theory Y" management. According to this theory, humans do in fact want to work and are looking for ways to match their interests with work. The manager need not tease motivation from workers but must instead create and sustain an environment that channels the motivation that is already present but dormant.

Theory Y neatly maps into Maslow's hierarchy and its recognition that people seek through work an outlet to satisfy their higher level needs. Work can become something much more than maintaining income for food, shelter, and transportation.

Think again about Marie Curie and her life's work. No one had to persuade or cajole her into investing long hours in the lab. The energy for her effort sprang from internal motivation.

■ Theory Z

It may seem that, in the extreme, Theory Y management can become laissez-faire and free form, making it unlikely that project objectives will be achieved. Where Theory X and Theory Y apply only to the supervisor, another approach places responsibilities on both the supervisor and the workers. William Ouchi of UCLA called this approach "Theory Z."

For the supervisor, the style of Theory Z is similar to the style of Theory Y. But Theory Z also has as a premise that workers are committed to the organization and to its objectives. Workers are provided goals and objectives and given limitations within which they can exercise authority. Theory Z is a practical way to strike the balance between the need for structure and the need for creativity on a project. It recognizes the partnership that must be forged between supervisors and workers for effective work to be accomplished.

■ Herzberg's Motivation Theory

What elements in the work environment motivate or demotivate people? Frederick Herzberg studied the subject with an eye toward differentiating factors that were beneficial to motivation from those that were detrimental. But his findings need to be considered in the context of Theory X/Theory Y and Maslow's needs hierarchy.

Herzberg found that various environmental factors will provide only weak motivation when they are present, but their lack can produce strong dissatisfaction with a job. Salary is one of these environmental factors: while a poor salary can be a demotivator, a wonderful salary does little to promote motivation. Other environmental factors include the health of relationships on the job.

Herzberg discovered that what really motivates people are factors intrinsic to the work: whether the work is interesting and rewarding, and whether recognition accompanies accomplishment.

In sum, if the intrinsic substance of work is lacking, people naturally lose interest and become more sensitive to environmental demotivators. If the intrinsic substance is enticing, environmental demotivators become less important. If I find my work rewarding in and of itself, a low salary may not bother me; if the work is not rewarding, it is easy for me to get irritated by a low salary.

Marie Curie could not only tolerate but ignore poor environmental factors because her work was so intensely rewarding in and of itself. The same can be said for the millions of people who volunteer their time to worthwhile causes.

■ Working in Groups

Whatever the project, whatever the team, individuals come together with differing, but hopefully complementary, needs and motivations.

Anyone who has been around organizational projects knows well that motivations often conflict. The customer wants the most product for the least expenditure. The performing organization wants the most income for the least work. The project manager wants to make the whole experience simple and predictable.

If a project is carried out adequately, the collective group's motivation becomes the least common denominator of their individual motivations. In many respects, the least common denominator approach is an adaptive and maintenance strategy, and that's not a bad thing. However, once again, it is worth asking, "Is that all there is?"

This is where leadership is needed. A primary job of a leader is to call upon the motivation of the team—to help the team move beyond the least common denominator to working on a project because it is important to do so. It takes leadership to summon—in the individuals and the group—those elements of passion that are most relevant and important.

■ Motivation Comes from Emotion

Motivation in the workplace has generally been viewed in rational terms, as if it can only be experienced according to calculated exchanges. Such considerations fail to recognize the essential need for emotion, which is the kind of enticement needed in Drucker's volunteer workforce.

Motivation is strongly related to investment in work. Three levels of personal investment, in increasing order, are: physical, cognitive, and emotional. At the physical level, a worker is a "warm body," there essentially for labor only. The cognitive level involves an investment of thinking. But at the emotional level, people become immersed in their work effortlessly.

This emotional investment is evident not only in an individual's personal devotion to work, but just as much in the quality of his or her relationships in the workplace. Emotional investment is marked by trust, care for others, and an open-ended commitment. "Strong motivation and psychological involvement are not possible without an emotional connection to the work or work context."[6]

Consider the intersection of the findings of Maslow, MacGregor, Maddock, Fulton, and Herzberg. Motivation is present in abundance when there is a rich purpose to work; managing such work is freed from persuasion and is redirected to facilitation and clearing the environment of obstacles.

The job of management becomes to create and facilitate energy that comes naturally. This energy springs from emotion, and it emanates from the right brain!

■ It's Contagious

Emotion is much more than the touchy-feely, Kumbaya sort. Emotion can run the spectrum of experiences. In fact, one of the most emotional workplaces is one where all-out aggression is rewarded: the hockey rink.

The National Hockey League (NHL) missed the entire 2004–2005 season because of a player strike. At the start of the 2005–2006 season, a ceremony was held to mark a unique addition to the Hockey Hall of Fame in Toronto: a green hard hat. We pick up the story back in 2003.

At the start of the 2003–2004 hockey season, the Calgary Flames were not expected to have a good season, having finished last in their division the previous year. Center Craig Conroy innocently began a ritual to recognize the play of a hard-working teammate after every game. The Saddledome arena where they played had undergone renovation, and Conroy found an abandoned hard hat. The hard hat embodied his ideals for the recognition of someone who played hard-checking, grind-it-out hockey: a "laborer" on the ice.

The dirty, battered hard hat soon became a coveted prize among the Flames players, and their level of play improved. The Flames made an improbable run into the playoffs, winning their division quarterfinals, semifinals, and finals. They progressed to the championship series for the coveted Stanley Cup, but lost in game seven to Tampa Bay. The green hard hat was credited by many with the Flames' unlikely success.

Such is the case with emotional investment, particularly emotional investment by a group. The phenomenon of emotional contagion is real. Team members "catch" emotions from one another. Emotions can be a force for either constructive or destructive purposes.

One of the key elements in the evolution of a group from a collection of independent individuals to a cohesive team is that members share strong emotional experiences. It is critical that, just as with the green hard hat, such experiences be genuine and not forced by the manager.

■ The Dark Side

There is an unfortunate dark side to unbridled motivation. It can lead to a life that is far out of balance, causing issues to arise in other areas of life. It can also be used for manipulation.

Individuals and groups that have discovered the energy of a driven purpose often encounter difficulty in relationships. This challenge is not unexpected: if one is "married" to work, it is understandable that a spouse will feel neglected. An addiction crowds out all other healthy pursuits.

It is not uncommon for those on high-performance teams to experience a higher rate of divorce and family problems. Other areas of life, such as health and finances, can likewise suffer.

While there is something noble about a life consumed toward a singular purpose, it can have an unattractive downside. In the case of Marie Curie, as well as her husband, prolonged exposure to high levels of radiation caused serious health problems.

One must maintain perspective and balance in the pursuit of the noble cause. Thankfully, the right brain can help out here.

The dark side of deep motivation has another pitfall: for those who lack integrity, it can be used to manipulate.

Consider a project sponsor who serves to gain financial reward or a promotion from the successful completion of an aggressive project. He sees an enormous opportunity for a personal windfall if the project team can pull off a miraculous result, but knows that conventional persuasion will not motivate the team. Needing driven motivation for the payoff, the sponsor cynically stimulates an enriching "spiritual" purpose to the work. But this purpose becomes the means, not the end.

This approach is at its core manipulative. Inevitably, situations will occur that will expose the ruse to the team, and its members will become cynical and bitter over being used.

In Chapter 2, we noted that higher stages of development bring growth in our morality or moral compass. With respect to right-brain project management, the most relevant aspect of this growth in moral maturity relates to morality in relationships on the job. Growth in maturity necessarily leads us to turn away from manipulation of others as being morally wrong.

■ Implications for Projects

The successful completion of a project depends on the motivation of the team. When the project is complex and aggressive, an even higher level of motivation is needed for the project to meet objectives. It is a significant challenge for a leader to articulate the purpose in a compelling way that evokes passion in the team members for the project.

But this is exactly what is needed for the project to succeed—a purpose that is compelling enough to call team members to stretch their limits. This situation requires change, and change requires leadership. ▪

■ ENDNOTES

1 Sharon Bolton, *Emotion Management in the Workplace* (New York: Palgrave Macmillan, 2005), p. 17.

2 Ibid., p. 18.

3 Richard C. Maddock and Richard L. Fulton, *Motivation, Emotions and Leadership: The Silent Side of Management* (Westport, CT: Greenwood Publishing, 1998), p. 20.

4 Ibid., p. 26.

5 Ibid., p. 28.

6 Blake E. Ashforth and Ronald H. Humphrey, "Emotion in the Workplace: A Reappraisal," *Human Relations,* Vol. 48, No. 2, 1995, p. 110.

CHAPTER 5

■ Projects Create Change, and Change Needs Leadership

■
■
■

Change is inevitable—except from a vending machine.

ROBERT C. GALLAGHER ■

A familiar theme in movies is time travel and the many complications it presents to the characters. A favorite involves Michael J. Fox as Marty McFly in *Back to the Future*, and his travels from 1985 to 1955. Playing guitar on stage in the past, he performs the "duck walk" à la Chuck Berry, for an audience who has never seen it before. Along the way, he throws in some equally foreign moves from Pete Townsend, Jimi Hendrix, Eddie Van Halen, and Angus Young. For his character, these moves are comfortable and familiar; for his audience, they are out of place and incomprehensible. Seeing their stunned reaction, Marty tells the audience, "I guess you guys aren't ready for that yet. But your kids are gonna love it."

A project brings about change.

It would be easy to change if we could peer into the future and see the results of the change. If we could experience time travel, we could comfortably experience the change without having to endure its attendant risks and trauma. We could jump straight to the robust Service Pack 2 without trudging through the bugs and crashes of the alpha and beta versions of our product.

If a project creates change, it is worthwhile to look at project management from a *change management* perspective. Such a perspective is valuable because it recognizes and appreciates the challenges associated with change for individuals and organizations.

In contemporary organizations, change is expected if not demanded by management and, more importantly, by the marketplace. We must become comfortable with—indeed, embrace—change. Because change can be chaotic and difficult, however, we need leadership to successfully initiate and navigate the change.

The process of change is very much a right-brain activity. Successful execution of a project, and the changes associated with it, depends on effective use of right-brain processing. Change is accomplished through the right brain in large part because it involves emotions, and because of the need to develop new patterns.

■ Projects Are Agents of Change

A project is defined as a unique endeavor that consumes resources to bring about a particular product. If we look through this definition, what is apparent is that projects bring about change.

"Project management ... provides business with a vehicle to implement change. Therefore, to adapt to changing business and environmental conditions, organizations require their project managers to lead strategic initiatives or projects."[1]

The effort put forth on a project by the project team is a change in itself. When trying to understand the concept of a project, we often differentiate the concept from *operations*, or activities that are regular and repeatable. A project therefore represents a change from the regular operations engaged in by team members, and furthermore, *this* project represents a change from all other projects.

What the project produces is also a change for the customer or user of the product. The outcome of a project may be a new product or process, and both represent changes from the past.

Those who are well attuned to the project environment also recognize that a project actually changes the organization: the organization is different for having executed the project. If inclined to do so, the organization can deliberately capture and understand what has changed. This is often done in a *lessons learned* process undertaken at the conclusion of a project. Other organizations may form a *community of practice* of their project managers to share best practices throughout the organization.

▪ Understanding Change

What elements are involved in the process of change?

Kurt Lewin, one of the first social researchers to study the change process in people, identified change as a transition through the states of "unfreezing, changing and refreezing."

If we consider that an individual is in some existing steady state or status quo, to initiate the change process, the individual must "unfreeze" this initial state. The next stage, or the "change" stage, is one that is dynamic and temporary—it is the stage in which we make the change. The "refreezing" state is the new steady state.

Upon closer examination, we can see that the change process, particularly the unfreezing stage, is dependent upon a *need* or *desire* to change. Why change unless the change offers some benefit? The change process is predicated on the recognition of a problem or dissonance in the current situation. There is also a recognition that the organization will be better as a result of the change.

In conjunction with this recognition, it is necessary to clearly identify the end result of the change. The organization identifies a *vision* or the representation of what it will become as a result of the change. The vision should be compelling enough so that those involved will overcome inertia and invest the effort needed to accomplish the change. Furthermore, the vision must be held in common in the organization or the various team members will pull in different directions depending on their own interpretations of the vision.

The revised model for change, depicted in Figure 5-1, addresses the steps involved in change. But we must look deeper to address the issues involved in *motivating* the change.

■ **Figure 5-1. Revised Model for Change**

■ Motivation: Internal or External

Why do people and organizations commit to change? While the specific reasons are numerous, the motivation can be boiled down to one dimension: internal or external. Internal motivation comes about through a decision to change based on the merits of the change. The external environment can also stimulate us to change; in this case, the decision process is more complicated. Humans often resist external change, at least until the motivation is internalized based on the perceived benefits of the change.

Change can become attractive to an individual or team when a transition is made from external motivation to internal motivation, or in other words, when the individual or team becomes willing to change. Without the internalization, a participant may either grudgingly go along with the change or openly resist it. Either scenario will impede the level of performance needed for a successful project.

What we are describing here is *alignment*—the congruence of the personal goals of individual team members with the collective goals of the group and with the vision. Alignment is both agreement with and commitment to the vision.

To achieve alignment, it is critical that project members understand and agree on the "why" of the project. This issue must go deeper than factual uses for the product or the casual, "Because the client needs it." Alignment is facilitated when we understand the reasons why this project is linked to the core spiritual survival motives of both the customer and the project organization.

■ Emotion: The Link from External to Internal Motivation

The key ingredient that makes an external motivation become an internal motivation is *emotion*. If our emotions concur with the change, we can muster the energy needed to accomplish the change. If our emotions resist the change, the change will be difficult if not impossible to accomplish.

I remember hearing about a cardiologist who expressed frustration over how to motivate his patients at risk for heart disease to change their lifestyles. He could talk until the cows came home about the merits of exercise and a healthy diet, but most of his patients simply nodded and continued to lead unhealthy lifestyles. However, if a patient had a heart attack and lived, he or she very often would make dramatic improvements in lifestyle. In the words of the cardiologist, the patient would suddenly become "teachable." When external motivation falls on deaf ears, sometimes it takes a crisis for internal motivation to come about.

No one would wish a heart attack on an individual, or the equivalent for an organization. But how do we go about making the transition from external motivation to internal motivation?

The answer involves leadership.

■ Leadership

The subjects of organizational change and leadership are inextricably connected. It is practically a given that change takes place in an organization only when leadership is exercised. Good leadership leads to healthy change while ineffective leadership produces mediocre results.

If we incorporate motivation into our model of change, and recast the steps to incorporate the role of leadership, the change process now consists of five stages:

1. Identify the need or recognize the problem.
2. Identify the vision.
3. Establish alignment.
4. Implement the change.
5. Make the change systematic.

The first three stages incorporate the "unfreezing" stage of Lewin's model. To unfreeze, we need to identify a need or motivation to unfreeze, identify where we will freeze next, and, as a group, agree upon the next freeze state.

It is quite common in organizations that a team leader or supervisor will initiate recognition of the need and establishment of a vision. From the perspective of individual team members, efforts by the team leader to promote change may be considered an external change and they may be resisted. This situation can make the leader's role more challenging. Only if everyone involved understands the "why" of the project can the deeper motivation that drives the need for the project be engaged.

■ What's the Problem?

In many cases, the problem is obvious and solving it is important to the group. In these matters, leadership is straightforward, if not easy. However, often the problem or need is not obvious, and members of an organization may find it difficult to see a reason to change. When this is the situation, leadership can be challenging.

Companies that experience success with a product or service often experience a common problem: their success fosters complacency, and complacency sets up their failure. In today's business environment, it is critical for organizations to continually change, adapt, and improve. When a company experiences success, it can be tempting to stick with the formula that brought about the success.

Attempts to lead change at such organizations are typically met with much resistance: if it ain't broke, why fix it? Meanwhile, the market and competition change, and what was once profitable can soon fall out of favor.

A particularly tough situation that cries out for leadership is the serious problem that no one wants to address. Perhaps the most common example of this is the project that is publicly portrayed as being on track while in reality it is in trouble. This denial of reality is emotional.[2] What is needed is for someone to take leadership— to publicly state what everyone avoids admitting, but in a way that prompts a shift to healthier emotions. Only then can a resolution be crafted to repair the trouble or, if necessary, to terminate the project.

To a large extent, the ability to recognize and admit to problems is a function of an organization's culture. An organization that values an honest understanding of itself and the environment and is comfortable with adaptation will be much more proficient at healthy change than one that suppresses such examination. This is one of the ways that an organization, much like an individual, can improve project management through development and maturity.

■ Vision and Alignment

A vision is a picture or description of where we would like an organization to be at some time in the future. It is a state that describes the organization after a change; it is the end point of the project. Without a clear vision, we do not know where to go; without consensus on the vision or alignment, team members may go in different directions according to their individual visions.

Therefore, a key aspect of leadership is establishment of the vision, which includes ensuring that all the relevant people agree with the vision.

Many common problems on projects, such as scope management, are symptoms of communication problems and the challenges of crafting a shared vision. It is worthwhile for a project team to invest time at the initiation of a project to be clear about the vision, and to continually be reminded of the vision throughout the project.

How do we go about identifying a vision? The answer resides in the right brain.

As we have discussed, the right brain is suited for recognizing patterns where patterns are not known. This will be the situation for any change of significance, including the development of an important new vision for an organization.

For example, an automobile manufacturer establishes a strategy to introduce a line of hybrid vehicles over a five-year period. This strategy will be implemented through a portfolio of related projects that together achieve the vision. While some similarities to previous model introductions are apparent, the development and sales of a hybrid present significantly new and unique issues that are not explained by prior practices. Necessarily, the company team members must apply right-brain techniques to develop new patterns to lead the company to its vision.

■ Change for the Better?

In the early 1960s, Bob Dylan was the leading artist in folk music. He had an acoustic sound with social consciousness, and for several years he was revered almost as a god. Perhaps weary of his status, or wanting to grow as an artist, in 1965 at the Newport Folk Festival, he shocked the audience when he appeared with an electric guitar. The festival had never before permitted electric instruments, and fellow musician Pete Seeger attempted to attack the electrical generator with an ax.

Many folk purists came to hate the new Dylan. In one 1966 performance, amid catcalls, a member of the audience yelled, "Judas!"

Dylan no doubt lost some of his folk-purist fans when he plugged in. But he also expanded his audience significantly with listeners who valued music with a message that was delivered with a rock sound—a market that would become substantial.

Change often challenges the status quo, and the status quo may fight back. Significant risks are involved in upsetting what already works; on the other hand, significant risks may also be involved with staying the same. It can be confusing, challenging, and anxiety-producing to determine a direction.

Does the idea of change elicit positive or negative emotions? Do we embrace the change, or resist it? Is it change for the better?

Wherever human beings are involved, the answer to such questions is often unpredictable and complex. Take any two people at random, give them the same choices, and they will reach likely reach opposite decisions. It is enough to make a manager run screaming from the office.

Effective leadership enhances the likelihood of achieving agreement about change, although the outcome may always be somewhat unpredictable. The central issue is what should change and what should remain constant. In their book, *Built to Last*, James Collins and Jerry Porras observe that companies that handle ongoing change well have made a set of unchanging core values part of their culture, but allow change for everything else about the company. This approach provides the proper balance between constancy and change.[3] The strategy is to preserve the organization's core purpose and values while stimulating change in cultural and operating practices as well as specific strategies and goals.

Consider the electronics giant Sony. The company's core purpose is: "To experience the sheer joy of innovation and the application of technology for the benefit and pleasure of the general public."[4] Sony started as a small company and its first product was a rice cooker. It has since grown into a powerhouse by continually changing and offering the market outstanding products, all in keeping with the company's core purpose.

In a similar way within an organization, employees can more readily adapt to change if consistent core principles create an environment of trust and concern for the staff.

■ Leadership and Emotions

If the left brain follows rules and procedures, a change to the rules will be processed first through the right brain.

Recall that the right brain assesses new situations and compares them with previously known patterns. In other words, the right brain *makes sense* of the new or changing environment.

The process of making sense of the environment involves accepting or rejecting the new situation according to the emotions associated with it, which is decidedly a right-brain activity. When the emotions associated with the change "make sense" and are agreeable, we can more effectively embrace or work with the change; conversely, negative emotions associated with the change tempt us to dig in our heels and avoid the change.

When we talk about recognizing a problem, crafting a vision, and developing alignment, the key element to address is the emotions of those involved. While a leader cannot manipulate the emotions of others, he or she can do much to create a positive environment.

The first step in a healthy interaction is simply to recognize that the people involved are going to have emotions and to allow those emotions to occur. It is a mistake to deny emotions or smooth them over, particularly for any change that may have negative repercussions or require significant adjustment. People are much more likely to come around to a constructive orientation if they are allowed to voice their objections and concerns.

If a company must issue layoffs because of a recession, for example, a tempting but faulty approach is to hand out pink slips and point to the door. A more effective approach is to deal directly with the various reactions—grief, anger, and anxiety—and then help people find new jobs.

The second step in a healthy interaction is to frame the positive benefits of achieving the vision. Doing this enables the team members to experience the positive emotions that will come with achieving the vision. Team members will often take emotional cues from the leader and from peers.

The third step in a healthy interaction is to emphasize how the change reflects the core, unchanging values of the organization. In the midst of change, it is important to highlight what will *not* change, to enable people to hold onto a sense of continuity while experiencing uncertainty.

In project work, a critical part of leadership is to highlight the core values that drive the project. Core values are deeply connected to emotions, which provide the energy to fuel project work.

NAVIGATING CHANGE

Bryan Webber

We cannot separate the consideration of people from project planning. When we deliberately plan for and address the needs and interests of the people involved, our projects have a much better prognosis for success.

My perspective comes from helping teams progress through change. In some cases, the change was not welcome. But I have come to believe that when a project is consciously structured to respect the emotions that the team will experience, even difficult change projects can be navigated successfully. This planning includes the specific allocation of budget for dealing with the distasteful "stuff" that comes with challenging change. You could call this budget item, "People Care."

This "stuff" includes the negative reactions that people have toward change; project leaders and sponsors often don't want to recognize or address these reactions. Dealing with the people stuff is an unavoidable, if not necessary, part of the project.

For example, one project I was heavily involved in dealt with upgrading the maintenance operations of a world-class paper mill to a computer-based system. Not only had the maintenance tradesmen always relied on paper-based methods for their procedures and communications, but many of them had never even operated a computer. This project was not just a technology upgrade; it was a major change in the lives of workers. When we approach a project with that perspective, we are able to empathize with the experiences of those affected by the change. As the tradesmen began to trust that the project leadership was concerned about their needs, they became more receptive to the change.

A balance needs to be struck between allowing people to be wherever they are in the change process and keeping focus on the vision. A significant part of facilitating change is helping people identify personally with the future state that the vision identifies. When this occurs, they can more easily let go of their resistance to the change. On unwelcome change projects, the team often does not trust in the vision. Group dynamics are such that various rumors and myths will get started—this is one way that people fight change. In such situations, it is important to perform "myth busting."

In one of my significant change projects, Weyerhaeuser Company conducted a hostile takeover of Willamette Industries. My responsibility was to help Willamette employees work through the takeover; we hoped they would choose to stay with Weyerhaeuser, but they could choose to leave as well. It was a challenging environment because the workers had organized a grassroots campaign to fight the takeover. Once we got onsite with our "People Care" approach, which demonstrated our intent to respect the needs, emotions, and experiences of the Willamette staff, we did not lose any employees during the tumultuous first three months of the takeover.

Anyone in a leadership position for a change process must realize that the impact of the change is just as significant for the leaders as it is for the workers. There is no textbook to follow; the process is complex, and navigating it effectively requires an organic and dynamic approach that is experimental.

Intuition and creativity are two very important ingredients in project work, especially when change is involved. The two domains that have dominated my career, IT and change projects, both have a high degree of ambiguity in the early stages. It is challenging to organize enough space in a project to allow intuition and creativity to operate to overcome the ambiguity. But I have seen time and again that when team members are allowed to apply creative solutions, their investment in a project rises dramatically.

Navigating change requires flexibility, not only for the solutions that come from the change, but also to proceed through the change process when both the destination and the path are ambiguous. Every individual and every group has to find their own way through this process; they need the freedom to find that path, but within a structure. It is a paradoxical process, and one that can occur only when the leader lets go and allows it to happen.

Bryan Webber *teaches in the Faculty of Management at Malaspina University-College in Nanaimo, British Columbia, Canada. He has worked for a number of years in industry on information technology and organizational change projects in the forestry business, most recently for Weyerhaeuser Company.*

■ Wanted: Skilled Leader with Emotional Intelligence

Research demonstrates that individuals with emotional intelligence (EI) skills make better leaders. Executives who scored higher on standard EI tests achieved better business outcomes and were rated as better managers by subordinates and superiors than peers with lower EI scores. Studies have also found that EI skill is a more reliable predictor of effective leadership than traditional personality and cognitive (IQ) tests.[5, 6]

The research should not be construed to suggest that the only skill a leader needs is emotional intelligence. Experience has shown that to reach a leadership position, an individual must generally demonstrate a high level of intelligence; once the individual is in that position, however, such measures do not predict relative performance as well as emotional intelligence measures do.[7] In other words, cognitive intelligence is the price of admission to a leadership position, but emotional intelligence most accurately matches performance once in that position.

These findings are not surprising. The most important elements of leadership are "soft," or people, skills. Leaders who work well with people will be more effective at leading groups through change and at leading project teams to successful outcomes.

■ Making Change Systematic

It is a tenet of contemporary work that change is a constant component of the marketplace. Industries and markets are in a continual state of upheaval. It is easy to see how workers can get fatigued and jaded as they deal with the high rate of change in the workplace. These marketplace realities are regularly impressed upon projects, with demands for aggressive scope, schedule, and resource outcomes.

Three strategies can be helpful in adapting to this contemporary reality; all three inherently rely on the right brain.

The first strategy is to accept, and even embrace, the reality of change. This strategy represents a fundamental shift in attitude, as well as the establishment of a certain sense of maturity and confidence, for both individuals and organizations. As we grow in personal maturity, we become better equipped to accept the ambiguity and internal challenges associated with change. Much as a chameleon can be at home in almost any environment, individuals and organizations thrive if they are agile and flexible in the changing marketplace.

The second strategy is to become adept at knowing what to change and what to keep constant. Again, we note that successful organizations have a set of timeless core values, which, for example, reflect a dedication to their customers and employees. While these values will be tenaciously held, everything else about the company is critically studied for change. Navigating this contrast keeps these companies both nimble and dependable.

The third strategy supports the other two: expertise with right-brain operation of an organization and with integrating right- and left-brain approaches.

If the left brain comfortably applies known patterns and rules, then the right brain is absolutely critical for thriving in a marketplace that demands change. Individuals and organizations need the ability to read the environment with an eye to discovering and creating new patterns. As new patterns are recognized, they can be converted into rules that the left brain can apply, for as long as those rules are helpful; understandably, it may not be for long in a world defined by change. The right brain/left brain partnership enables both individuals and organizations to thrive when the world is dynamic.

■ Distributed Leadership

The Orpheus Chamber Orchestra, based in New York, has recorded nearly 70 albums, performs at Carnegie Hall, and has been awarded two Grammys. The orchestra has performed with great artists such as Yo-Yo Ma, Isaac Stern, and Itzhak Perlman.

Orpheus is unique because it has no conductor.

Consider the organizing principle behind this uncommon group. "Orpheus is a self-governing organization. Central to its distinctive personality, is its unique practice of sharing and rotating leadership roles."[8]

Orpheus has become a role model for sharing leadership in organizations. The "Orpheus Process" has been implemented by major business schools and corporations, and Orpheus offers a number of leadership seminars.

In a performance industry known for its prima donnas and idiosyncratic personalities, how can a conductor-less orchestra succeed? As Orpheus has proven, shared responsibility and leadership promote ownership and empowerment.

We must be clear at this point about what we mean by leadership. Forget for a moment the common image of a leader as a singular charismatic individual who wisely knows the right direction through change and has the perfect combination of interpersonal skills to persuade others to follow. While such people may be worth their weight in gold, they are rare; what's more, having them doesn't really address what the organization needs.

Our culture places too much importance on individual leaders, wanting them to be omniscient and clairvoyant superheroes.[9] There is a growing realization that this expectation is not realistic, and furthermore, is not best for the organization.

What is far more valuable is to have an organization that has the skills and motivation to lead itself through change to worthy destinations. In other words, it is better to have a number of individuals throughout the organization who exercise leadership in various ways. This is why Theory Z hits the mark more effectively than Theory Y. The development of an organization made up of many individuals who are comfortable with leading is largely dependent on the culture of the group and the signals people receive when they exercise leadership.

The concepts of distributed leadership and self-organization run counter to Descartes' prevailing view. If the organization behaves like a machine, necessarily there must be someone who designs, operates, and maintains the machine; a machine cannot self-organize. This worldview excludes any effort at leadership by the cogs in the machine: the cogs are incapable of changing the machine, and therefore are incapable of leadership. In the contemporary project, such a worldview is counterproductive. Success with a complex and aggressive project demands the creativity, motivation, and leadership of many, not just the project manager.

In the project management short courses I teach, I talk about the need for team members to step up into appropriate leadership roles. From time to time I casually seed suggestions for how this can be done when the group returns to work, but I avoid shameless pleading or asking for volunteers. It is a turning point in the course when, without prompting, the first participant takes the initiative and commits publicly to take the lead on an issue at work. It is an event for which I give gushing praise, as I do for each subsequent act of leadership for the remainder of the course.

We can choose to have an organization that behaves as a predictable machine, but the result is typically business as usual. It is far better to have an organization that engages the hero that is in us all.

In essence, this is a new paradigm for leadership and for an organization. It represents a transformation from a *rank-based* organization to a *peer-based* organization.[10]

If an organization values distributed leadership, it must be prepared to give up some control over the work. If the team members really do have ownership of the work, they will have substantial control over the outcome of the work. This attitude necessarily demands trust.

Distributed leadership is a critical ingredient of the high-velocity project in an ambiguous environment. It is a key tool for agility when decision-making must be nimble.

■ Transformational Leadership

To conclude our examination of change and leadership, let us contrast two styles of leadership: *transactional leadership* and *transformational leadership*.

Transactional leadership is a more conventional style, as embodied in the traditional military style of management. Transactional leaders direct tasks and either coerce or cajole team members to perform, using a combination of carrot and stick strategies. Transactional leaders work with MacGregor's Theory X style. While work can be accomplished, it does not engage the energy of the workers and it brings little or no inherent change for the workers or the organization.

In contrast, transformational leadership changes the fundamental relationship of workers to the work and in the process changes the organization. It is founded on the belief that people want to contribute their energy to meaningful work, which is consistent with MacGregor's Theory Y and Ouchi's Theory Z management styles.

Transformational leadership is directed toward the accomplishment of something truly worthwhile: to *transform* the individual workers and the organization. It recognizes that work can and should be structured according to the highest levels of Maslow's needs hierarchy and is consistent with the deep motivation of spiritual survival.

Where transactional leadership intends for workers to meet goals, transformational leadership seeks to inspire workers to perform beyond expectations. This is accomplished in any one of three interrelated ways:

> *(a) An increased level of awareness by subordinates about the importance of designated outcomes, (b) by getting individuals to transcend their own self-interest for the sake of the team, and (c) by altering the subordinates' need levels on Malsow's hierarchy or expanding the set of needs.*[11]

Contemporary project teams have much in common with research and development organizations, considering the ambiguous and risky nature of many projects. With this in mind, research has demonstrated that the transformational leadership style is more effective among such teams. Transformational leadership correlates more significantly than transactional leadership with better project quality and budget and schedule performance.[12] These findings make sense because aggressive projects demand considerable innovation in technology or in human processes; in other words, these projects require transformations. Less aggressive or incremental projects can be completed satisfactorily without transformational leadership.

There is a well-known story of the construction of a large cathedral centuries ago. Two workers at the site were asked what they were doing. One answered, "Laying bricks." The other answered, "Constructing a grand cathedral that will serve as a place of inspiration for many."

The two answers capture the contrast between transactional and transformational leadership. With transformational leadership, it is much easier to engage the energy and positive emotions of workers to accomplish something worthwhile. In the process, they grow personally as well.

■ Individual and Organizational Change

One of the hallmarks of effective leadership and change is that they bring about growth and maturity in both the organization and its individuals. While it is worthwhile to identify new skills, capabilities, or products that result from projects, it is perhaps more important to strive for and recognize how the group has grown in pride, agility, resilience, and emotional intelligence. Far from being inconsequential fluff, these developments are valuable assets—with significant economic value—for the organization.

Projects do bring about change. When performed well, they bring about change that transforms people and their organizations for the better. ■

■ ENDNOTES

1 William Leban and Carol Zulauf, "Linking Emotional Intelligence and Transformational Leadership Styles," *Leadership and Organization Development Journal,* Vol. 25, No. 7, 2004, p. 560.

2 Jeffrey B. Schmidt and Roger J. Calantone, "Escalation of Commitment During New Product Development," *Journal of the Academy of Marketing Science,* Vol. 30, No. 2, 2002, pp. 103–118.

3 James C. Collins and Jerry I. Porras, *Built to Last* (New York: HarperBusiness, 1994).

4 "Building Your Company's Vision," http://www.jimcollins.com/lab/buildingVision/p2.html. Accessed October 2006.

5 David R. Caruso, Brian Bienn, and Susan A. Kornacki, "Emotional Intelligence in the Workplace," from *Emotional Intelligence in Everyday Life, 2nd Edition,* Joseph Ciarrochi, et al., Editors (New York: Psychology Press, 2006), pp. 187–205.

6 David Rosete and Joseph Ciarrochi, "Emotional Intelligence and Its Relationship to Workplace Performance Outcomes of Leadership Effectiveness," *Leadership and Organization Effectiveness Journal,* Vol. 26, No. 5, 2005, pp. 388–399.

7 Ibid.

8 Orpheus Chamber Orchestra website, http://www.orpheusnyc.org. Accessed July 2006.

9 Amanda Hay and Myra Hodgkinson, "Rethinking Leadership: A Way Forward for Teaching Leadership?" *Leadership and Organization Development Journal,* Vol. 27, No. 2, 2006, pp. 144–158.

10 Jeffrey S. Nielsen, *The Myth of Leadership* (Palo Alto, CA: Davies-Black Publishing, 2004).

11 Robert T. Keller, "Transformational Leadership and the Performance of Research and Development Groups," *Journal of Management,* Vol. 18, No. 3, 1992, pp. 489–501.

12 Ibid.

■ Tools of the Trade: Working with the Right Brain

We shape our tools and thereafter our tools shape us.

MARSHALL MCLUHAN ■

A s an indication of the power of right-brain processing, consider the following story.

One morning, Paul McCartney awoke from a dream in which he had composed the entire melody of a song. He quickly wrote it down and recorded it before losing it to fading memory. The experience of writing a song while asleep seemed so bizarre and unexpected to him that he initially believed he must have heard the tune somewhere before. Although he liked the melody, he did not want to plagiarize someone else's work.

In the coming weeks, he played the tune for a number of people; perhaps someone else would recognize the melody and put an end to the matter. But no one else had heard it before. Finally, McCartney accepted that the song must be his own.

He eventually put words to the tune. The other members of the Beatles initially disliked the song, in part because it was such a departure from their existing work.

McCartney's creation has since become the most "covered" song ever. More than 3,000 other versions of the song have been recorded, and the clearinghouse BMI estimates that it has been performed some seven million times.

Certainly, only a composer as gifted as McCartney could write "Yesterday." But what is so amazing about the song is that he slept through the act of composing it. While he slept, his right brain was truly busy constructing the pattern of notes that would become one of the most memorable songs of our time, and in his own words, "the most complete song I have ever written."[1]

It is unlikely that a project sponsor would understand if I said I needed to get some sleep to work on her challenging project. Since there are few McCartney-esque project managers around, we mere mortals can benefit from a set of tools that enables us to take advantage of the right brain during our waking hours.

Work on a phenomenal project demands a high degree of right-brain processing. Drawing on motivation from emotional energy, we apply creative abilities to sort and apply new patterns, using rich communication and decision-making skills.

Such a project exercises the right brain to an extraordinary degree, but this does not mean that the left brain takes a vacation. On the contrary, if we look a bit more closely we can see that the two hemispheres are working together. The left brain is quickly applying the new patterns the right brain is creating.

One of the elements that may feel surprising when we exercise the right brain more fully is the agility with which this process of right brain/left brain coordination happens. Our brains are wired for this kind of processing, and we have much to gain by working with these natural processes.

As with any other skill, we become more proficient in the tools of the right brain the more we use them. So how can we take advantage of all that these "tools of the trade" have to offer?

■ Second That Emotion

Emotion. The mere mention of the word in the workplace makes people uncomfortable.

Isn't the office a place where emotions are kept in check? The workplace culture allows appropriate, reserved expressions of emotion, but frowns upon emotional outbursts. There is nothing intrinsically wrong with this culture: emotional "freedom" is culturally regulated in many places we frequent depending on context. However, the key issue with emotion in the workplace is not the expression of emotion so much as it is the appropriate acknowledgment of emotion.

The marketplace is overwhelmingly a place where rationality is valued over emotion; Descartes would feel very much at home there. Emotionality is regarded as the "antithesis of rationality."[2] Companies view the components of organizational work from a rational perspective, whether the topic is strategy, compensation policies, competition, or any of a host of other issues.

But the reality is, humans experience emotions throughout the workday. While we may keep our emotions in check inside the office or factory, we certainly do not leave them outside the door. Organizational life cannot be separated from emotion.

Recall the studies we discussed in Chapter 3 concerning fMRI scans of individuals who were presented with various images. Their neurons fired automatically, resulting in basic and moral emotions. Other individuals presented with hypothetical moral decisions also exhibited neurons that fired and caused moral emotions. In the office or on the shop floor, we are constantly presented with images and situations that form both basic and moral emotions.

For humans, emotions serve very important functions. Fear keeps us out of danger, anger can bring about change, and joy is the essence of what makes life worthwhile. If that is not enough reason to value emotion, remember that emotion is necessary for making decisions, even the most trivial ones.

On the other hand, emotions can get us in trouble. An individual with excessive fear can become virtually paralyzed. Inappropriate rage can be cause for termination, and out-of-place boisterous laughter will lead to ridicule.

This potential for dysfunctional experiences with emotions has contributed to the dominance of rationality in the world of work.[3] But excessive reliance on rational thought can likewise be dysfunctional. For example, in a crisis situation, a robotic reflection on the pros and cons of various response options is likely to result in failure or tragedy. What is needed in crisis situations is quick action that is thoughtful but heavily dependent on emotion and intuition.

Consider also that humans avoid activities and environments that seem robotic and devoid of emotion or idiosyncrasy. While *Star Trek's* Mr. Spock was a "fascinating" character, few people could stand to be around him all the time. There is something inhuman about extreme rationality.

Both emotionality and rationality therefore serve important functions, but they can be dysfunctional depending on the context. When we rely too heavily on rational thought, we tragically fail to take advantage of the many benefits of appropriate emotional energy. This blind spot is particularly relevant to contemporary, complex projects because they sorely need appropriate emotion to succeed.

So how we can best use and apply emotion in the workplace? It is helpful to acknowledge the role of emotion. It is even more beneficial to recognize that rationality and emotionality are very much linked and work together powerfully.

The key to using emotion to advantage in project management is emotional intelligence. "Emotional intelligence essentially describes the ability to effectively join emotions and reasoning, using emotions to facilitate reasoning and reasoning intelligently about emotions."[4] In other words, what we seek is not the absence or neglect of emotion, but the active partnership of the rational and emotional worlds.

The ingredients of emotional intelligence can be summarized as:[5]

- The ability to know one's emotions
- The skill to manage one's emotions appropriately

- The means to motivate oneself
- The perception to recognize emotions in others
- The skill to handle relationships competently.

This perspective is foremost a recognition and acknowledgment of the value of emotion in the life of the organization as well as in the lives of individuals. The significant shift in thought is from a generalized "all emotions are irrational" to the more targeted "appropriate emotions are beneficial while dysfunctional emotions are harmful."

Consider a brief example of how emotional intelligence applies and is important on the contemporary, complex project. Suppose there are two projects with two project managers, Emily and Lee. The projects are exactly the same, and they are both considered to be complex and on aggressive schedules. The project managers have the same domain knowledge and overall cognitive intelligence. The only difference in the two scenarios is that Emily has a higher level of emotional intelligence than Lee. Emily has learned to know and manage her own emotions appropriately, while Lee has some difficulty in this area.

When faced with the ambiguity and pressure of this type of project, many people will understandably feel anxious. As someone with a low EI, Lee might have difficulty comprehending this anxiety and taking steps to address it. Also, Lee might be unable to help team members work through their anxiety. A persistent high level of anxiety is likely to cloud good decision-making on the project and drain away energy that is needed to work effectively. Emily, the project manager with a higher EI, is more likely to recognize and acknowledge the anxiety appropriately and lead the team through it effectively.

In both cases, anxiety is present. When the project manager possesses emotional intelligence skills, he or she will be able to channel the emotion of anxiety in conjunction with rational thought.

Considerable research backs up the beneficial effects of applying emotion appropriately. Executives who demonstrate higher levels of EI have been shown to be more likely to achieve desired business outcomes and be judged as effective leaders by both subordinates and superiors.[6] Enhanced emotional intelligence for a project manager has been shown to have a positive impact on project performance.[7]

Project success is enhanced by a motivated team, good team processes, good communication, and effective team decision-making. These elements are all facilitated by high levels of emotional intelligence.

Interestingly, these elements are also components of leadership abilities. Contemporary, challenging projects need good leadership, and furthermore, they need good distributed leadership. While it is great to have an outstanding leader as project manager, it is far better to have an entire team of individuals who are competent leaders. Not coincidentally, research shows a linkage between maturity in emotional intelligence and leadership abilities.[8] This should come as no surprise because good leadership is so dependent on people skills.

As one example of the appropriate and effective use of emotion, consider the progression of messages on safety signs. A number of years ago, a safety sign near an electrical facility may have simply said, "Danger – High Voltage." In recent years, it has become standard practice to include on the sign the action to be avoided and the consequence of interacting with the hazard. When one reads that an action "... may result in death," the message becomes very powerful. The content of the sign does not explicitly include emotion, but it clearly engages strong emotions.

The management of emotion is an important element of effective projects and right-brain project management. While emotion is important in many ways, let us focus on five benefits of exercising emotion appropriately on projects:

- *Motivation.* Work on challenging projects requires considerable mental energy and commitment—in other words, motivation. While rational thought helps, the true source of motivation is emotion.

- *Team processes.* Humans are creatures with emotions. Aware-ness of one's own emotions and the emotions of others is critical for team communication and interactions to be productive.
- *Cohesiveness.* A collection of individuals can work together, but the transition to becoming a cohesive team is made when the individuals share important experiences with sig-nificant emotional content.[9]
- *Performance.* Individuals and teams perform best when emo-tions are healthy and positive.
- *Decision-making.* If an individual needs emotion to make decisions, so too does a team. Group decision-making is facilitated when the emotional component of options is taken into account.

Maturity in emotional intelligence is a skill that can be improved upon much like any other skill. The process begins with the acknowledgement of emotion in the workplace and an apprecia-tion of its benefits. While such an approach may run contrary to the dominance of rationality in the workplace, the advantages to be gained are significant—and are therefore well worth our rational consideration! They are advantages that are absolutely essential for the contemporary project.

■ Creativity and Pattern Discovery

Creativity is at its core divergent thinking. It is the decision to take a known pattern or rule and break it in the quest to find a new and useful pattern. To a large extent, this is an experimental process, but the process starts with breaking the old pattern.

The greatest challenge to creative thought is temporarily turn-ing off conscious or left-brain, rule-based thinking so that new approaches can be considered and tried. At times, these patterns are so ingrained and so automatic that it is necessary to perform delib-erate interventions to access the right brain.

Malcolm Gladwell, in his book *Blink*, talks about the unconscious processing of the right brain as activity that goes on behind a locked door. But be certain that the processing is occurring. Our task is to access it.

A number of interventions can stimulate creative thought when attempting to solve a problem; the objective is to purposely bypass the left brain and its rules. One set of interventions involves contradicting known patterns and assumptions to determine if new patterns may work. This process is often called *provocation*.

For example, on a project, consider the assumption that "Task A will take at least 15 days to complete." To start the creative process, we break this assumption by saying, "Task A must take less than 15 days to complete."

Suddenly, the left brain is out of commission. It doesn't have a pattern to apply to the new condition, and so it turns the problem over to the right brain. This handoff starts a series of creative "what if" questions in the right brain: What if we add staff to the task? What if we use some new, efficient technology? What if we completely rethink the task from a different perspective?

The creativity guru Edward de Bono identified a continuum of provocation, from the gentle "What if?" to a more extreme revision of known reality—cases that seem impossible or illogical. He even coined the word "po" (provocative operation) as a function to introduce such an extreme provocation. Po is a signal to those involved in the creative exercise that the premise to follow is really wacky.[10]

In one example of this process, we start with an assumption of something familiar, something we take as a given, and then we violate it. For example:

Cars have headlights.
Po, cars do not have headlights.

Creatively, we attempt to construct systems that might fill the functions formerly performed by headlights. Perhaps cars might be coated with paint that glows in the dark. We might include a sonar-type instrument to alert us of an obstacle in the road ahead. We won't necessarily choose these options, but suggesting them may uncover a breakthrough concept.

Pattern discovery goes hand in hand with creativity. If creative thought is divergent thought, then pattern discovery is the effort to bring the creative process to converge on something useful to the need at hand.

One of the keys to appreciating pattern discovery in the right brain is to recognize that we search for patterns according to context and expectations.[11] For example, letters can be distinguished faster and more accurately when they appear in the context of a known word rather than as a set of random letters or alone.

When this concept is applied in the project context, we search creatively for new patterns for the problem we are solving. We do so based on the context of the project as well as what we know has worked in the past.

Pattern recognition within a context is directed toward a goal: to solve the problem at hand. Once a suitable pattern is found, it becomes part of the repertoire of the left brain for practice and skill. It also becomes part of memory that the right brain can access in the future for other pattern-discovery tasks.

■ Metaphor

Suppose a spacecraft of friendly Martians landed and I wanted to describe to them various aspects of life on earth. When I arrived at the subject of a rose, I could convey the concept in several different ways.

I could quote them the definition of a rose: "Any of numerous shrubs or vines of the genus *Rosa*, having prickly stems, pinnately compound leaves, and variously colored, often fragrant flowers."[12]

I could show them a photograph of a rose.

I could hand them a rose and let them smell it and feel the soft petals and prickly thorns.

Finally, I could quote Shakespeare from *Romeo and Juliet*:[13]

What's in a name? that which we call a rose
By any other name would smell as sweet.

My new friends might say, "Whoa, back up. You were describing a rose and you lost us when you got into names and such."

My friends are not familiar with the power of metaphor. In two lines, Juliet uses the sweet smell of a rose to make a powerful statement of her love for Romeo. The love between Romeo and Juliet is forbidden because of their families of origin; for love of Juliet, Romeo states that he will renounce his family and change his name. She loves the person regardless of his name. The "thing" that we call a rose will still be the same "thing" and will have the same essence no matter what name we give it. But more than that observation, Juliet's passing reference to an arbitrary designation for a flower speaks volumes about the identity and character of a person, as well as how the love in a relationship remains even when people change their names.

This is the amazing power of metaphor. Had Juliet chosen a left-brain approach, this passage might have taken several pages using logical constructs to convey what she said in 18 words. Even then, the logical description would not capture the richness of the metaphor.

The left brain can process only the literal meaning of Juliet's words and would completely miss her expression of love and profound truth about identity. Metaphor is one of the most powerful and economical ways to communicate and to understand using the right brain.

A metaphor can be used in a straightforward manner, perhaps in the form of a simile. For example, if our project is to design a new electronic language translator, we could say that it will have a user interface like that of an iPod. Right there, we have cut to the chase and connected what is familiar with something that does not yet exist.

The metaphor can be more indirect, conveying information that is emotional in nature, and perhaps be more effective when it comes to marketing. "Our translator is a door to foreign lands. Walk through the door and onto the Champs-Élysées."

That approach will connect back to the design project in terms of features and interface. But the way that the user experience is communicated has an emotional impact on the development team as well. What is it about the translator that enables this virtual trip to Paris? Is it a visual interface with scenes of Parisian streets? Does the computer include the chatter of street sounds and Parisians talking? Perhaps an olfactory generator pumps out those unique molecules that create the aroma of freshly baked baguettes.

Using the metaphor and imagery, we have transformed a language dictionary into an experience replete with sensory and emotional richness. Advertisers work this magic on us all the time. One can of beer becomes a winning touchdown, another is a pleasant conversation with good friends, yet another is a drink from a pure mountain stream.

Yes, it is magic—pure right-brain magic.

■ Tell the Story

Closely related to metaphor is the rich communication style of storytelling, which is an outstanding tool of the right brain. We will look at stories in more depth later, but for now, let us briefly note the reasons for adding storytelling to the project manager's toolkit.

Storytelling is a powerful way to communicate complex ideas or establish a case for change. It is also an excellent way to transmit values and to encourage people to work together quickly and enthusiastically.[14] Complex and aggressive projects need these benefits of storytelling.

When we talk about storytelling in an organizational setting, we do not mean something that starts with, "Once upon a time ...." Rather, it is the natural telling of events, objectives, and what they mean. While good storytelling involves certain elements, anyone can tell a story. The case studies of exceptional projects included in this book are examples of storytelling.

Members of Generation Y, the children of baby boomers, are particularly receptive to stories, and they are familiar and comfortable with the informal exchange of stories through, for example, blogs.[15] That's a promising sign, as many believe that storytelling is one of the most important skills needed by present-day and future leaders.

■ Non-Verbal Communication

While the left brain processes information verbally, through words, the right brain can process information non-verbally, through pictures, sensations, and spatial relationships. We generally attempt to solve problems with verbal techniques, but it is often helpful to switch to another form of communication to engage the right brain. In many cases a combination technique is quite helpful.

One such technique is a mind map. A mind map is a visual representation of the components of an issue and the relationships and dependencies among the components. The visual aspect of this tool helps engage the right brain more than words alone. This technique engages not only left-brain sequential processing but also right-brain spatial processing. A mind map tool is also available in software that enables a user to organize ideas visually.[16] An example of a mind map is shown in Figure 6-1.

Some problems are far easier to solve visually than verbally. When James D. Watson and Francis Crick cracked the genetic code by determining the structure of DNA, they solved the problem spatially. They approached the problem by asking which atoms like to sit next to each other; their main tools were a set of molecular models that resembled children's toys.[17]

■ **Figure 6-1. Mind Map for a Project Planning Retreat Meeting**

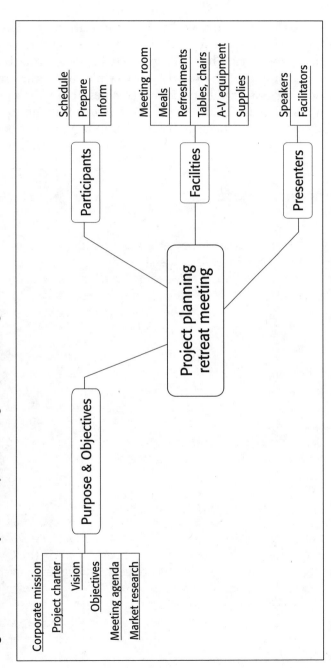

An important form of non-verbal communication is what is commonly known as "body language." If we are present with someone and listening to him or her talk, the left brain is processing our literal understanding of the words. Meanwhile, the right brain is picking up on various visual and auditory clues about the emotional content associated with the words. It is estimated that 80–90 percent of the content of a message is received in the form of body language.

Visualizing the Project

Matt Glei

I find it very helpful to use visual approaches in project management. One of my favorite techniques is to visualize an image of the end product or service and work backwards to decompose the parts and the order of attack. Sometimes this approach helps people flesh out the totality of the project goals and remember them on a daily basis. It also humanizes the goals, so they become much more than the elements of a project plan or checklist.

This visualization approach is instinctive. When we were kids and wanted to build a dam across a creek, we didn't stop and do a drawing, a work breakdown structure, and so forth. Instead, we would visualize and discuss what we wanted to do, and how cool it would look when complete. The image enabled us to see where the spillway or waterfall would be, and how we could catch crawfish, fish, or bugs in the "reservoir."

Visualizing the final product allowed us to think naturally about left-brain items—I need rocks, sticks, leaves, and mud—for resource management and staging. It also prompted questions about how the work would be accomplished: Do I need to get a bucket or can? (tools) What size rock can I carry? (resource capabilities) How far away are the rocks? (resource logistics) Can I get some help? (resource planning) Are there snakes around? (risk analysis) Kids don't need project management training to do this—it comes naturally. Of course, we would make mistakes and learn better ways; then we would adapt and change strategies before proceeding too far with the project.

I often intermingle right- and left-brain styles. For example, I may start with product visualization and decomposition, and then switch to traditional task analysis, work breakdown structures, and resource leveling. Once this is done, I identify the milestones (or yardstones) and use the yardstones to help guide and evaluate progress. Although disconnected information can result, it is often better to use the plan as a guide rather than completing the proper steps in order (unless the specific order is critical to success). In this way, I use the plan to make sure that no key part goes undone and I gauge progress from achieving the yardstones. This is more efficient than tracking whether my plan was flawless.

Risk analysis is another method that can be used in both left- and right-brain ways. We can easily brainstorm the riskier parts of a product or project at a high level and use that knowledge to think about how to mitigate risks at the appropriate time in the project. Most of us don't need to prepare a 36-page, formal probability/severity/mitigation risk document to understand what parts of the project are the riskiest and what can be done to reduce or mitigate those risks.

One challenge that project managers often face occurs when a new team member comes on board in the middle of a project. While the new member may have a basic understanding of the project, he or she lacks the detailed context of how decisions have been made. Some excellent tools are available to assist a project team in visualizing the process. One approach that I particularly like is to use a mind-mapping tool for documenting key decisions. This tool captures the alternatives, and pros and cons, in the decision as well as who participated in the decision. Mind mapping makes it easy to document the decisions and provide important context. This tool is great for helping explain to a new team member what key decisions were and why they were made.

It is also important to convey to new team members the philosophy and purpose behind a product or project. Any approach that uses images and metaphors to connect to emotions can be very powerful. Rather than saying "this device measures blood oxygen levels non-invasively," it is much more powerful to say "this device can prevent the anesthesiologist from accidentally killing the patient."

In short, many of the most successful and innovative projects include techniques from both sides of the brain. Right-brain approaches are incredibly powerful, but they can't do all the heavy lifting. What they can do is help drive thinking in new ways, spotting possible risks and opportunities that a left-brain approach alone may not uncover.

Matt Glei is Executive Vice President of Operations for Hoana Medical in Honolulu, Hawaii. Hoana develops and markets medical devices for non-contact patient monitoring systems. Matt has over 30 years of experience in the medical industry, with a focus on device product marketing and research and development. His career has included positions with Honeywell Medical, Hewlett-Packard, and Nellcor Puritan Bennett.

■ Intuition

In 1969, The Who released what was billed as the first rock opera. *Tommy* featured the story of a fictional "deaf, dumb, and blind kid," rendered that way by a traumatic childhood experience. Tommy discovers that he has astounding skill at playing pinball and becomes the champion "Pinball Wizard," puzzling his competitors because he "plays by intuition."

To a certain extent, on the complex project we all operate as the "deaf, dumb, and blind kid." We encounter situations that are unfamiliar, forces that seem to defy our control. We need a way to see through the fog and operate with mastery.

An important technique in this environment is to play by intuition.

If emotion is the ignored child in the workplace, then intuition must be its first cousin. Whatever you call it—gut feeling, instinct, or sixth sense—it is a form of guidance that is not consciously derived. Intuition is "... direct knowing without any use of conscious reasoning."[18]

Intuition seems inexplicable, mystical, ephemeral, and at times random or serendipitous. In other words, it is not rational. Although anything that is not rational is generally avoided in the workplace, intuition is actually used quite often (if not publicly acknowledged).

Intuition is real, and it is very valuable (if misunderstood). It is one of the powerful tools of the right brain, one that is exquisitely tailored to the complex project.

To understand and appreciate intuition, recall that the right brain can process vast amounts of information and do so holistically, in contrast to the stepwise left-brain style. The right brain often does this work quietly, in the background, under the radar of consciousness. It works particularly on those problems or challenges that involve some novel element, and it is directed toward pattern recognition and solution. To arrive at the solution, intuition draws heavily on experiences and the emotions associated with those experiences. In many cases, the processing occurs with astounding speed.

The way the solution is reported may be puzzling to many. For some people, intuition results in an emotion associated with a thought. Intuition works through a part of the brain that is wired into the viscera. A solution derived through intuition is communicated into the torso through this channel. So when someone says that they have a gut feeling, they do in fact have a feeling in their gut!

Left-brain, rational thinking analyzes; right-brain, intuitive thinking synthesizes. Intuitive thinking synthesizes disconnected pieces of information and experience into an integrated picture.

Intuition can be divided into two types. Expert intuition is the result of years of experience. When a slightly novel situation arises, an expert can intuitively know how to react, without analytical thought. As an example, an individual who has operated the same industrial plant for 25 years knows its functioning intimately. If one day, an area of the plant shuts down unexpectedly, he will likely experience a gut feeling about the cause.

The second type of intuition is entrepreneurial intuition, which we experience in an entirely new situation. We have no definitive rules or framework to operate from, but we do have our own personal years of experience. The right brain searches that experience for patterns that are analogous in some way.

Intuition is highly valuable, if not necessary, in complex environments, especially those that are characterized as "high velocity." These situations require that many options be processed based on limited information. Intuition is needed when the problem is ill-defined and has no precedent[19]—a description that could easily serve as the definition for a contemporary project! For stable, familiar environments, intuition is not needed, and can actually be detrimental. In such situations, a rational, analytical process works best.[20]

Once we rented the DVD for *The Bourne Identity*. After watching the movie, we watched the commentary by the director Doug Limon. He made the comment that, when it came to filming, he didn't want to think too much—he believed it was important to be instinctive.

In many cases, thoughtful planning and execution lead to a good product. But after the planning is done, acting on intuition or instinct may produce even better results.

It is important to note that intuition should not be relied on to the exclusion of rational analysis. On the contrary, such analysis plays an important role in making decisions; it is one of the mechanisms that intuition uses to synthesize all that is known and understood about the problem at hand.

Intuition relies to a large extent on emotional memories associated with experiences. This linkage is one of the critical elements in the growth in maturity from novice to expert, whatever the skill. If our experiences were detached from emotion, we would have little motivation to push through our limitations and improve. But when we deeply feel pride in accomplishment, or feel the remorse of mistakes, those emotions lay the foundation for expertise. In other words, it is because we care about the outcome that we progress toward maturity.[21]

Interestingly, research has shown that memories associated with negative emotions, such as shame or remorse, carry more weight than those associated with positive emotions. For example, while we might expect that investment decisions would be made rationally, most people pay far greater attention to losses than to gains. In fact, the emotional effect of a $250 gain is about the same as the emotional effect of a $100 loss.[22]

It is believed that intuition can be developed by repeated expo- sure to the complexity of real problems.[23] It is also helpful to develop ways to access intuition more reliably. Here is a simple trick to do so: flip a coin.

The coin flip sounds silly, but it is a powerful tool. If you are faced with a tough, complicated decision, it can be easy to get para- lyzed by the ambiguity because analytical techniques will go only so far. While agonizing over the decision in the conscious mind, the right brain is processing patterns in the background. The coin toss trick is what enables us to access what intuition has to say.

The trick works like this: the result of the coin toss is used to trigger a feeling at the outcome. Our job is to be attentive to the feeling triggered immediately on the result; this is the intuitive, gut reaction. If "heads" means that we complete the troubled project, and "tails" means we terminate, what is our immediate reaction when the coin lands? Do we feel relief when the coin lands on tails? Do we feel renewed purpose if the coin lands on heads and the proj- ect is given a new lease on life?

Shortly after our third child was born, my wife and I started looking for a new, larger house for our growing family. We fell in love with a beautiful property on two and a half acres. It was a little out of our price range, but we put in an offer and signed the contract. We were elated at the prospect of moving into our dream house.

A few days later we did a walkthrough with an inspector. His first words were, "The prior owners have been hard on this house." He went on to show us several major problem areas, including some evidence of water damage on the ceiling. Our dream house suddenly became one that needed nightmare repairs.

We had one week from signing the contract to back out of the deal and lose only a small fee. After this time, we would pay a hefty penalty for terminating the deal. This deadline approached only 24 hours after the news from the inspector. For 23 hours we agonized over the decision but were unable to decide. With one hour to go, I pulled a coin from my pocket ... heads we proceed, tails we back out of the contract.

Nervously, I flipped the coin—tails. I didn't know what I felt. I was so agitated over this decision that it was difficult to access my feelings. To get past my paralyzed left brain, I knew I had to keep trying. I flipped again—tails again, but still no direction. By the third toss, and the third result of tails, I was starting to perceive relief. I wanted to be sure, so I continued.

Eight flips, and eight straight times the coin landed on tails. This was not a cosmic message telling me to quit the deal; a coin flip has an equal likelihood of hitting heads or tails on any given toss. But after eight flips, I strongly *felt* the answer. I experienced a definitive sense of relief and calmness for what I came to know was the right choice: terminate the contract.

After 23 hours of decision paralysis, within two minutes the coin toss revealed the answer. While this technique often illuminates a direction on the first toss, for particularly tough situations, it may take several attempts, as happened in this case.

The coin toss enables us to experience the *feeling* of different outcomes of the decision. The coin toss is a trick, but it is merely a trick to quickly bypass conscious thought and all its ruminations, to access the valuable insights that intuition has to offer.

■ Striking the Balance

As we close this brief look at a few of the tools for engaging the right brain on projects, let us note that it is the partnership between the right brain and the left brain that serves us most beneficially for our complex projects. For insight on this balance, let us turn to the individual who has been recognized as the greatest genius in the history of the world, Leonardo da Vinci.[24]

Da Vinci was both an outstanding artist and an outstanding scientist. In our specialized world, we see these personas separately. But in the human brain, they are intimately related and feed upon one another. Da Vinci was an outstanding scientist because he was an outstanding artist, and vice versa. This is yet another manifestation of Kant's outlook.

The tools of the right brain and the tools of the left brain are complementary in purpose. Working together, they accomplish amazing feats in project management. ▪

▪ ENDNOTES

1 "Yesterday," *Rolling Stone,* http://www.rollingstone.com/news/story/6595858/yesterday. Accessed October 2006.

2 Blake E. Ashforth and Ronald H. Humphrey, "Emotion in the Workplace: A Reappraisal," *Human Relations,* Vol. 48, No. 2, 2000, p. 97.

3 Ibid., pp. 97–125.

4 Jennifer M. George, "Emotions and Leadership: The Role of Emotional Intelligence," *Human Relations,* Vol. 53, No. 8, 2000, p. 1033.

5 Daniel Goleman, *Emotional Intelligence* (New York: Bantam Books, 1994), p. 43.

6 David Rosete and Joseph Ciarrochi, "Emotional Intelligence and Its Relationship to Workplace Performance Outcomes of Leadership Effectiveness," *Leadership and Organization Development Journal,* Vol. 26, No. 5, 2005, pp. 388–399.

7 William Leban and Carol Zulauf, "Linking Emotional Intelligence Abilities and Transformational Leadership Styles," *Leadership and Organization Development Journal,* Vol. 25, No. 7, pp. 554–564.

8 Jennifer M. George, "Emotions and Leadership: The Role of Emotional Intelligence," *Human Relations,* Vol. 53, No. 8, 2000, pp. 1027–1055.

9 Blake E. Ashforth and Ronald H. Humphrey, "Emotion in the Workplace: A Reappraisal," *Human Relations,* Vol. 48, No. 2, 2000, pp. 97–125.

10 Edward de Bono, *Serious Creativity* (Toronto: Harper Collins, 1992).

11 Nick Lund, *Attention and Pattern Recognition* (London: Routledge, 2001), p. 75.

12 *American Heritage Dictionary of the English Language, Third Edition* (Boston: Houghton Mifflin), p. 1568.

13 *Romeo and Juliet* (II, ii, 43–44), *The Complete Works of William Shakespeare, The Cambridge Edition Text,* edited by William Aldis Wright (Garden City, NY: Garden City Books, 1936), p. 325.

14 David Rymer, "Powerful Storytelling: Rich Connections Between Leaders and Generation Y," *Leadership Compass,* Banff Centre, Summer 2006, p. 25.

15 Ibid.

16 MindJet MindManager, http://www.mindjet.com. Accessed October 2006.

17 Roger N. Shepard, "Externalization of Mental Images and The Act of Creation," *Visual Learning, Thinking and Communication,* edited by Bikkar S. Randhawa and William E. Coffman (New York: Academic Press, 1978).

18 Marta Sinclair and Neal M. Ashkanasy, "Intuition: Myth or Decision-Making Tool?" *Management Learning,* Vol. 36, No. 3, 2005, p. 353.

19 Ibid., pp. 353–370.

20 Naresh Khatri and H. Alvin Ng, "The Role of Intuition in Strategic Decision Making," *Human Relations,* Vol. 53, No. 1, pp. 57–86.

21 Hubert L. Dreyfus and Stuart E. Dreyfus, "Expertise in Real World Contexts," *Organization Studies,* Vol. 26, No. 5, pp. 779–792.

22 Kenneth L. Fisher, *The Only Three Questions That Count* (Hoboken, NJ: John Wiley & Sons, 2006), p. 88.

23 Naresh Khatri and H. Alvin Ng, "The Role of Intuition in Strategic Decision Making," *Human Relations,* Vol. 53, No. 1, pp. 57–86.

24 Michael Gelb, *How to Think Like Leonardo da Vinci* (New York: Dell, 1998).

CHAPTER 7

■ Doing What Works: Contemporary Projects in an Accelerated World

■
■
■

Never interrupt someone doing what you said couldn't be done.

AMELIA EARHART ■

In Chapter 3, we presented one of the dimensions of personality type as Judging and Perceiving. In essence, this dimension addresses the degree of structure and organization that is comfortable for a person: a Judging person prefers structure while a Perceiving person prefers flexibility. Another way to describe this dimension is according to time: a Judging person prefers that matters be decided and then implemented, while a Perceiving person is comfortable with deferring decisions to take in later information.

The characteristics of this dimension can be used to illuminate how people and organizations approach projects. Put simply, project work can be planned in a fully structured fashion and then executed, or it can be approached in an experimental, adaptive way. Of course, these "extremes" fall along a continuum of approaches that incorporate both methods.

Both approaches are worthwhile, but both also have their disadvantages. The structured approach offers predictability but suffers if conditions change. The adaptive approach readily handles changing information but can miss opportunities by deferring action.

While it may seem obvious, it is worthwhile to highlight that a combination of approaches is most helpful. The most effective combination will change based on the particular needs and environment for the project.

But hold on a minute! The profession of project management leans heavily toward the structured model. And this gets us back to where we began .... What's wrong with project management?

A large part of what is wrong with project management is that external forces on the project demand flexibility and high performance while the dominant model for applying project management is structured. That model delivers great performance when the need is familiar and predictable, but struggles when the need is novel and ambiguous.

It is helpful to review how the profession got to this point and then to recognize the need to evolve from here. To start our review, let's go back in time.

■ Ancient Project Management

While the formal discipline of project management is considered to have started in the last 50 years, humans planned and executed massive projects thousands of years ago. For evidence, consider the construction of the Pyramids.

It is estimated that the Great Pyramid of Egypt took approximately 20 years to build and was staffed with perhaps more than 300,000 workers. Obviously, a project of this magnitude required considerable planning and management.

In addition to such structured projects, humans have also been capable of carrying out projects that involved a great deal of adaptation. As an example, the colonization of the Americas by European explorers and settlers required considerable flexibility for new environmental conditions.

■ Rational Projects

To understand conventional project management, it is important to see its origins in the context of management thought at the time.

Recall the predominance of scientific management and Taylorism in the early 20th century. The whole of work came to be viewed much as the workings of a machine, with workers serving as cogs in the machine. It was in this period that Taylor's associate Henry Gantt developed planning and control techniques, including the Gantt chart that is still used extensively in project management today.

While the ultimate goal of scientific management is economy, it relies entirely on predictability. It is thus most suited for work that can be analyzed completely and planned thoroughly in a predictable fashion. Even when management practice began to incorporate human relations in the 1930s, analysis and predictability remained compelling.

■ Origins of Modern Project Management

Modern project management is typically dated to the 1950s, when mathematical models and computer programs were first applied to schedule projects. These models were the program evaluation and review technique (PERT) developed as part of the Polaris missile program, and the critical path method (CPM) developed by DuPont and Remington Rand for plant projects.

Without going into their details, these techniques formed the perspective that projects can be managed rationally, analytically, and predictably. The left-brain perspective has since dominated the project management discipline.

This approach to project management offers great benefits. Projects that are substantial in size and complicated in execution lend themselves beautifully to analytical methods; it would be challenging and time-consuming to manage these projects any other way. Whereas in the past such projects were understandably allowed much freedom in scheduling, modern demands necessitated shorter schedules—and analytical techniques delivered. Large-scale military and space projects made extensive use of these project management approaches with considerable success, and industry quickly harnessed their capabilities as well.

The project model widely applied was sequential in nature, and it came to be known as the waterfall model (depicted in Figure 7-1). The stages of a project were identified in various ways according to the application, but they can be classified as follows:

- Initiation
- Planning
- Execution
- Control
- Closing.

In the waterfall model, stages flow one after another in a predictable, reliable manner. Projects progress through what is essentially a sequential path. The elements within these phases and within the overall project flow, in essence, downhill. For example, once a

---

▪ Figure 7-1. Waterfall Model

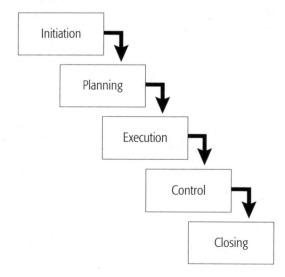

project plan and specifications are developed, it becomes possible to implement specifications in a design, and then to build what has been designed. This approach to project execution is logical, linear, and sequential. Once the project starts, change is viewed as undesirable.

■ The Project Management Profession

As technology and markets developed, organizations needed to bring new products to market on a more accelerated schedule. These products were often more complex and development teams were more likely located at dispersed sites. While many who managed projects in the past did so without formal training, the marketplace demanded a higher level of skill among project managers.

This need has largely driven the maturation of project management as a well-defined, international profession. With it the Project Management Institute (PMI) grew and became the dominant professional organization. PMI has grown dramatically, with a current membership of about 250,000. PMI has invested extensive effort in codifying the practice of project management, in its *A Guide to the Project Management Body of Knowledge (PMBOK® Guide)*.[1]

■ The *PMBOK® Guide*

The *PMBOK® Guide* consists of 44 processes, each structured with an input, an output, and an operation. The system is highly structured, formal, and logical, and its illustration in the *PMBOK® Guide* looks like the subdivision of a project.

The *PMBOK® Guide* is a masterpiece; it is in many ways the ideal. If the *PMBOK® Guide* could be implemented well in all its details, project management would be more successful. Unfortunately, in a real organization, with the pressures and realities of the workplace, it is challenging to implement the full extent of the *PMBOK® Guide* and its principles.

As an example, Figure 7-2 depicts the "Perform Quality Assurance" process as represented in the *PMBOK® Guide*.[2] This process (as do many other *PMBOK® Guide* processes) specifies documenta-

- **Figure 7-2. "Perform Quality Assurance" Process of the *PMBOK® Guide***

Inputs	Tools and Techniques	Outputs
Quality management and process improvement plans Work performance, metrics, and quality control measurements Implemented change requests, corrective actions, repairs, and preventive actions	Quality planning tools and techniques, audits Process analysis Quality control tools and techniques	Requested changes and corrective actions Updates to organizational process Updates to project management plan

tion. Given adequate time, it may be possible for a project manager to complete this documentation and follow the *PMBOK® Guide*, but most project managers struggle to keep up.

The *PMBOK® Guide* is the gold standard for how the profession believes project management should be practiced, and it is overwhelmingly a left-brain document. It is structured, linear, formal, logical, and very appealing in its formality.

For the purposes of this book, we will refer to the waterfall project model and the *PMBOK® Guide* as "conventional project management" because they represent the most widely used method—and the one that the profession has identified as the standard. Conventional project management is powerful and beneficial when practiced well and when used for appropriate projects. Research studies have shown a correlation between the use of project management best practices and the avoidance of many problems that commonly arise on projects.

Other Project Models

Nevertheless, the waterfall model does not fit well with many projects. This is particularly true in software development, which seems susceptible to difficulties with estimation. This model has been modified to include multiple, serial waterfalls in the form of phases. At the start of each subsequent waterfall section, what has been learned in the previous section is applied through updated planning. This approach addresses some of the issues of uncertainty that may be present at the start of the first waterfall.

The modified waterfall is often a good fit for projects such as research and development leading to a product. On the other hand, for other projects, notably software development, the uncertainties at the start of the project are more focused on features and implementation. These issues lend themselves to successive passes or iterations at the objective. Accordingly, an alternative project model, the spiral model, was developed for such situations.

The spiral model can be visualized as water going down a bathtub drain. Project execution proceeds in an iterative, spiral fashion, swirling around a core. The spiral represents the learning and the associated reduction in uncertainty that takes place as the project proceeds. Therefore, it is usually necessary to revisit initial assumptions and plans: as new facts are learned and new information develops, the plan is changed. This image of project execution accepts change as an inherent part of the project. The spiral model includes techniques that promote agile development, such as creating short, time-boxed iterations.

Many individuals, notably those in software development, found conventional project management models to be cumbersome and ineffective. This frustration led to the development and implementation of agile project models and associated techniques. Agile project management shares certain features with the spiral method in that development is planned as a series of iterations, but agile iterations are quick and focused, with each iteration lasting a few weeks. Where conventional approaches emphasize prediction of project tasks, agile approaches emphasize adaptation. Agile projects are deliberately kept small and fast, in contrast to conventional projects, which can be scaled up to large, multi-year efforts. Finally, agile techniques are centered on people and communication, whereas conventional approaches emphasize tasks. In these respects, agile methods share considerable common ground with the principles of right-brain project management.

This evolution in project management recognizes the need to adapt management techniques to the realities of projects.

■ Risk and the Organization

Let's look at the practice of project management from a different perspective. Many people, and perhaps most organizations, tend toward left-brain approaches, and a predominant reason involves perceptions of risk. It is uncomfortable for many to leave the future to chance, and therefore we seek dependability in outcomes. This risk-averse behavior is particularly in play in companies that trade on the stock market; if stock analysts perceive too much risk-taking, they can trash the company in the market. Our organizations demand to know the cause that can produce the desired effect, so we have a propensity to plan and then to implement the plan.

Brian Tate, who teaches leadership, says "Organizationally, I think because we're so terrified of ambiguity, we over-structure everything."[3] This attitude is applied throughout management, including project management, and it often works well. But the attitude can be problematic when applied inappropriately, and it is counterproductive in a rapidly changing environment.

■ New Realities

With rapidly developing technological capabilities in recent decades, what once could be planned thoroughly has become chaotic and difficult to predict. Technology changes overnight, markets exhibit upheaval, and customers change their minds at will.

This is the reality of the contemporary project environment. Unfortunately, the processes that organizations use to manage projects presume a much more stable environment, one in which plans can be made and executed with predictability.

As someone who has provided corporate training to project managers, I am struck by how many feel overwhelmed by this situation. They clearly feel the pressure to finish aggressive projects while operating within a hurricane of dynamic forces. Rather than admit the incongruity of it all and risk career fallout, they and their organizations exhibit an alternative universe, where publicly the project is on track but in secret everyone knows it is a train wreck.

Conventional project management has many strengths and works well in many circumstances. When a project is well defined and where the risks are manageable, it is predictable, reliable, and repeatable.

But conventional project management also has weaknesses. It does not effectively address the critical people issues involved in project work, and it has trouble with many common issues such as chaos, accelerated projects, new technologies, and dispersed teams.

■ Applying the Appropriate Approach

Conventional project management is exceptionally successful where it is applied appropriately. But other approaches have much to offer depending on the need and context.

In the end it is important to keep our brains engaged in project management and apply what works for the situation in question. If conventional techniques rely more on the left brain, much can be gained by integrating right-brain techniques into project management.

Research has shown that large projects need the structure and predictability that conventional techniques supply. Likewise, projects that involve familiar components do best with conventional techniques. Many projects, such as those that involve public or consumer safety, or that carry a high degree of administrative accountability, absolutely need formality. Often such projects do not stretch the bounds of novelty and speed.

On the other hand, projects that involve new technologies or other unknowns, or that are subject to aggressive schedules, are best managed with non-conventional approaches. Dwight Eisenhower, who led the allied forces in World War II and was later President of the United States, observed, "I have always found that plans are useless, but planning is indispensable." In war, plans change once the bullets start flying.

These guidelines make perfect sense. If it is not possible to confidently plan the progression of a project, why give any credence to a detailed project plan? Projects in volatile or dynamic environments need experimentation and uncertainty early in the project to allow adaptability and agility.

In other words, do what works.

Another way of stating this perspective is that we need to pay attention to project processes. Process design or process management is the conscious and deliberate effort to define and agree on the processes that team members will use to interact and make decisions on a project. The process is how the team works together, or the rules of the game that the parties will follow during the project.[4] In one survey, one of the top reasons cited for project failure was poor project management processes.[5] In a project, it is easy to become overly focused on the product at the expense of attention to the process.

■ How We Work

A project is an important endeavor undertaken by people. With a project, we strive to accomplish something of value, something worthwhile. The completion of a project should be an accomplishment that brings pride as well as economic reward for the organization.

Because projects are human endeavors, it is important to return often to an understanding of what ingredients promote good work.

To summarize what we look for in our work, let's turn to the book *How We Work*, by Roderic Gray. Gray offers nine ingredients that together bring about a successful outcome at work:[6]

1. I know what I'm expected to do and why it needs to be done.

2. I want to do it.

3. I have the ability to do it.

4. Someone who matters to me will notice if I do it.

5. I know how well I'm doing it.

6. Processes help me to do it.

7. I have the resources to do it.

8. The environment is right.

9. I can do better next time.

These nine ingredients make a lot of sense, but we must be careful about the conclusions we derive from them. It can be tempting to look to executive management to put these ingredients in place and, if an ingredient is lacking, to criticize management.

In reality, it is a rare organization that gets all nine ingredients right every time, given the nature of human beings and the pressures of the marketplace. It is far better to get a critical mass of ingredients right, and then give workers the green light to fill in what is missing. This is what is suggested in Ouchi's Theory Z. It is the essence of distributed leadership, and it is the stuff of which exemplary projects are made.

This movement toward the right brain represents a radical shift in how management is practiced. It is also a major shift in attitude for many workers who would rather avoid responsibility for decisions and motivation, preferring to criticize management for whatever goes wrong. Scott Adams has parlayed this attitude into a successful career through his *Dilbert* comic strip.

When we accept and believe in distributed leadership, we recognize that the project leader is not a hero; no manager is omniscient and can structure the project work so well that execution is easy. We understand that everyone on the team must step up to accept responsibility for the outcome.

In the real world of projects, there is often so much ambiguity and chaos that many of the ingredients on Gray's list cannot be defined or even addressed at the beginning of the project. And that's okay. When we all accept this foundation as part of the process, as the rules of the game, and when we are motivated and allowed to excel, amazing things can happen.

These simple tenets become the basis for the critical mass needed for people to work well in the complex world of contemporary projects. Let us now restate the nine ingredients offered by Gray:

1. I know what is most important to do, and why it is important. I am able to learn the details and adapt as appropriate.
2. I *really* want to do it.
3. I have the ability and the authority to experiment to learn what will work.
4. Someone who matters to me will notice if I do it, especially my peers.
5. I will learn how well I'm doing it.
6. I have the authority to mold the processes to help me do it.
7. I have the authority to find the resources I need to do it.
8. I have the ability to recreate the environment to do it.
9. I will do it well this time, because this opportunity will likely not come again, and I will learn things from this experience that will help me on the next.

The critical mass for establishing a project focuses on the first two elements. When we know what is most important and when we are truly motivated, it is possible to undertake a project. The remaining ingredients constitute an attitude that adaptation is critical, and that leadership is expected and valued in everyone on the project team. This is the essence of *process management*.

It is critical that we be clear on the rules of the game. Moreover, the rules we apply must be directed toward allowing adaptability, distributed and transformational leadership, and the human element of work.

These attitudes animate right-brain project management.

■ Taking It to the Extreme

Many in the project management profession have undergone an epiphany of perspective about projects and project management.

It is a familiar story. A professional (pick from any number of disciplines) enters a career and within a few years is promoted to the position of project manager. With luck, the fledgling project manager is given training in project management and perhaps is encouraged on the track to a PMP® certification. Armed with conventional techniques, the fledgling applies those techniques on his or her projects.

But many conventional projects don't fit the template for conventional techniques to work. In many instances, the project environment is so volatile that plans become obsolete as soon as they are made. Conventional project management answers this situation by calling for more discipline—more training, more planning, and more documentation.

More discipline takes more time and stress increases, with more meetings and longer workdays. Project managers and their teams work longer hours to somehow tame the chaos.

The epiphany eventually reached is that real-world projects have external forces that will not wait for this type of discipline. Something else is needed.

Doug DeCarlo, a project management consultant, trainer, and speaker, is one such convert. His book, *eXtreme Project Management*, is an entirely fresh approach to managing contemporary projects, and offers extensive insights on the change from Newtonian or conventional projects to quantum projects.[7]

Of particular note is DeCarlo's flexible project model. The overall theme to his approach can be simply stated as "Do what works."

If we understand that conventional project management has limitations for many contemporary projects, we need a foundation to master the many project challenges we face. It is time to make the complex simple. ▪

■ ENDNOTES

1 PMI, PMBOK and PMP are registered trademarks of the Project Management Institute.

2 *A Guide to the Project Management Body of Knowledge,* Third Edition (Newtown Square, PA: Project Management Institute, 2004), Process 8.2, p. 188.

3 Katie Daniel, "Improvising Leadership: Finding Comfort in Ambiguity," *Leadership Compass,* Banff Centre, Summer 2006, p. 29.

4 Hans de Bruijn, Ernst ten Heuvelhof, and Roel in't Veld, *Process Management: Why Project Management Fails in Complex Decision Making Processes* (Boston: Kluwer, 2002).

5 "Global IT Project Management Survey," KPMG, 2005, www.pmi.org. Accessed June 2006.

6 Roderic Gray, *How People Work* (Harlow, England: Prentice Hall, 2004).

7 Doug DeCarlo, *eXtreme Project Management: Using Leadership, Principles and Tools to Deliver Value in the Face of Volatility* (San Francisco: Jossey-Bass, 2004).

CHAPTER 8

Making the Complex Simple

*Everything is simpler than you think and at the same time
more complex than you imagine.*

JOHANN WOLFGANG VON GOETHE

W hen my wife was in labor with our second child, things were happening way too fast. Even though we were hurrying to leave the house, she felt the need to push and was certain the baby was ready to come out.

The situation clearly called for creative driving to get to the hospital in time. I drove way over the speed limit and ran red lights. We made it to the hospital with little time to spare; the nurse delivered our daughter in the exam room long before the doctor arrived. Had I followed the rules of the road, I would have had the unique experience of delivering the baby in the car.

The challenge of driving to the hospital was at the same time very complex and very simple. The task was complex because the car had a manual transmission and I needed to help my wife breathe through contractions while she squeezed my hand (tightly). I had to navigate safely while driving aggressively and keeping her calm so she wouldn't start pushing as her body wanted to do. I had to be concurrently hyperalert for traffic and hyperinvolved with my wife.

This was a complex and unique project, and yet it was somehow simple. The objective was crystal clear, and it *had* to be accomplished.

Sometimes, the only way to get something done is to break the "rules"—in this case, the rules of the road.

What thought processes come into play when we need to break the rules? In our mad dash to the hospital, I did violate a number of traffic laws, but in doing so, I tenaciously tried to follow guiding principles that would maintain safety for those in our car and in other cars. For example, I looked very carefully before proceeding through the red lights.

In other words, there are rules, and then there are *Rules*.

The project management profession has been successful at learning how to expertly manage a large number of projects—those projects that are familiar, predictable, and even those that are major endeavors.

But the profession has struggled to tame those projects that embody the unfamiliar, the unpredictable, and the urgent. Conventional techniques cannot successfully handle aggressive and dynamic needs in a volatile environment. We can either attempt to apply existing rules more emphatically or we can better understand the *Rules* behind the rules.

In this light, let us offer a fresh approach—not to discard what works, but to augment it with a new perspective and new tools. In exploring right-brain project management, we will not tear down left-brain approaches, but will attempt to supplement them in areas where they are limited. With this fresh approach, we will build a partnership between right-brain and left-brain approaches to develop powerful capabilities in managing projects.

We need to make the complex simple.

■ Where Are We in Project Management?

The main perspectives we have covered so far highlight the needs of projects in contemporary organizations.

Perspective 1. The needs and characteristics of people and groups are the most important ingredients of project management.

To improve the practice of project management, it is helpful to study and understand people, how they work and interact. This view does not in any way discount the need for domain expertise or the need to understand the tools of project management. Rather, what is most relevant to the improvement of project performance is individual and group performance.

> *Perspective 2. Projects struggle with uncertainty, complexity, and pressure.*

Conventional techniques excel at executing projects that deal with the familiar using sufficient resources and an adequate schedule. These techniques fail in the face of uncertainty, complexity, and pressure. To make significant improvements with such projects, we need to understand and accommodate these typically challenging forces. Projects need creative thought, experimentation, and sense-making to respond adequately.

> *Perspective 3. Projects in organizations must achieve a reliable and predictable standard of performance, even in the midst of uncertainty and seemingly unreasonable expectations.*

While project managers and their teams understandably complain about runaway scope changes, insufficient project resources, and unrealistic schedules, these are the realities of the workplace in which we operate. It is too late (if it was ever possible) to constrain the world to fit project management methodologies. We must adapt to the world as it is and work with it.

Numerous projects have overcome daunting challenges—improbable deliverables, inexperienced teams, impossible schedules—and delivered the goods. What is it about a project that makes it a phenomenal performer? The answer to this question forms the principles of right-brain project management. These principles can be applied (as appropriate) to help any project.

To understand how the right brain can improve project management, we must understand and address the issues of complexity and uncertainty in projects.

■ Understanding Complexity

The descriptive term "complex" is often used to describe projects. Complexity implies a project that is challenging to manage because of size, complicated interactions, or uncertainties. Often, anxiety goes hand in hand with complexity.

Although complexity will ultimately mean different things to different project managers, we can develop a framework for categorizing types of complexity. Doing so will help us better understand and manage project complexity, which is a significant aspect of handling the problems that plague contemporary projects.

■ Categories of Complexity

Complexity can be viewed in terms of two major dimensions: structure and uncertainty.[1]

Structural complexity concerns the composition of the project elements, in particular the number of elements and their interdependencies.[2] For example, a major construction project with many task dependencies is structurally complex. The concept of structural complexity can also be applied to the project organization (e.g., how many stakeholders are involved in decisions) and to the product or technology (e.g., the integration of subassemblies in the product).

Many project managers believe that uncertainty also dramatically compounds the complexity of a project. While the concepts of complexity and uncertainty are somewhat different, we can readily see how uncertainty increases complexity.

As an example, consider a general contractor who builds both custom homes and "spec" houses. A custom home is built to the requirements of the owner while a spec house is built to the requirements of the builder, typically without having a buyer identified until after the house is complete. The custom home building process is considerably more complex because much is uncertain prior to and even during construction. More exploration of options and costs, more negotiation, and more rework are typically involved. The builder must schedule more coordination with the subcontractors to ensure that specific features are incorporated. In contrast, the builder controls all aspects of the spec house, so much less uncertainty—and therefore complexity—is involved.

It can be enlightening to quantify the overall level of uncertainty for a project. Baccarini and Archer offer one method that specifies 23 dimensions of a project and provides scores for characteristics of each dimension.[3] For example, on the "Uniqueness of the Product," a score of 5 could be given to a project that includes a "Prototype Incorporating New Techniques," while a score of 1 could be given to a project that is intended to deliver "One of a Series of Repetitions." The higher the numerical score, the higher the uncertainty on the project.

The aggregate score can provide an excellent representation of the degree of uncertainty involved in the project. Such a tool can greatly assist the project organization in scoring candidate projects and adapting management styles accordingly.

■ Adapting Management to Complexity

When an organization faces a complex project, it is often tempting to smooth over the complexity and manage the project with conventional approaches. Uncertainties are not adequately addressed and major issues are deferred in the hope that they will resolve themselves. While known issues are problematic enough, issues that are unknown or just under the surface can be crippling for a project.

It is important to be clear and honest about the project's level of complexity, and then to apply a management approach that is appropriate to the complexity.

Turner and Cochrane provide an excellent way to categorize uncertainties on projects. They divide types of uncertainties into two categories: goals and methods. The goals of a project are its objectives. The methods are the processes used to manage and execute the project.

Let us highlight one aspect of the uncertainties in methods. A significant source of uncertainty, and one that may be somewhat hidden, is the uncertainty associated with team interactions, especially for those teams that are distributed geographically or that include members who are new to each other. Regardless of what process may exist on paper, the progress of work for such teams is tenuous until informal working relationships are established in practice.[4]

Uncertainties in both goals and methods have profound implications for projects. If project objectives are ambiguous, for example, inconsistencies may be evident in the deliverables. Uncertainties in methods can have a significant effect on the progress of a project. For example, one team member may believe she has the authority to make a decision unilaterally, while the project manager may believe otherwise.

Turner and Cochrane categorize projects into four types, as summarized in table 8-1.[5]

Conventional project management techniques and tools necessarily fit into the Type 1 project category. Once goals and methods become certain, a project enters the Type 1 category and can be managed with conventional techniques. Until that certainty is achieved, however, the management styles for each of these categories will be accordingly different at the start of the project.

▪ **Table 8-1. Classification of Projects according to Uncertainties in Goals and Methods**

Type 1	Both goals and methods are well defined (construction project).
Type 2	Goals are well defined, but methods are not (product development).
Type 3	Goals are not well defined but methods are (software development).
Type 4	Neither goals nor methods are well defined (R&D).

Turner's and Cochrane's suggestions for project start-up are listed in Table 8-2.[6] The metaphor noted in parentheses for each option represents a model for the project manager's role in each case.

■ Complexity and Uncertainty in Organizations

In my first career position in industry, I worked for a division of General Electric that was developing a new computer-based power system product. (I worked elsewhere in the division and was not on the project team.) In the early 1980s, this was a state-of-the-art development, and many significant technical and market issues represented unknowns throughout much of the effort. Management approached what was clearly a research project as a product design project, focusing on schedule to market. The result was a train wreck that caused the sponsor to fire the entire development team. The project was finally completed four years late.

In one study, project managers "... rated the ability to handle ambiguity as very important in the performance of their roles as project managers."[7] While ambiguity creates stress, this stress is more manageable than the stress that comes with trying to act like a project is predictable when it is not.

■ **Table 8-2. Start-up Focus for Projects as a Function of Uncertainties in Goals and Methods**

Type 1	Focus on refining the definition of goals and methods into detail (conductor).
Type 2	Focus on defining the scope of work and process for the team (football coach).
Type 3	Focus on defining objectives and purpose (sculptor).
Type 4	Must address both goals and methods, using creativity and inspiration. The process is inevitably iterative and should be directed toward moving the project into either a Type 2 or Type 3 category (eagle).

To a significant degree, project difficulties arise from the mismatch between project complexity and the management model used. Conventional project management methodology is predicated on a project being orderly and predictable. This approach is entirely understandable: when the environment is complicated, it is natural to want to make it orderly and predictable. This tendency is particularly evident in an organization where decision-making tends toward safety and predictability.

Let's look at this from a different perspective. An organization is most often modeled as a system in the aggregate: it has inputs, it performs functions on the inputs, and it produces outputs. From a macro perspective, there is cause and effect. Everyone associated with the organization wants the operation to be as understandable, profitable, and predictable as possible.

In many organizations, predictability is preferred over enhancements that are unpredictable. Through a collection of risk management strategies, an organization seeks to minimize financial risks that arise from the volatility of the environment; however, it is more challenging to address an unpredictable internal process.

Organizations apply this overall philosophy naturally to projects and project management. We want to believe that disciplined processes will convert a project's complexity into something that can be planned reliably.

While it is better to acknowledge the complexity of the project and plan accordingly, it is much more common to gravitate toward the rational management style espoused by Taylor:

> *Many managers continue to manage by using reductionist approaches (separating things into parts); by devising complex planning activities based on the notion of a predictable world; and in believing that cause and effect processes produce fairly foreseeable results .... [A] considerable number of managers appear to have a mindset similar to the Taylorist model developed at the beginning of the last century."*[8]

■ Describing the Uncertain

It is certainly possible to plan for uncertainty even if our plans cannot articulate definitively the outcomes of that uncertainty. The key to this planning is to use the right approach, and the right approach begins by accurately describing the uncertainty.

Let us consider three different classes or representations of projects: orderly, chaotic, and complex. These classes of projects can be considered representations of systems.

For a project, the cause-effect relationship is embodied in the project plan. From a macro perspective, if we provide inputs to the project in the form of resources, the execution of the plan will supposedly result in the intended output. The plan is the transfer function, or the cause-effect operator.

An orderly system has a well-defined cause-effect relationship. Input-output relationships are well understood and plans can be formulated that rely on these relationships. In a chaotic system, there is no cause-effect relationship. What happens is seemingly the result of chance (or the cause-effect relationship is so tenuous that it is unusable).

For complex systems, the cause-effect relationship is not initially known, but it can be discovered. We can see the patterns of causality with the benefit of hindsight. In such systems, order emerges, but it may not be explicitly repeatable.[9]

An orderly project is one in which the process to complete the objectives is familiar, the team process is understood and has been in practice, and there are no significant risk issues, such as with technology or schedule. In other words, the process from start to finish is known, understood, and logical. Such a project can be successfully managed with conventional project management practices in a reliable and predictable manner. As an example, when an experienced contractor pours a concrete sidewalk, the project can be considered orderly.

A chaotic project is one in which the environment is so unfamiliar and dynamic that it challenges the very notion of management. A chaotic project may be a serious and unique crisis that suddenly presents itself, such as the terrorist attacks of September 11, 2001. Such events can only be addressed through immediate action to gain some control over the chaos.

A complex project may involve an unproven technology, team members who are unfamiliar with one another, an aggressive schedule, or other significant risks. At the initiation of such a project, one cannot (and should not) attempt to state the cause-effect relationship of the project in the form of a reliable project plan. Yet that is exactly what typically happens.

A far better "plan" is to begin by making sense of the complexity—by exploring what is uncertain, making it certain, and making the transition from what is complex to what is orderly.

The crux of the difference between managing orderly projects and managing complex projects is the difference between exploitation and exploration. If a cause-effect relationship is known and reliable, it can be exploited. If the relationship is ambiguous or not reliably known, the environment must first be explored to determine the relationship. Only then can it be exploited.

Certainly, projects fall along a continuum of orderly and complex characteristics. Along the continuum are projects for which there is *hidden order*[10] or for which a cause-effect relationship is at first unknown but is discoverable. The management approach for these projects is like that for complex projects, but planning is somewhat more predictable.

■ Management Approaches

It is important to characterize a project's type or level of order and then apply an appropriate management approach. This is in essence a macro or big-picture step that should be taken very early in a project or as part of a project office.

Table 8-3 summarizes the macro methods for managing the various types of projects.[11]

Risk versus Uncertainty

The terms "risk" and "uncertainty" are sometimes confused when discussing the complex project.

In conventional approaches, risk management is a fundamental and well-known element of project management. A risk has been defined as "an uncertain event or condition that, if it occurs, has a positive or negative effect on a project's objectives."[12] In other words, a risk is a potential *future* event that can affect the achievement of the project objectives—*if it occurs*. The concept of risk is an important one to address and consider in a project plan, but it does not quite address the landscape of the complex project.

In contrast, uncertainty is best understood not as a future possibility but as a *present reality*. For example, we are uncertain *now* about the features the customer values for product X. Typically, for a project to progress, we must take steps to reduce the uncertainties. These steps are different from those commonly practiced to manage risk.

We might say that there is a *risk* (future) to achieving project objectives if we do not resolve the *uncertainty* (present and ongoing until resolved) in product features.

▪ Table 8-3. Project Types and Corresponding Management Approaches

Project Type	Characteristics	Management Approach
Orderly	Projects that are well defined	Conventional techniques
Complex	Projects that have uncertainties	Explore to determine relationships
Chaotic	Projects that are completely novel and dynamic, or out of control (e.g., crisis situation)	Act quickly to bring the situation under control

In conventional approaches, it is implicitly assumed that all (or nearly all) ambiguity is resolved *before* the project commences. While straightforward choices may be made during the course of the project, the stakeholders have resolved substantive questions about objectives or methods prior to approving the project plan.

In real organizations, many projects begin with considerable uncertainty in play. Recognizing this (possibly inevitable) situation, teams need a framework and tools that enable them to successfully navigate projects in this environment.

Management of uncertainty on a project is often mixed with management of risk, but it is better to address the concepts separately. Risk management involves planning to accommodate future events that may or may not happen. Uncertainty management is the proactive effort to make sense of the project and reduce ambiguity in the present. Experience has shown that a key success factor for projects is the recognition and proactive management of complexities.[13]

Uncertainty Management

In conventional project management, uncertainty is often considered a synonym for *variability*. For example, in the planning stage, when estimating task durations, we can account for the probabilities of variations in the estimates. For our purposes, we will assume that existing tools are more than sufficient for managing issues of variability.

A critical source of uncertainty on many contemporary projects is better understood with the synonym *ambiguity*. While variability can be somewhat challenging, ambiguity has the potential to have significant impact on the project.

The techniques for managing this concept of uncertainty are primarily about sense-making—skills that are considerably different from skills for managing risk and managing variability.

Uncertainty management "... implies exploring and understanding the origins of project uncertainty before seeking to manage it, with no preconceptions about what is desirable or undesirable."[14] This is the essential meaning of sense-making.

Making Sense of Complexity

In essence, sense-making is the process of coming to a common understanding of the appropriate direction forward.

As an example, in a product development effort, there is a common tension between the engineers and the marketers. The engineers, if they are true to stereotype, want to include technical elegance in the product and take their time in development. The marketers want a lot of features and to get to market quickly. It is critical that the leader of this effort help the team collectively *make sense* of the product, preferably giving the customer's needs priority. If sense is not made, team members inevitably pull in different directions.

Sense-making is predominantly a right-brain activity: it requires seeing and developing patterns where no clear patterns exist. However, it is not a shot in the dark because the team relies on the collective values and purpose that form the foundation for the effort. This stage of the effort requires some experimentation to determine patterns.

This is an entirely different approach to project management, and one that is well-suited to the right brain.

A Fresh Perspective

Conventional project management "... is supposedly a systemic approach to management of change but its foundation lies in the traditional rational managerialism thus facing an increasing threat of irrelevance unless newer models are developed to respond to change and complexity."[15]

The reality of projects in contemporary organizations demands, and can benefit from, a fresh perspective. There is no argument that conventional project management approaches are excellent for managing projects that are well-defined. But complex and aggressive projects need a different framework and assumptions for progress to be made.

The framework and assumptions for complex projects are best handled through the right brain. To move toward the principles that form the foundation of right-brain project management, we will first study the factors that contributed to the phenomenal performance of five projects. ▪

■ ENDNOTES

1 T. M. Williams, "The Need for New Paradigms for Complex Projects," *International Journal of Project Management,* Vol. 17, No. 5, 1999, pp. 269–273.

2 David Baccarini, "The Concept of Project Complexity—A Review," *International Journal of Project Management,* Vol. 14, No. 4, 1996, pp. 201–204.

3 David Baccarini and Richard Archer, "The Risk Ranking of Projects: A Methodology," *International Journal of Project Management,* Vol. 19, No. 3, 2001, pp. 139–145.

4 Stephen Ward and Chris Chapman, "Transforming Project Risk Management into Project Uncertainty Management," *International Journal of Project Management,* Vol. 21, No. 2, 2003, pp. 97–105.

5 J. R. Turner and R. A. Cochrane, "Goals-and-Methods Matrix: Coping with Projects with Ill Defined Goals and/or Methods of Achieving Them," *International Journal of Project Management,* Vol. 11, No. 2, May 1993, pp. 93–102.

6 Ibid.

7 Jane Helm and Kaye Remington, "Effective Project Sponsorship—An Evaluation of the Role of the Executive Sponsor in Complex Infrastructure Projects by Senior Project Managers," *Project Management Journal*, Vol. 36, No. 3, September 2005, p. 56.

8 Elizabeth McMillan, *Complexity, Organizations and Change* (London: Routledge, 2004), p. 56.

9 Dave Snowden, "Strategy in the Context of Uncertainty," *Handbook of Business Strategy*, Vol. 6, Issue 1, 2005, pp. 47–54.

10 Ibid.

11 Ibid.

12 *A Guide to the Project Management Body of Knowledge,* Third Edition (Newtown Square, PA: Project Management Institute, 2004), p. 373.

13 Ali Jaafari, "Management of Risks, Uncertainties and Opportunities on Projects: Time for a Fundamental Shift," *International Journal of Project Management,* Vol. 19, No. 2, 2001, pp. 89–101.

14 Stephen Ward and Chris Chapman, "Transforming Project Risk Management into Project Uncertainty Management," *International Journal of Project Management,* Vol. 21, No. 2, 2003, pp. 97–105.

15 Ali Jaafari, "Project Management in the Age of Complexity and Change," *Project Management Journal*, Vol. 34, No. 4, December 2003, p. 56.

CHAPTER 9

■ That's Incredible: Case Studies of Phenomenal Projects

■
■
■

An invasion of armies can be resisted, but not an idea whose time has come.

VICTOR HUGO ■

C hatting with working project managers in industry, we get the impression that many projects finish late and over budget, and that they struggle to meet their objectives. This level of performance seems to have become the norm.

Occasionally we encounter a project that not only meets its objectives but goes far beyond them. What makes such projects tick?

In this chapter, we examine five such *phenomenal* projects. All far exceeded what would have been predicted by conventional wisdom.

These five projects are all "right-brain" projects, in that their success secrets have decidedly right-brain ingredients. This does not imply that left-brain, formal practices were not used on these projects, but rather that their extraordinary success was linked to right-brain principles.

We will describe these projects and then examine the right-brain principles that drove their unusual success, particularly those elements that were observed in common on the five projects. These elements form the principles of right-brain project management.

■ The Skunk Works[®1]

During the long days of World War II, Allied intelligence indicated that Germany was working on the development of a jet fighter. At a time when propeller planes were state-of-the-art, the jet fighter would offer a strategic advantage in the sky. With the continent of Europe still securely in German hands, Germany's development of a jet fighter first could dramatically tip the balance of war in its favor.

In this context, in 1943 the U.S. Army Air Force authorized Lockheed to develop the first U.S. jet fighter, the P-80 Shooting Star. Work was begun on a handshake; the project was underway for four months before a contract was signed.

In the midst of the many important and strategic initiatives underway at the time, the importance of the jet fighter initiative cannot be overstated. War has a way of focusing attention, and that was certainly the case with this project.

The effort was placed under the direction of Clarence "Kelly" Johnson, a young Lockheed engineer with a reputation for no-nonsense leadership. The choice of Johnson was perhaps the first element in the success of this project. He established control and set the culture for the project from the start. Johnson made known a number of principles that would guide his leadership of the project (see Table 9-1).[2] During a time of war and with an important strategic mission, Johnson insisted that nothing stand in the way of achievement.

Under Johnson's direction, the project team was organized in ways that were unusual for the time. First, the entire team was located away from Lockheed facilities. This helped ensure that the team's work would not be interrupted. Second, Johnson selected team members with a proven track record of superior performance. Third, he insisted that the team members not be assigned to any other project, so they could devote their attention entirely to the jet fighter.

The facilities for the team were austere to say the least; the team was actually housed in a circus tent. The facilities were located next

■ **Table 9-1. Kelly's 14 Rules from the Lockheed Skunk Works®**

1	Give virtually complete program control to the Skunk Works® manager, who should report to a division president or higher.
2	Provide strong but small project offices for both the military and the contractor.
3	Ruthlessly restrict the number of people connected to the project, using a small number of good people (10–25 percent of the number used on conventional projects).
4	Use a simple and flexible drawing and drawing release system.
5	Keep reports to a minimum, but thoroughly document important work.
6	Stay current with cost accounting and provide the customer a monthly cost and projected budget review.
7	Allow the contractor more than typical responsibility for vendor bids for subcontracts on the project. (Commercial bid procedures often surpass military procedures.)
8	Push more basic inspection to subcontractors and vendors, and avoid duplication.
9	Delegate the authority to test the system in flight to the contractor.
10	Ensure that hardware specifications are agreed to well in advance of contracting.
11	Ensure timely funding for the program to prevent financial pressure on the contractor.
12	Promote mutual trust between the military project organization and the contractor, as well as their close cooperation on a daily basis, thus reducing misunderstanding and correspondence.
13	Strictly control access to the project by outsiders through appropriate security measures.
14	Provide appropriate awards and recognition for performance, and do not link rewards to the number of personnel supervised.

door to a plastics factory, which gave off a vile stench. It is believed that this odor was the reason for the informal name of the group. In the popular Li'l Abner comic strip, there was a "Skonk Works" that cooked up a smelly brew made of skunks, old shoes, and other nasty ingredients.[3]

While it is always nice to have pleasant facilities and tools, the Skunk Works® is an example of how teams will tolerate and overcome unpleasant conditions to accomplish project goals. Conventional project management wisdom estimated that it would take 18 months to develop a prototype of the jet fighter. Incredibly, the team completed the prototype in *143 days!*

The Lockheed P-80 never actually flew in combat. The project nevertheless stands as a testament to the leadership principles of Kelly Johnson and the motivation and energy offered by a compelling purpose.

The success of the P-80 development prompted Lockheed to maintain the Skunk Works® as an ongoing division for advanced development projects. Since the P-80, the Lockheed Skunk Works® has successfully completed a number of other development projects, including the SR-71 Blackbird, the advanced, long-range Mach 3 reconnaissance aircraft.

The group's name is now associated more generically with a project team that is organized to achieve extraordinary results, using means that are outside the usual rules and policies, with minimal bureaucratic restraint. These projects are often set up as informal, quasi-legal, off-site entities, and may be carried out secretly. Usually, a strong champion leads the group—someone who can protect the team from the inevitable heat from the bureaucrats.

■ Apollo 13

"Houston, we have a problem."

Other than the transmissions from the first lunar landing, these five words form the most memorable sentence communicated from space. They initiated the most challenging and dramatic crisis ever encountered in space exploration—an event that seemed to stop the world for three intense days.

In May 1961, President John F. Kennedy proposed a bold mission for the country: to land a man on the moon and safely return him to earth before the end of the decade. This mission was issued in the context of the Cold War. The conquest of space and the achievement of a manned moon landing was seen as a way to gain strategic military advantage as well as bragging rights over the Soviet Union.

In July 1969, the Apollo 11 mission fulfilled Kennedy's dream, and astronauts Neil Armstrong and Buzz Aldrin walked on the moon. The National Aeronautics and Space Administration (NASA) planned several more moon missions focused on gaining scientific knowledge about the moon.

After the landings of Apollo 11 and 12, on April 11, 1970, Apollo 13 was launched with astronauts James Lovell, Fred Haise, and John Swigert. The astronauts entered orbit around the earth and performed the burn of the spacecraft engine that would break them free of earth's gravity and set them on a course to the moon.

On the evening of April 14, while on course for the moon and nearly 200,000 miles from the earth, the astronauts experienced an explosion on their spacecraft. In the hours and days after the explosion, little was known about what had happened. Many feared that the unthinkable would come true—that the astronauts would perish in space.

It was only much later that the cause of the explosion would become known. On board the spacecraft, liquid oxygen tanks were used for life support for the astronauts and also to produce electricity from fuel cells. The liquid oxygen had to be "stirred" from time to time to maintain proper consistency. As a result of a combination of factors, the insulation had failed on wires to the stirrer in one of the tanks. When the stirrer was activated, a short circuit caused the liquid oxygen tank to explode.

The spacecraft consisted of three components: the command module (CM), the lunar module (LM), and the service module (SM). The explosion occurred in the SM and critically damaged another oxygen tank. The failures of the oxygen tanks threatened not only the astronauts' life support, but also the power supply for the CM. The CM had batteries, but they would be needed for reentry.

Hurtling away from the earth and unable to perform a spacewalk or repair the craft, the astronauts turned off power to the CM and entered the LM as a "lifeboat." Over the next three days, the astronauts encountered one major crisis after another.

To conserve power, they endured freezing temperatures inside the ship. To limit the discharge of waste, which would require an offsetting fuel burn to maintain course, the astronauts cut back on consumption of water, to the point that Haise became sick.

To return to the earth, the astronauts performed a course correction that would use the moon's gravity for a single pass around the back of the moon, a maneuver much like the flight of a boomerang. This correction required the burn of the LM descent engine, which was never intended for this use.

One of the most threatening problems was the buildup of carbon dioxide from respiration. The cabin air system was taxed because the LM was designed to support two astronauts, not three. The ground crew improvised an apparatus for the scrubbers that removed carbon dioxide from the air, which the astronauts were able to implement.

Throughout the crisis, NASA ground personnel worked tirelessly to creatively solve all the many problems faced in the mission, focused on one goal: the safe return of the astronauts.

The spacecraft hobbled home. In the final crisis, the astronauts manually performed the engine firing that would put them on the proper course for a safe landing. To great relief, Apollo 13 landed safely on April 17.

One cannot overstate the degree of difficulty and risk inherent in the many solutions that were invented and improvised in the harrowing three days of the Apollo 13 crisis. The astronauts and the NASA ground team made extensive use of a specific creative skill called "bricolage," which is the process of creatively adapting whatever is at hand to solve a pressing need. Bricolage makes heavy use of the right brain.

It is a testament to professionalism, creativity, and commitment to the objective that Apollo 13 became NASA's "most successful failure."

■ Linux

In 1991, graduate student Linus Torvalds began work on a kernel for the UNIX operating system. Naming his kernel Linux, he posted the source code to other programmers for comments. This thread began what has come to be called the open source software movement.

Torvalds' associates shared their ideas with others, and the sharing process grew. A number of programmers contributed sections of code or made improvements upon existing code, all in a free and transparent manner. In the coming years, thousands of programmers contributed to the effort.

Linux became much more than the technical implementation of an operating system: the word "revolution" was often used to describe development of the software. Where commercial software companies, notably Microsoft, closely guarded source code and sought profit, Linux became the vanguard for free and open distribution. Many saw Linux as a social movement as well as software development.

Linux is an excellent example of a grassroots effort driven by sheer passion on the part of the developers. Linux is also an example of a development that stretches the definition and meaning of a project.

When there is a grassroots effort, with no definitive end point, a project can begin to look a lot like "operations" or "continuous improvement." The work on the project can take on the characteristics and workings of a living organism. When this is the case, the host organization may have difficulty managing the endeavor. While such a project has considerable power and value, only an adaptive management style will allow the effort to proceed with defined intermediate points.

We will come back to the Linux story later because it offers some excellent lessons on motivation and what fuels emotional involvement in a project.

■ Hurricane Katrina Shelter at the Houston Astrodome

Hurricane Katrina struck the Louisiana and Mississippi Gulf Coast on the morning of August 29, 2005. As a category 4 hurricane with winds of 145 mph, it caused widespread damage at landfall in Mississippi. But it is what dramatically unfolded in the city of New Orleans over the next two days that captivated the attention of the world.

Below sea level and surrounded by water, New Orleans is protected by levees. Knowledgeable people in the city had long feared what would happen if the levees were breached during a hurricane. This time, the unthinkable happened.

Initially, it was believed that the city had dodged a bullet. The storm passed seemingly without widespread damage. Then, after the hurricane was well inland, puzzling reports came in to authorities that water was flooding into the city. People literally had to fight for their lives to escape the rising water.

Levees had failed in multiple places, and soon 80 percent of the city was under water. Thousands of people were rescued dramatically by helicopter and boat.

As a shelter of last resort, the Louisiana Superdome held over 20,000 people. When it became damaged and lost power, shelter evacuees took to the streets.

Images of the suffering that ensued moved the nation and the world. The need became compelling and monumental: immediately evacuate the estimated 100,000 people who remained in the city. It was a logistical nightmare.

As the drama unfolded, officials elsewhere in the region realized that New Orleans needed help. At 3:00 a.m. on August 31, a phone call came in to the official in charge of the Houston Astrodome: would it be possible to use the stadium as an evacuation shelter?

Once billed as the "Eighth Wonder of the World," the Houston Astrodome was the first domed stadium. Over 40 years old, the Astrodome was a semi-retired facility. No longer used for professional sports, it had not been used for any significant event for 18 months. Certainly, it had never been used as an evacuation shelter. In fact, there had never before been a shelter to care for 25,000 people. In the early morning hours of August 31, the commitment was made, and the plans for such a facility were set in motion.

While the area authorities had executed plans and staged mock exercises for hurricane shelters, the enormity of this endeavor had no precedent that even came close. All the provisions and elements—food, cots, medical facilities—had to be assembled immediately. Based on the initial commitment, buses packed with evacuees left New Orleans bound for Houston. There was no turning back.

This was another crisis that called for creative solutions. Site security was essential, including identification for each evacuee. The Kroger supermarket chain donated enough magnetic affinity cards and scanners to fill this need; shopper discount cards were adapted to serve as ID cards.

Nineteen hours after the 3:00 a.m. phone call that set the process in motion, the first cots arrived from out of state. Ten minutes later, the first bus arrived from New Orleans. As evacuees stepped off the bus, Mayor Bill White greeted them with "Welcome to Houston."

Only one significant omission occurred in the process of readying the shelter. In all the chaos, no one thought to arrange for towels for the evacuees to use after showering. This oversight was remedied by the next day.

The Astrodome served as temporary housing for several weeks while more permanent arrangements were being made. During this time, the 25,000 evacuees were served by nearly 60,000 volunteers from dozens of agencies. In another first, the evacuation shelter was assigned its own zip code.

Establishment of the Hurricane Katrina evacuation shelter at the Astrodome demonstrates the logistical feats that can be accomplished when people are moved by compassion over the suffering of others.

■ Red, White, and Blue Out

The terrorist attacks of September 11, 2001, prompted a number of heroic responses. The incredible bravery and professionalism of the responders in New York and the courageous improvisation of the passengers on United Flight 93 stand out for our recognition, our homage, and our gratitude.

In the days after the attacks, another project evinced a strong sense of community cohesiveness. Powerful project management principles seem to work intuitively when the purpose of the project is compelling.

From a personal perspective, this project was pivotal for me. I had managed a number of projects in my career and had spoken with many project managers. I had become somewhat jaded about the profession of project management and its challenges. Like many others, I wondered if there was any real hope for the profession to overcome its perceived mediocre performance. While I had nothing to do with this project, observing it in action renewed my faith in project management.

This project took my understanding of project management and turned it completely upside down. In fact, this one project served as the genesis for this book.

To call this a project in the conventional sense of the word is actually quite a stretch. There was no designated project manager, not even a project organization. Those who led the effort had no training in project management. No one was paid for their time working on this endeavor. There was no project plan, and the objective evolved gradually. Only within hours of the schedule deadline was the scope of the project communicated to a large number of participants.

In other words, this project violated just about every rule of conventional project management. It was an "accidental" project—and it was a phenomenal success.

In the days after the September 11 attacks, the nation grappled with the enormity of what had happened and struggled with how to react in a meaningful way. Many people and groups organized events to raise funds for victims and their families. Many wanted to make a statement of values.

At Texas A&M University, one student wanted to do something that would raise money and make a statement. After giving it some thought, he settled on the idea of selling patriotic T-shirts for fans to wear at the next home football game, which was nine days away. The proceeds of shirt sales would go to responders in New York.

The student shared the idea with a few other students, and the concept began to evolve into a more dramatic event. Wouldn't it *really* make a statement if the colors at the stadium could be coordinated into three sections: the upper deck red, the middle deck white, and the lower deck blue? With this simple vision, five students embarked on an impromptu and unlikely project. They thought their initial objective—to sell a few thousand shirts—was ambitious but achievable.

The event was called the Red, White and Blue Out,[4] kind of like a "white out" in a blizzard. As the five students shared the idea, it spread like wildfire. Students were eager to help the cause, and many wanted to buy shirts. The makeshift group could hardly print shirts fast enough for people to buy.

As the demand increased, scores of students devoted all-nighters to making T-shirts. Soon the local stock of T-shirts was exhausted.

Here, I think, is one of the most amazing parts of this story. One of the project leaders phoned a T-shirt vendor in Dallas and asked for 10,000 shirts. The makeshift student group had no line of credit, could offer no payment up front, and had no way to arrange delivery. Catching the buzz of the project, the vendor agreed to the request on a verbal promise to pay later, and even offered a truck to deliver the shipment overnight.

That's the power of a compelling purpose.

Game day arrived on September 22. While many shirts had been sold earlier, a number of out-of-town fans arrived with no knowledge of the event. It was only when they arrived at the stadium that they learned of the Red, White, and Blue Out and felt the electricity in the air.

The project volunteers sold an astounding 30,000 shirts in the four hours prior to the game (about two shirts per second), for a total of 70,000 shirts sold by kickoff.

The view from above was moving. Each deck of the stadium was a nearly solid color, just as envisioned. While the scene itself was inspiring, what was really inspiring to me as a project manager was how a group of college students—amateur project leaders—could pull off the improbable.

Perhaps the most appropriate word to characterize this project is "organic." It demonstrated a number of important principles, including: (1) a project can be successfully completed with intuitive skills, (2) a compelling vision provides the energy to overcome project challenges, and (3) trust brings significant agility to a project.

The Red, White, and Blue Out raised approximately $200,000 for responder relief funds in New York City. To honor the five project leaders, an alumni group paid for them to fly to New York to deliver the check personally to police and firefighters. The group also donated a $1,000 scholarship for each of the five leaders.

This is the nature of a phenomenal project.

■ Lessons Learned

The famous quote from Victor Hugo at the start of this chapter may capture a fundamental truth about phenomenal projects.

When a group of people really want a project to succeed and they put forward a compelling purpose, they inspire nearly boundless and unstoppable energy and creativity.

These five projects all demonstrate in different ways the possibilities for projects, and they all exhibit various characteristics of right-brain approaches. We will now introduce the seven principles of right-brain project management to call upon the powerful techniques that made these and other phenomenal projects work so well. ▪

▪ ENDNOTES

1 Skunk Works is a registered trade mark of the Lockheed Martin Corporation.

2 "Kelly's 14 Rules," http://www.lockheedmartin.com. Accessed October 2006.

3 "How the Skunk Works® Got Its Name," http://www.lockheedmartin.com. Accessed October 2006.

4 B. Michael Aucoin, *From Engineer to Manager: Mastering the Transition* (Boston: Artech House, 2002), pp. 259–260.

■ Principles of Right–Brain Project Management

■
■
■

Mind unemployed is mind unenjoyed.

CHRISTIAN NESTELL BOVEE ■

W e have now laid the groundwork for the principles of right-brain project management. Before proceeding, let us summarize a bit and briefly review the foundations of project needs, the nature and value of right-brain approaches, and ways to facilitate right-brain processes.

Foundation 1. Two brains are better than one.

Conventional project management techniques rely predominantly on the left brain, and they work exceptionally well for appropriate projects. The right brain houses powerful capabilities that can dramatically improve work performance on projects. In short, two brains are better than one.

Power and stability come from using more than one perspective on an issue. This tenet is true not only for organizations as a means of promoting diversity of ideas, but also for the individual who can access two perspectives and processing styles.

Foundation 2. The needs of projects map well to right-brain capabilities.

Organizations struggle with projects in complex and ambiguous environments. Project teams often lack motivation and enthusiasm for their work. Groups face challenges in making sense of the work and the various pressures placed upon it. These are all areas in which the right brain excels.

> *Foundation 3. Right-brain approaches are natural elements of human thinking.*

Right-brain techniques are natural processes of the human brain; they are intuitive, even instinctual. They are also commonly underused and largely dormant on project work. By applying these powerful capabilities, project teams can make significant improvements in project performance.

To overcome any sense of intimidation or discomfort, project managers should proceed objectively and dispassionately in examining how the right brain may help a project. The objective is to improve project effectiveness; if right-brain approaches can help this effort, they are certainly worth exploring.

> *Foundation 4. The benefits of right-brain techniques are well-supported.*

The concepts that underlie right-brain project management are well-supported by research and experience in organizations. Many projects have achieved phenomenal results by applying right-brain approaches.

> *Foundation 5. To be effective, right-brain approaches need to be applied in an environment that values their contributions.*

Right-brain techniques work best with management and leadership styles that value the creativity and motivation of team members. It is counterproductive to expect creativity from team members while applying project processes that prevent the application of new ideas.

By its very nature, right-brain project management incorporates a high level of trust and belief in the abilities of team members. Organizations that value and practice the Theory Y or Theory Z style of management and transformational leadership will be better suited to implement right-brain techniques with a team. In this context it is also helpful to understand Maslow's needs hierarchy and the human need for worthwhile work that engages our passions.

Above all, these attitudes and practices of project managers must be genuine. If right-brain techniques are used in a disingenuous and manipulative manner, team members will inevitably see through the ruse and will react with resentment and retaliation.

> *Foundation 6. Right-brain project management is one tool in the project management toolkit.*

Right-brain techniques are not intended to substitute for or supplant left-brain approaches to project management. Right-brain approaches augment good conventional approaches and apply in areas where left-brain approaches are not sufficient or fully effective.

Right-brain project management is not a step-by-step recipe or prescription approach to projects. By nature, "right-brain" work on projects requires experimentation and adaptation. It will make sense to emphasize certain principles on one project but not on another. The effective way to apply right-brain project management is to understand and internalize the attitudes it incorporates and then to use what works most appropriately on a given project.

While right-brain approaches can help any project, it makes no sense to apply them cavalierly on all projects. We have noted that large projects should be managed using conventional left-brain approaches. A project that involves extensive coordination of tasks with numerous players demands a methodology that is analytical and rational. A project that concerns public safety would likewise be best approached with a well-defined set of rules. A project that requires administrative oversight and accountability must also adhere to formal procedures and processes.

Right-brain approaches will help most significantly on those projects that are set in complex environments, those that require innovation (either for product or process), and those that are urgent. Right-brain approaches can also help *any* project with respect to motivation, purpose, and sense-making for team members.

What Do Project Teams Need?

Because projects operate in a world that is complex and impatient, teams need tools that enable them to overcome challenges creatively and innovatively. Teams also need a decentralized structure with distributed leadership to speed decision-making and task execution, as well as to promote ownership.

Perhaps most importantly, teams need tools that are accessible by a broad spectrum of people. Training in conventional techniques—and individuals with PMP® certification—will always be needed. But organizations also need tools that virtually anyone can use, especially tools that are essentially intuitive. Right-brain project management works because it draws upon simple, natural, and familiar concepts.

Principles of Right–Brain Project Management

Right-brain project management is based on seven key principles, which are summarized in Table 10-1.

> *Principle 1. Find the compelling purpose.*

▪ **Table 10-1. Principles of Right-Brain Project Management**

	Principle	*Description*
1	Find the compelling purpose	Finding emotional energy and motivation
2	Make sense of the project	Exploring what the project should be
3	Experiment and adapt	Adapting to what is learned
4	Create the new reality	Discovering new and useful patterns
5	Exercise and fulfill trust	Making decisions that foster leadership
6	Hit the sweet spot	Improvising within the project framework
7	Leave a legacy	Developing and fulfilling a lasting vision

At the core of right-brain project management is the significant benefit that arises from having a compelling purpose to drive the project. A compelling purpose is an objective that is so important it *must* be accomplished. A worthy goal provides energy to engage the intellect and the soul on the project. It is also the kind of purpose that helps us tolerate the imperfections of any organization.

When team members recognize and internalize such a purpose, a powerful emotional connection is created. While projects need plans and processes, what they really need is energy—*human energy*. Human energy and motivation spring directly from emotion. With a compelling purpose, projects that are seemingly impossible can achieve extraordinary results. Without a compelling purpose, a project can become tiresome.

The energy that drives a successful project starts with right-brain emotion. It is engaged by understanding and attending to each person's need for spiritual survival.

Contemporary projects are much like the Olympics in that they demand a high level of commitment and mind space. We wouldn't expect an Olympic athlete to compete without top-notch nutrition; in the same way, project teams need sufficient fuel. The fuel that is needed most is a compelling purpose.

Ultimately, we seek to give value to others in a way that relates to our own values; we seek to do that which engenders pleasing emotions. When an organization finds the compelling purpose, it creates the environment for executing successful projects. The abundant energy that is generated finds a way to overcome obstacles.

This, then, is a fundamental requirement for all projects: identify the *compelling* purpose!

Principle 2. Make sense of the project.

A significant problem with contemporary projects is that they literally do not make sense. I don't mean this in a facetious way, but rather that the collective forces on the project simply do not add up; they are too complex. If we can make sense of the project, then we can move forward effectively. If we do not collectively make sense, we will not progress, or we will move erratically.

The right brain excels at discovering patterns from fragmented and disjointed pieces of information or new situations. The left brain is good at testing these insights for validity and then applying them predictably. Working together, these two hemispheres make sense of the world and its complexities and then apply this sense productively. In this holistic way, the right brain creates and sees the big picture, and the left brain puts the picture to work.

Project sense-making is a broad topic, and it is closely connected to finding the compelling purpose. When we have a compelling purpose, we are better able to make sense of the environment and guide the project to completion. Above all, the purpose provides the context that is critical to sense-making.

Sense-making involves finding patterns where there appear to be none. In this way, an environment that is initially complex can be turned into one that has order.

Sense-making applies not only to product and task issues, but just as importantly to processes. In many cases, team members are working together for the first time, or they may be geographically dispersed. It is important for team members to make sense of the interactions and relationships that form the foundation for their project work.

One of the most important ingredients of sense-making is the broader context of why the project is important. When we have a deep understanding of the purpose and the "spiritual survival" elements of the project, we are energized to work on the project.

Primarily a right-brain process, sense-making uses rich forms of communication, such as metaphor, story, and visuals. Intuition is particularly useful for sense-making efforts, as it is one of the most valuable tools for making sense of what is complicated or difficult.

One of the most valuable opportunities for using intuition as a sense-making tool is on the troubled project. It is often difficult to sort through the complicated and challenging facts and emotions associated with such projects. Intuition can often quickly enable us to see through the forest to reach the needed answer.

Intuition, and more generally sense-making, are directed toward discovery of the truth, to help us understand reality more completely. When we embark on the complex project, we do not have a complete grasp of what we need to know; that can only come through exploration—once sense is made.

Principle 3. Experiment and adapt.

The conventional project model assumes that once planning is complete, everything about the project is known. How else is it possible to identify the tasks and durations that will form the project execution phase? In other words, the conventional model assumes that all experimentation is over once the project plan is formalized. While this may hold true on some projects, the high degree of complexity and ambiguity found on many contemporary projects demands considerable experimentation during the course of the project.

This approach to a project requires a considerable shift in attitude and a sense of comfort with ambiguity. With experimentation naturally comes adaptation. We continue to learn more about our destination and throughout the project close the gap of what is unknown.

Projects would proceed more effectively if teams experimented before committing significant resources. Many bad projects go on for too long because commitments were made before experimenting. Perhaps the problems on these troubled projects weren't predictable: all the more justification to experiment!

Principle 4. Create the new reality.

It is essentially axiomatic: if there is not a familiar path for a project, one must be created. Contemporary projects demand a high level of creativity and innovation. To be sure, this does not mean that they must always create something that is absolutely novel. Instead, we use creativity to build upon prior knowledge in new ways.

Creativity is not solely the province of artists and musicians. *Every* professional in a contemporary organization must be creative in some way. Moreover, creativity is called for not only in a professional domain, such as electronics, but just as importantly for improvements to human processes.

Here we should distinguish between creativity and innovation. While creativity involves bringing about a novel idea, innovation means applying a novel idea in a productive or profitable manner. Creativity is a necessary element of innovation, but it is innovation that organizations value.

Not every creative idea is useful or profitable; in fact, most are not. Once the right brain provides the new idea, the left brain tests the idea for usefulness in the relevant context. The right brain can generate a winning idea, but it also is responsible for many dogs. This is where the left brain performs its valuable role as tester and critic. This is one of the important ways in which the two brains work together on projects.

The right brain creates because of its processing style: it excels in discovering patterns from fragments of information. It is unencumbered by rules and conventional logic, so it can break new ground and think outside the box.

From an organizational perspective, we need a process that encourages creative ideas yet quickly determines if they are worth pursuing. Such a process provides an excellent balance between right-brain creativity and left-brain frameworks.

Principle 5. Exercise and fulfill trust.

An important ingredient promoting right-brain techniques is trust.

If trust is not part of a relationship, those in the relationship must rely on set rules of behavior to interact and accomplish anything. Deviations from the rules are viewed with suspicion.

When trust is present, it is possible to allow more freedom of behavior, believing that the other will ultimately have the best interest of the relationship in mind. This framework permits more creativity, ownership, and pride. It is the goal of Theory Z management.

Trust offers other substantial benefits as well. When team members operate in an environment of trust, decision-making and leadership can be exercised throughout the group. This approach on a project can dramatically improve the speed and quality of solutions.

Trust also makes it possible to reduce the amount of monitoring needed. With little trust, a bureaucratic approach is appropriate to monitor behavior and performance—and we all know how bureaucracies grind work to a crawl. When people operate in an environment of trust, they can make decisions and act in a timely and agile fashion.

Principle 6. Hit the sweet spot.

A complex project needs both left- and right-brain approaches in operation: it needs both structure and freedom; it needs both framework and improvisation. The sweet spot is a place of balance and harmony between the left- and right-brain styles, a place where we achieve powerful, synergistic performance.

When we get into a great place in our work, everything becomes effortless—we don't have to think about what we're doing. Many professionals get lost in their work; it is said that they're "in the zone." This place is reached largely by putting into action the other six principles, with repetition, practice, experimentation, and adaptation.

Principle 7. Leave a legacy.

It is too limiting to describe a project only in terms of technical deliverables, task durations, and earned value. A project is a human endeavor that in the end delivers something of importance and tells a story. Will the story be one of accomplishment, or will it be one of bitter defeat? Will the story be told with pride, or with cynicism? Will we look back on this project as a lasting testament to how we worked together for something worthwhile, or will we wish our names had never been associated with it? What is the metaphor that best describes our project?

This is the project legacy. When we think about the project legacy, the right brain focuses on what is most important and most lasting. This is ultimately what our work is about. It not only makes our project human, but it helps us become more fully human as we manage our projects. ▪

CHAPTER 11

■ Discovering Fire: Finding the Compelling Purpose

■
■
■

Find purpose, the means will follow.

MOHANDAS GHANDI ■

How do you *feel* about your projects?

Do some projects feel like a dead weight around your neck? Do you wish they would go away? Do some projects get you so excited you can't wait to work on them?

What about the challenges you encounter on these two types of projects? Do you avoid them or do they seem to be no big deal?

The answers to these questions to a large degree determine the level of energy we devote to a project. The energy for project work, or the lack of it, comes predominantly from the emotions we experience about the project.

It may at first seem tempting to correlate positive emotions for a project with a wish list of project perks. How about a project with an unlimited budget? Wouldn't it be nice if the boss allowed you to finish the project whenever you felt like it? Perhaps your project would be more exciting if you had a bigger office, a faster computer, or lattes delivered to your desk.

Some people have many or all of these perks and still find their projects distasteful. Others have none of these perks, yet can't wait to get to work every day to jump into their projects.

Project energy springs from positive emotion, and the source of positive emotion—and therefore the fuel for projects—is a meaningful sense of purpose. It is a sense of spiritual survival that animates our project work. Substantial energy radiates from a *compelling* purpose.

Finding a compelling purpose to a project is much like the excitement our ancestors felt upon discovering fire: we experience a sense of enthusiasm and awe at the power that can be unleashed.

■ What Is the Most Important Resource?

It is a tenet of project management that projects run on resources; ultimately, resources are tied to money. While that is true at face value, the right-brain project manager knows a hidden and powerful truth: projects run on human energy.

Take a moment and consider the many projects you have worked on and observed. Would you agree that some projects just muddle along, while others are noted for their ability to grind everyone down with some inescapable bad karma? On the other hand, a precious few projects generate so much enthusiasm that they are literally unstoppable.

Dr. Patrick Dixon, author of *Building a Better Business*, has said, "I would rather work with five people who really believe in what they are doing rather than five hundred who can't see the point."

It is worthwhile and important to understand and evaluate the many parameters of projects that facilitate their success. But to really find the fuel that the drives projects, we need to delve deeper into the core of human motivation.

Quite simply, when people really want to do something, they will overcome any obstacle. When people lack motivation, they will find a variety of excuses, thinly disguised as valid reasons, why something can't be done.

Organizations need people who have the motivation to face the considerable challenges of contemporary projects with energy, confidence, and creative thought. This is exactly what a compelling purpose can do for the team.

A compelling purpose is intimately tied to human motivation, which arises from emotion or passion. Passion comes from becoming involved in something meaningful, something that engages our sense of spiritual survival.

The tagline to the movie, *The Blues Brothers*, captures the motivation of a compelling purpose: "They're on a mission from God."

■ What Is Compelling?

Does your project have a compelling purpose? If not, why not? More to the point, why work on the project at all? Does your project make you want to jump out of bed in the morning and get to work? If the answer is no, then something needs to change.

So many things compete for our attention in the workplace that we will naturally gravitate toward those that have a compelling purpose.

The phenomenal projects we have highlighted all had a compelling purpose. Of course, they all had deliverables that could be specified. Beyond their deliverables, though, each had identified a strong human need or benefit. This human need translated powerfully into an emotional connection and thus a compelling motivation to achieve the project objectives.

One of the dominant themes in our case studies was a powerful sense of urgency. There is no question that urgency demands a compelling purpose. In some cases, it is a matter of life and death; in other cases, it is an important external deadline. This urgency creates an overwhelming sense that we must succeed, and must succeed quickly. But in these cases the urgency was genuine, not just the directive of an impatient sponsor.

There is a line in the movie portrayal of *Apollo 13* that captures the meaning of the compelling purpose. Even though the line was not verbalized during the mission, it crystallizes what everyone at NASA understood at the time. Flight Director Gene Kranz tells the team, "Failure is not an option."

Commitment to a compelling purpose goes far beyond a rational choice; it is the complete dedication—rational and emotional—to fulfill the objective. Commitment engages both the left and the right brains.

■ Values: Change or Inertia

If we look beyond a singular project in an organization, we will find a set of values, or interests that are collectively held to be important. Often, the individuals in the organization are not consciously aware of these values, but they underlie the work environment. One organization may value entrepreneurship, another bureaucracy. One organization may place importance on state-of-the art, high-end products, another on low-cost products.

It is often the case that what an organization values most is "not rocking the boat." There may be good reasons for this mindset, but these reasons stifle the ability to fulfill some other worthy purpose.

This gets us to the crux of the compelling purpose. The established rules and behavior patterns of an organization can stand in the way of accomplishing the purpose of a project. In other words, when a project has a compelling purpose, previously held organizational rules may have to be broken. Some in the organization may not think kindly about this approach; thus, the Skunk Works® was deliberately buffered from the rest of the bureaucracy at Lockheed.

Organizations need both inertia and change, and there will always be tension between the two. Without continuity of practices, there is no framework to guide interactions or work. Without change, there is stagnation. It therefore becomes a challenge for an organization's leadership to balance constancy and change.

The most successful organizations have a strong set of core values or purpose that is unchanging (or that changes only in incremental steps). Everything else about the company is fair game for change, however.[1]

The Search for Meaning

Let us revisit Maslow's needs hierarchy. The majority of us working in contemporary organizations have our needs in the lower three levels of the hierarchy met. Our needs then move into the areas of recognition, esteem, self-actualization, knowledge, and aesthetics.

The common thread in these needs areas is meaning or purpose. We endeavor to do things that validate ourselves and our contribution; in doing so, we become more complete. In a similar way, Maddock's and Fulton's idea of spiritual survival holds the key to connecting passion with the project purpose.

What prompted so many people to volunteer their time to contribute to the development of Linux? On the surface, it was the goal of developing a functionally superior and robust operating system. But the energy for the project really came from three deeper sources:

- The desire for recognition from peers
- The excitement of creating open-source software, which would represent a true revolution in large-scale software development
- The thrill of being a David who would slay the Goliath Microsoft.

That is the real story of Linux.

It is sad that too many people at too many organizations go through the motions. For them, what happens in the workplace is only loosely connected, if connected at all, with these deeper needs; those needs are satisfied elsewhere. We will work hard, but we park our passion at the office door.

There is nothing unethical or disingenuous about this arrangement—it works for the parties involved. But it is a terrible waste of talent and a terrible waste of opportunity.

Something special can be accomplished through our projects when we endeavor to give them meaning and purpose that transcend factual project objectives.

■ My Projects Are Just ... Boring

What about those many corporate projects that are just ... boring?

I won't be so naive as to say that every project justifies over-the-top enthusiasm, but do so many projects have to be so uninspiring? How can we engage deeper motivation and emotion to pump inspiration and human energy into a project?

Emotion and passion are linked directly to our values—what we consider important. Again, let's get past the simple and necessary statements about important product features to a transcendent set of values that engage the spirit.

We can start to make the transition to a compelling purpose by asking important questions, such as:

- What do I consider important?
- In our team, what do we collectively consider important?
- What is *really* important to our sponsor and to our customer?
- What do we value, and what are our values?
- What characteristics of projects has experience shown to be motivating?

If we keep seeking what is important, we will begin to discover the deeper purpose that drives the involvement of the various actors on the project; we will discover a worthwhile purpose. Everything else is secondary.

It is important to differentiate the "what" of a project from the "why." The "what" of the project includes the conventional project objectives, primarily the scope. This is the logical, left-brain explanation of the project. The "why" of the project provides its deeper reasons and purpose. "Historically, organizations do a sound job of communicating the 'what' and a poor job of outlining the 'why.'"[2]

Statements of Core Purpose

While each of the phenomenal projects we highlighted had a strong sense of urgency and passion, we know that many projects in the workplace do not, at least not at first glance. We need a way to tease from these projects a deeper sense of purpose, to identify what they are *really* all about.

We are explorers; we are on a mission to uncover the secrets of the project that animate its purpose. Table 11-1 provides some example statements of core purpose for some well-known organizations.[3]

Three common themes underlie these descriptions of core purpose:

- High ideals
- Explicit or implicit service to humanity

Table 11-1. Statements of Core Purpose for Well-Known Companies

3M	To solve unsolved problems innovatively
Cargill	To improve the standard of living around the world
Fannie Mae	To strengthen the social fabric by continually democratizing home ownership
Hewlett-Packard	To make technical contributions for the advancement and welfare of humanity
Mary Kay Cosmetics	To give unlimited opportunity to women
Merck	To preserve and improve human life
Nike	To experience the emotion of competition, winning, and crushing competitors
Wal-Mart	To give ordinary folk the chance to buy the same things as rich people
Walt Disney	To make people happy

- Strongly positive emotions, as well as a desire to feel the emotions associated with fulfillment of the purpose.

Many corporate or governmental projects express their purpose in terms of product features. Would you get excited about working on a project "To convert Route 243 from two lanes to four between Route 5 and Route 7"?

But what if you thought for a moment about the effects of this project on the people who will benefit? Perhaps the real purpose of the project is to improve the lives of those who will use the highway by making the driving experience safer and more pleasant.

What if the highway is seen as a metaphor for the various journeys taken by all the drivers and passengers for years to come? The highway is the journey of the anxious couple to the hospital for the delivery of their first child. It is the trip to the Little League game and the family vacation. It is the journey of the teens to the senior prom and graduation ceremony.

We are not just adding lanes to a highway; we are making possible the journeys of life.

Simple and powerful statements of core purpose help guide team members on decisions and tasks. But more than that, they engage the soul. Where project objectives focus on goals, statements of core purpose describe who we are and where we stand. They define our *identity:*

> *When people in great organizations talk about their achievements, they say very little about earnings per share. Motorola people talk about impressive quality improvements and the effect of the products they create on the world. Hewlett-Packard people talk about their technical contributions to the marketplace. Nordstrom people talk about heroic customer service and remarkable individual performance by star salespeople.*[4]

Recall the story of the two bricklayers. The one worker lays bricks to collect a paycheck; the other does so to make a lasting contribution to the good of the community. In the process he too becomes more fulfilled. Which worker will be more motivated to invest energy and creativity in the project?

The story of the bricklayers is a good example of the contrast between "high-road" work and "low-road" work, as described by the author Tanis Helliwell.[5] High-road work recognizes how what we do impacts other people, and how our work is interdependent with their lives. Low-road work simply fulfills a checklist and serves short-term needs that are usually disconnected from benefiting others. When someone says that they go to work to get a paycheck, they are referring to low-road work.

High-road work can be our ideal job, a vocation or calling. But it can also be an otherwise low-road job that we view as a vehicle for high-road purposes.

Needless to say, it is easier for someone to feel motivated on their project if they are involved in high-road work or if they view their project from a high-road perspective. We can more easily see the high road when we look for the connections of our project to the emotional and spiritual survival needs of those we serve: how will it impact them in a truly meaningful and positive way?

Let us return for a moment to our revised list of elements that help people work:

1. I know what is most important to do, and why it is important. I am able to learn the details and adapt as appropriate.
2. I *really* want to do it.
3. I have the ability and the authority to experiment to learn what will work.
4. Someone who matters to me will notice if I do it, especially my peers.
5. I will learn how well I'm doing it.
6. I have the authority to mold the processes to help me do it.
7. I have the authority to find the resources I need to do it.
8. I have the ability to recreate the environment to do it.
9. I will do it well this time, because this opportunity will likely not come again, and I will learn things from this experience that will help me on the next.

As we mentioned, it is critical that the project organization fulfill the first two elements on this list; this is exactly what the compelling purpose accomplishes. With appropriate Theory Z attitude and processes in the organization, the project team can then structure the environment to fulfill the remaining elements on the list.

Genuine Purpose

It is important to be genuine when expressing the purpose of a project. While it is possible to manipulate team members to be passionate about the cause, being disingenuous is certain to lead to failure and bitterness. Individuals eventually sense the scam; once they do, it is almost impossible to regain trust.

Here's a little test. Describe the compelling purpose of your project to the customer and ask if it is being fulfilled. Ask the same question of the team members. The answers will let you know how genuine the purpose is.

Morality is an important component of emotional intelligence. Being genuine about the compelling purpose of a project involves an important moral choice to respect the others on the team.

Right-Brain Toolkit: Purpose

So how can we make the transition from a set of uninspiring project objectives to a description of core purpose that is meaningful? One tool we can use is an exercise called the "Five Whys."

If you've ever been around a four-year-old for very long, you have likely seen this exercise in action. Curious to understand the meaning behind everything, four-year-olds have a proclivity for asking "why?" over and over again.

This exercise is a simple way to find the meaning and motivation behind a project. Suppose you are the project manager at a billing software company. For an upcoming project, you start with the following project objective: "To complete the conversion of legacy software to the customer's new platform." Now ask, "why is that important?"

The initial answer may be something to the effect that the customer has upgraded equipment, and we want to keep their business. That answer is okay, but why is *that* important? A number of worthwhile endeavors can pay the bills, but why is *this one* important? We might say that it is important to remain up-to-date with our products. Again, why? If we remain current, then we can better serve the customer. If the customer's needs are met, they can better serve their markets. What if we were to say something like:

We strive to be our best so the customers we serve can be their best.

Now we are getting somewhere. A legacy software update doesn't necessarily excite anyone. A quest for excellence, service, and teamwork does.

For the Five Whys exercise, continue to ask "why is this important?" in sequence, until you find an answer that resonates. Experience has shown that it takes about five cycles of this exercise to come upon the answer that will get you eager to work on the project.

Once our group develops answers to these questions, it is important to remind ourselves regularly what is important. The simple recitation of the project purpose at the start of every project team meeting can lead to more successful project completion. This approach can be called "centering." As we all arrive at a meeting, our minds may be elsewhere on other concerns. Centering helps pull the focus to our common purpose and reminds us all why we are there.

This line of questioning may prompt a serious evaluation of our work and our organization. While conventional thinking holds that the purpose of a business is to make money for its shareholders, Art Kleiner, author of *The Age of Heretics*, believes that its purpose is to change the world.[6]

■ The "Cool" Factor

Genuine and healthy pride plays a key role in project motivation. To continue with our legacy software example, a wonderful feeling comes with serving the customer. But look a little closer and we also see the pride that comes with a job well done. This sense of pride includes internal pride, but perhaps more importantly, it involves the pride that comes from recognition by others. Recognition from a superior is valuable, but it doesn't hold a candle to the pride that comes from peer recognition.

Here we get into the "cool" factor. I don't know anyone on the Apple team that designed the iPod, but I would imagine the team members take a great deal of pride in the kudos they have received for such a "cool" product, one that was far ahead of its time in function and design.

While we are asking ourselves why something is important, it is helpful to explore whether there is something really special, or really "cool," about the project. This is a valuable question to ask because, quite simply, team members jump at the opportunity to work on a cool project.

So what is cool about a software update? Perhaps it can be done in a way that has an engaging user interface—maybe similarly to a video game (of course done in a way that is consistent with the customer's operation and culture). The point here is not to explicitly answer the question, but rather to start asking the question and seeking fresh answers ... to discover fire.

Airline passengers who have flown Southwest Airlines regularly get to observe the creativity and playfulness of the staff. In one of the airline's trademark stories, a flight attendant used the typically boring safety briefing to announce that anyone who didn't follow safety rules during the flight would be asked to immediately leave the plane!

Southwest is known for low fares. With any other airline, low fares could be an excuse for mediocre service. At Southwest, the culture and core purpose of the organization are to entertain and to make travel fun.

■ Distributed Purpose

Among the many benefits of identifying a compelling purpose for a project, here is a big one: a compelling purpose makes distributed leadership possible. In fact, a compelling purpose practically demands that many individuals step forward and exercise leadership.

In a sense, discovering a compelling purpose for a project is akin to letting the genie out of the bottle. Once it happens, and the team internalizes the project's purpose, it is difficult to stop team members from taking the initiative to solve problems, make decisions, and achieve the desired outcome.

Contemporary projects are complex and typically have a short fuse. Accordingly, they dearly need the distributed leadership that a compelling purpose inspires. Because this approach to a project demands a change in attitude and an abdication of control, it is threatening to many people and organizations. If I am a project manager and I allow—or even promote—team members to make decisions, doesn't that potentially threaten the project? What if they make the wrong decisions or take the project in the wrong direction?

These legitimate concerns can be addressed in two ways. The first approach is making sense, which we'll address in detail in the next chapter.

The second approach gets back to being clear and simple about the core purpose. Go back to the company purpose statements provided as examples, and notice how direct they are. They embody the high-level principles from which details can be readily derived.

For example, with the Hurricane Katrina shelter at the Astrodome, we could state the overall purpose as:

Our friends in New Orleans have suffered greatly. We will quickly create a temporary home that is safe and comfortable while we help them find more permanent homes. We will have a fully functional home ready before the first of our friends arrive.

This sample statement of purpose establishes the human need and communicates some important human values. Even the choice of wording conveys meaning. We could have selected the word "shelter," but "home" has a stronger emotional connotation. Our "friends" could have been called "evacuees," but which term is more likely to strengthen the connection? It is clear that because of the urgent need, distributed decision-making was imperative. With this statement of purpose, many individuals were empowered to make detailed decisions and be confident that those decisions would be consistent with the project's overall objectives.

Distributed leadership also includes the initiative to communicate. Compelling projects prompt people to cut through bureaucracy and confusion to seek answers and convey information.

■ Making the Human Connection

One of our fundamental observations has been that projects are inextricably connected to people. We can talk about product features and project objectives; clearly, they are important. But when we talk about the needs and aspirations of our associates and customers, we put ourselves in the position to structure something meaningful and special together.

What will be the human connection between what we do on our project and the emotions the customer experiences when using the output of our project? The ultimate purpose of every project should be to put smiles on the faces and pride in the hearts of all those associated with the project.

Compelling motivation ultimately comes from making the human connection on projects—finding the common purpose that describes our collective needs and desires for something meaningful. Finding the compelling purpose leads us to our next principle: making sense.

THE PROJECT'S EMOTIONAL ENVIRONMENT
Jill Irwin

We function with incomplete information every moment of our lives. In project management, I think this is one of those truths that is not fully appreciated: a project manager never has enough information. This is particularly true with respect to people.

When it comes to interactions with people on projects, I accept what's on the table at face value, but also understand that the reality may turn out to be a bit different. If someone says, "This is black or this is white," I will accept that as the best current information; however, I am aware that the issue may turn into a shade of gray. This right-brain attitude prepares the entire team for change and adaptation as information becomes more complete.

Similarly, I create a project plan based on the best information I have at the time, while understanding that what I know or assume during planning may change dramatically. For example, I assume that a staff member will be available throughout the project, but if she wins the lottery, she may decide that the villa in the Italian countryside is more appealing than my project.

I enjoy the right-brain aspects of projects, particularly the excitement of having a new team come together. While much of project management can become the application of rote techniques, forming and motivating a cohesive new team is both challenging and fun.

There is no question in my mind that the moving force on any project is the attitude and temperament of each individual on the team. Project managers must fully comprehend and appreciate that, on any project, we are dealing with people who have emotions, hormones, and other outside issues that arrive with them on the project. The biggest mistake that a project manager can make is to assume that a team member is a task-oriented, "left-brain" resource. We cannot separate the "person" from the "resource." I strongly feel that it is dysfunctional to avoid and deny the human element of project work.

This subject hit home for me in a project meeting some time ago. In late fall, we were scheduling project work into the next year. I noted the need to accommodate the holidays and how it would be unreasonable to expect typical productivity in light of the many distractions of the season. My comment irked my boss, who asserted that we can't put war, famine, and pestilence into the schedule—we should assume that the team members will continue to give 100 percent regardless of holiday festivities and demands.

I was completely taken aback by his comment. When we try to force the human element out of the project, the results are often damaging. Project work is affected by the life of the person as a whole.

I believe that we are better off focusing first on the project people and then on the project task. In project team and one-on-one meetings, I make a point to first check in with people. While this reflects my attitude of caring about people, it is also pragmatic. If someone is having a bad day, it can significantly color their work, their comments, and their decisions. It is hard for people to feel motivated at work if something is troubling them. That is information I need to know as a project manager.

It occurs to me that this attention to the human element of project work is somewhat like the preparation and staging that go into a construction project. In construction, considerable preparatory work must be performed at the site to ensure that equipment and supplies are in place prior to actual construction. A framing crew cannot erect a wall without lumber, tools, and fasteners. If their tools are in disrepair, the work will suffer.

Similarly, our project tasks are facilitated when we attend to the complete person, ensuring that each team member has an environment that will promote healthy emotions and motivation. This emotional preparation and staging work is a daily, ongoing effort.

This approach to working with people on projects helps put the project in perspective. From my experience, when we attend to the project's emotional environment, the contractual project proceeds more successfully.

Jill Irwin is the founder of Jill Irwin and Associates, a San Jose, California, firm that specializes in technical writing for the medical device industry. Jill has over 20 years experience in project management, mechanical design, and technical writing in the medical device community. ▪

■ ENDNOTES

1 James C. Collins and Jerry I. Porras, *Built to Last: Successful Habits of Visionary Companies* (New York: HarperBusiness, 1994).

2 David Rymer, "Powerful Storytelling: Rich Connections between Leaders and Generation Y," *Leadership Compass* (Alberta, Canada: Banff Centre, Summer 2006), p. 25.

3 James C. Collins and Jerry I. Porras, "Building Your Company's Vision," *Harvard Business Review,* September–October 1996.

4 Ibid.

5 Tanis Helliwell, *Take Your Soul to Work* (Ontario, Canada: Random House of Canada, 1999).

6 Art Kleiner, The Age of Heretics (New York: Currency Doubleday, 1996).

■ Solving the Mystery: Making Sense of the Project

.
.
.

It is better to ask some of the questions than to know all the answers.

JAMES THURBER ■

Picture for a moment an author of fiction going into a meeting with a publisher. The author is there to ask that the manuscript of her latest mystery novel be accepted for publication.

The publisher says, "We can't accept a mystery novel because when readers start the book, they won't know how it ends."

After absorbing the initial incredulity of the comment, the author replies, "That's the whole point of reading a mystery novel. Readers like to take part in solving the mystery. It's what fiction is all about—getting involved in the story."

The publisher stands firm. "How does the reader know that the mystery will be solved?"

Unwittingly, the publisher has stumbled on a profound truth. A reader believes that the mystery will be solved, but the occasional author throws a curve and does not solve the mystery by the end of the book.

The author gives the only answer that can be truthfully given. "The reader believes that the experience will be worthwhile, and that the mystery *can* be solved."

Such a conversation between an author and a publisher is unlikely, because publishers know the value of mystery fiction. But change the author to a project manager, the publisher to a sponsor, and the mystery novel to a complex project, and the interaction describes project management all too accurately.

This metaphor of the mystery novel directs us to one of the central issues of what is wrong with project management: the model of the project. The prevailing project model assumes and expects no uncertainties once the plan is prepared. But we could use a different model, not unlike the model of the mystery novel. With this model, we assume and expect uncertainty at project start. We plan to the extent that we can and we seek to identify the significant objectives of the project, but we remain aware that the details will emerge. We believe that the endeavor will be worthwhile and that it will successfully converge on something of value.

Just as we can stop reading the novel, we can terminate the project at some point if we conclude that the effort is not beneficial. This model is entirely valid and intuitive. We have come to expect and feel comfortable with this model for a mystery novel; nothing prevents us from adopting it as appropriate for projects.

■ Destination and Journey

It is an uncomfortable truth of contemporary project management with complex projects: at the start, we do not know the explicit destination or the precise path, but we believe we will reach a worthwhile destination and that the journey will be rewarding. This reality stands in stark contrast to the preference of some stakeholders to know in advance the exact roadmap for a known destination.

The conventional answer to this dilemma is to seek and impose order, to develop more certitude in the path and destination, or at least to make it appear that way. Significant value is assigned to *the plan*, and the measure of success becomes how well we execute the plan, regardless of whether or not the plan is appropriate.

In a complex project world, this entire premise is flawed. There is no possible way to plan explicitly for what is not yet known.

The contemporary project environment is not chaotic, despite the fact that it may feel that way to the participants. Rather, it is complex. It may not be ordered, but it is capable of order once the nature of the project is learned.

A better approach is to plan what we can and prepare to learn what is not yet known. The project objectives and processes are mostly known, and what is not known can be learned through deliberate steps. We call this model "sense-making."

Sense-making is a well-developed group methodology that offers an excellent approach to managing the complex project environment. It recognizes the inherent unknowns of the project and it includes specific strategies to learn how to convert what is unknown into what is known.

You don't drive with a map pasted to your windshield. You consult it before setting out or when you get disoriented. The joy of a journey is not reading or following a map, but exploring unknown places and wandering off the map now and then. It's only by getting creatively lost, beyond the boundaries of tradition, that new discoveries can be made.[1]

It is only when we accept and embrace complexity, adapt to it, and prepare appropriate approaches to it, that we can successfully navigate complex projects.

We will approach sense-making from two directions: making sense of different perspectives, and making sense of the unknowns.

■ Truth Be Told

We cannot overemphasize the importance of being truthful when the project and the environment are ambiguous. It is crucial that we be honest about what is uncertain, even if that admission is not politically popular.

In the early stages of the Apollo 13 crisis, NASA engineers explicitly acknowledged that they did not know specifically what was wrong or how they would get the astronauts home safely. One researcher, Mark Stein, found that this acknowledgment was an important ingredient in the ultimate success of the rescue.[2]

In stark contrast, in the Three Mile Island (TMI) nuclear plant accident, the participants were more intent on calming an alarmed public than on mitigating the accident. This face-saving stance caused the response team to ignore critical information. Incredibly, the reactor was within 30–60 minutes of a full core meltdown. Meltdown was prevented only through an incidental action by an off-duty operator who thought his action had nothing to do with the crisis.[3]

With Apollo 13, the purpose was to get the astronauts safely home. Sense was made according to that objective. At TMI, the purpose was to avoid blame and not tolerate ambiguity; the actors attempted to create reality rather than make sense of it.

An important step in sense-making is acknowledging both the present reality and what is not known, even if that acknowledgment is uncomfortable.

■ Learning to Perceive

A synonym for the term "sense" is perception. When a proposed project is orderly, familiar, and well-defined, team members can draw upon considerable experience to understand the project. The perceptions or perspectives of the various stakeholders overlap overwhelmingly. These projects "make sense," so it is possible to develop a plan in considerable detail and then to execute that plan.

The rational, Cartesian approach to a project is based on the assumption that we understand the project environment, that the environment makes sense. For an uncertain environment, we must avoid the temptation of this assumption, because it is false. Instead, we must learn to perceive—to read and explore the environment until it makes sense.

One of the ambiguous areas of a complex project is the typical divergence in perspectives and perceptions of the various stakeholders. At the onset, these projects do not make sense, and certainly not in a collective manner. On such projects, we must learn to perceive order, in contrast to the conventional project where we are already aware of order.

Often, the stakeholder with the most political clout is the one whose "sense" predominates. Although the need to respect political power can't be ignored, sometimes one person's perspective can be difficult to achieve, and, more importantly, is not necessarily a good solution. Perhaps a better approach is possible.

One of the fundamental challenges of complex projects is addressing the different perspectives of stakeholders. How can we find a common ground? The term "common ground" implies that we reach a collective understanding of what is known. But common ground doesn't help us with the unknowns of complex projects. A more helpful approach, and a more relevant question, is "How can we make sense of the project?"

■ Finding a New Perspective

The first reason that projects are complex is that the different stakeholders come to the project with different perspectives. To a certain extent their perspectives overlap, which is what makes the project possible at all. Where the perspectives diverge is where things get complicated.

Often these perspectives are mutually exclusive. At a macro level, the customer wants to fulfill a need for their operations, and they want it now. The project organization wants to maximize profit. The engineering team wants to enhance the technical elegance of the product, while the marketing team wants a lot of features and an attractive design.

Each stakeholder comes to the table with a different *story*. The human tendency in this situation is to optimize *my* story and to negotiate what I can tolerate with respect to the other stories. From a sense-making perspective, we need to shift the focus to *our* story, or the story that will come to be the project.

This part of the sense-making activity is itself a complex and paradoxical effort. We develop the common story by starting with the individual stories. Many of the later elements of sense-making depend on this foundation. We can do something special together only when we understand and value all the diverse perspectives that come to the table. What will result is not so much a common ground (as in least common denominator) but a fresh, new perspective.

One of the best ways to recognize when "sense" is made is a resulting intuitive perception of "rightness." As an example, consider another crisis event, the Tylenol product tampering scare.

In 1982, seven deaths were linked to consumption of the popular pain reliever, Extra Strength Tylenol, made by Johnson & Johnson. Investigators determined that someone had opened bottles of Tylenol, added arsenic to the product, and returned the bottles to store shelves.

Johnson & Johnson reacted decisively. Through the media, the company told customers to stop taking Tylenol and organized an immediate recall of all Tylenol products. The company recalled approximately 31 million bottles of Tylenol, at a cost of over $240 million.[4]

Faced with public fears over the safety of its products, Johnson & Johnson took an unusual step. It became the first company to develop and introduce tamper-resistant packaging for its pharmaceutical products, and such packaging quickly became the industry standard. This move ensured product safety, but it also communicated to the public that the company's foremost concern was for its customers. Once the new tamper-resistant packaging was introduced, sales of Tylenol quickly rebounded.

Nothing had prepared Johnson & Johnson for this crisis. However, the company's guiding principle in its response was a long-standing credo that made the company's responsibilities to its consumers and the community its highest priority.[5] The company chose its response because *it was the right thing to do.*

Johnson & Johnson could have justifiably taken a different path that followed more "conventional" wisdom. The company could have performed a limited, targeted recall. Even with a complete recall, Johnson & Johnson could have immediately returned to the market with Tylenol in the existing package.

But for Johnson & Johnson, neither of these approaches was "right" and neither made "sense." Johnson & Johnson made sense by consulting and applying its core values, the mission and passion that gave the company a deep purpose. It was the right business decision for the long term.

◼ Stuff Happens

The Tylenol product tampering case and Apollo 13 are extreme examples of the unexpected—situations that cause us to scrap the plan and address an immediate crisis. Many of our projects get hit with unfortunate outbreaks of Murphy's Law to varying degrees of significance.

When "stuff happens," it is an important time to make sense. When the "stuff" is relatively minor, we can roll with the punches and adapt. But with a serious situation, confusion and anxiety may hinder our ability to make sense and find a path. The value of a high level of maturity and emotional intelligence becomes clear at such a critical time; it does not help to curl into a fetal position and wish the problem would go away. The ability to tolerate ambiguity and anxiety, as well as to manage emotions effectively, often makes the difference between a successful outcome and a train wreck.

As we have seen, when we are faced with a crisis, a fundamental element of making sense is focusing on the core purpose of our endeavor. The Tylenol and Apollo 13 cases also show that it is the human connection of the core purpose that can most successfully guide us toward making sense.

Before we talk in detail about making sense of complexity, let us recapitulate the model of complexity that describes contemporary projects.

■ Making Sense of Complexity: Emergent Order

Earlier, we introduced descriptors for types of organizational systems according to their degree of functional predictability: ordered, complex, and chaotic. Along this continuum of states, the area that is of most interest for project management is the region between ordered and complex.

In this region, we find three systems: those that are already ordered, those on the border that display emergent order, and complex systems.

Project environments that are ordered can be managed effectively with conventional approaches. The cause-effect relationships are familiar and applicable.

Projects with emergent order are capable of attaining order, but at their start, we do not know the cause-effect relationships. Many technology and product development projects fit this category. Once the relevant questions are answered, we can rely on the learned cause-effect relationships thereafter.

For complex systems, the cause-effect relationships are tenuous, and those that are learned on one project may not be applicable on the next project. This does not mean that the project environment is chaotic, but rather that the order is specific and cannot be generalized. Team and marketplace dynamics are excellent examples of complexities that are often unique to a project.

Management approaches are well-developed for ordered projects. For emergent projects, techniques such as the spiral project model are often helpful. However, for many emergent projects and certainly for complex projects, we need a new management framework. We need a way to make sense of complex projects.

■ Analogy: The Party

Dave Snowden has presented an excellent analogy for contrasting management approaches. The analogy involves a party for children.[6]

In the conventional project management approach, the parents plan the party in specific task detail, along with specific objectives. Any parent who has tried this approach recognizes its futility. A group of children is a complex system: they can exhibit order, but it is not necessarily predictable.

Using the sense-making model, parents view the goal of the party as for the guests to have enjoyable experiences, but will not attempt to be specific in advance about those experiences. The parents will establish boundaries for behavior and redirect unwanted patterns. They will also use certain activities (e.g., games) to seed and encourage pleasing (and largely self-organizing) experiences. Snowden concludes the analogy as follows: "At the end of the party you would know whether it had been a success, but you could not define (in other than the most general terms) what success would look like in advance."[7]

Five themes from this analogy shed some light on the challenge of managing complex projects:

- The overall objectives cannot be described in explicit detail at the start.
- Boundaries must be established and recognized (although they may, by agreement, change during the course of the project).
- Learning experiences can be prompted through "attractors" or deliberate seeding exercises. However, what will be experienced or learned is not explicitly known ahead of time.
- The team is self-organizing to a considerable extent.
- "Control" is exercised through the correction of negative patterns and transgressions beyond boundaries. It is not related to deviations from the original plan.

■ The Challenge of Making Sense

The analogy of the children's party highlights one of the central challenges of sense-making: the tension of rationalism versus empiricism, even Judging versus Perceiving. The rational perspective is to plan the project; the empirical approach is to explore what the project should be.

If an organization operates from the rational perspective, it will be uncomfortable with the concept of making sense. We could say that for such an organization, sense-making makes no sense!

Once again, we come to the need for a fundamental shift in perspective and worldview. For sense-making to make sense, the team members and the organization must believe that an empirical approach to the environment is as valid and appropriate as a rational approach.

■ Learning Projects

Let's look at sense-making from a slightly different angle. Projects can be characterized according to how much learning must take place during their course. Again, the continuum of experiences reaches from familiar and well-known project environments that involve little or no learning, to complex projects that involve a high degree of learning.

In one study,[8] projects were analyzed and characterized according to the extent of learning that occurred. A.J. Shenhar formed a continuum of four project categories: A, B, C, and D, with A projects having a high level of certainty and D projects having a high level of uncertainty. The results of the study were intriguing. As uncertainty increased, the management of projects became more flexible and communications became more intense:

Type A projects were managed in a very formal and rigid way, with cost control and completing to schedule the priorities. Communications were quite formal. Type D projects were managed with high levels of flexibility, with a high tolerance for change.

Communications were very intensive, and did not just follow formal channels.[9]

Here is the important takeaway: flexible management and intense communication are the most efficient and the most cost-effective ways to learn when there is much learning to be done.[10] As the research shows, these styles arise naturally and intuitively.

When there is much uncertainty and much to be learned, management's primary activity is sense-making. The sense-making model for managing complex projects is the most effective and lowest cost approach to successful project conclusion. It is also the way that groups will organize and execute such a project, when allowed or encouraged to do so.

■ Organizational Complexity

All human organizations, including project teams, are complex systems to some degree. On a project, one of the most important areas of complexity to address is the complexity of its human system. Simply put, we cannot know with certainty how the team will act, particularly prior to the start of the project. The level of uncertainty is the product of many factors, including the familiarity of team members with one another.

As an important case, consider a team composed of members who have never before met. Some learning must take place to determine the nature of their interactions. Whatever the project communications plan may say, if Bob repeatedly does not respond to phone messages I leave, I quickly learn not to depend on Bob.

This is a natural process. Groups of people learn processes of interaction with one another and adapt. We experience and determine patterns, and we begin to make future plans based on what we learn.

This concept of "interactional uncertainty"[11] states that if there is uncertainty in a relationship, the participants will tend to withhold information and calculate the effects of sharing information. Such preoccupations take emotional energy away from work on project tasks. On the other hand, when trust, or certainty, is present, both vertically in the project hierarchy and horizontally with peers, team members can focus their energy directly on task-oriented activities.

Sense-Making Model

The process of sense-making is iterative, but iterations do not occur as might be understood in the conventional meaning of the term. Referring to the five elements of sense-making depicted in Table 12-1, going through step 5 does not necessarily imply a return to step 1 for the next iteration; the process is fluid and dynamic. Learning that occurs may suggest different seeding for the next time, or it may indicate that new rules have been learned and can be reliably applied.

Let's apply the sense-making model in an example. Consider an R&D project made up of team members who are not familiar with one another. Boundaries will be established for budget and duration, as well as for behaviors within the team. We may also establish certain boundaries of performance for the product or technology we are investigating.

Many organizations use team-building exercises at the start of a project with a new team. Essentially, these seeding activities are meant to help members develop a facility for interaction. Seeding activities can also be introduced simply by getting to work on some element of the project. While we are experimenting with the technology, we are also experimenting with the dynamics of the group.

▪ Table 12-1. Sense-Making Model

Identify boundaries.
Seed the system with attractors.
Sense the reaction of the system.
Learn from the observations.
Exploit the knowledge learned and adapt or correct as appropriate.

We then sense the outcome of the seeding activity—in this case, what did the experiment tell us about the technology, and what did it tell us about the workings of the group? Based on this information, we incorporate what we have learned and adapt or correct as appropriate.

Once again, this is a natural, intuitive process that we apply whether we do so deliberately and consciously or not. We do not follow this sense-making approach to the exclusion of conventional project management approaches, but recognize that it is a more appropriate choice for complex project situations.

In many ways, the sense-making process involves processing incomplete or inaccessible information. We don't always know completely what we are sensing or what it means—we make educated guesses based on the information we have. The right brain is highly engaged in this process to identify patterns that were not previously known. Intuition often comes into play extensively in sense-making processes.

Sense-making is a skill that can be learned and practiced, and it flourishes in organizations and cultures where it is valued. Although not opposed to rationality, sense-making stands in clear contrast to it. As practiced in many organizations, the rational model of management values and finds meaning in data, analysis, and dispassionate decisions. Sense-making values experiences and finds meaning in them. It is more akin to inspired guesswork and experimentation.

■ How to Fight a War

A compelling study[12] shows the benefits of sense-making over rational decision-making in a complex environment.

Paul Van Riper ran the leadership and combat development program for the U.S. Marine Corps in the 1990s. At the time, the training focused on rational decision-making processes and checklists for combat. But when applied in simulations or in combat, the approach seemed to fall short of the expected results.

Van Riper teamed with psychologist Gary Klein and ran an experiment in which a group of Marines traded securities on a simulated trading floor, competing against a group of securities traders. This setting was picked because the trading floor of a stock exchange exhibits many similarities to the situation of combat, where decisions must be made based on incomplete information. To no one's surprise, the traders beat the Marines.

Then the experiment resumed, but this time the Marines competed against the traders on a combat simulator. To everyone's surprise, the traders won again. The securities traders performed better in combat situations without any combat training than the Marines did with extensive combat training!

The implication was that the traders were more skilled and comfortable operating in a complex and ambiguous environment. As a result of this experiment, the Marine Corps made significant changes to its training programs. The rational model of analysis and decision-making is ill-suited for dealing with complexity and ambiguity. Sense-making is a much better model.

■ Acceptable Sloppiness

All across human endeavors we see the tension between the need for order and predictability and the need to adapt and learn. In many ways, this is the tension between the left brain and the right brain.

This tension is not manifested as rigid rules versus complete anarchy, but rather as a challenge to determine the appropriate application of *flexible rules*. When we apply rules flexibly, we allow room to learn and to adapt to new situations. In essence, we use "meta-rules" to guide the specific rules we learn during the project.

This is the reality of how humans operate.

Blogger Adam Bosworth captured the essence of this approach in a presentation to the Second International Conference on Service

Oriented Computing, where he changed the KISS acronym ("keep it simple, stupid") to "keep it simple and sloppy." While his comments concerned software user and programmer models, they also apply to project management:

> There has been, of course, an eternal tension between that part of humanity which celebrates our diversity, imperfectibility, and faults, as part of the rich tapestry of the human condition, and that part which seeks to perfect itself, to control, to build complex codes and rules for conduct which if zealously adhered to, guarantee an orderly process ....
>
> It is an ironic truth that those who seek to create systems which most assume the perfectibility of humans end up building the systems which are most soul destroying and most rigid, systems that rot from within until like great creaking rotten oak trees they collapse on top of themselves leaving a sour smell and decay .... Conversely, those systems which best take into account the complex, frail, brilliance of human nature and build in flexibility, checks and balances, and tolerance tend to survive beyond all hopes.[13]

■ Right-Brain Toolkit: Hitting the Box

Several years ago, PBS ran a series called *The Wayfinders*, a documentary on the fascinating people of the Pacific Islands and how they populated the scattered islands of the Pacific Ocean.[14] These islands were once thought to have been colonized by chance; we then learned that the process was very sophisticated. It also happens to be a great example of sense-making.

Thousands of years ago, these people sent out parties in boats to explore and look for new islands. Even without modern instruments, they developed sophisticated methods for following the stars and reading subtle signs in the ocean to determine position and course. They established parameters for each trip. If they found nothing, the group returned and the information was retained for future planning; if they found land, the group returned and a second group embarked to settle on the newly discovered island. In this way, they systematically explored and populated islands across a vast area of the Pacific Ocean.

The skills of the culture developed so that over time, voyages of several months and thousands of miles could be successfully completed.

The present-day descendants of these people are attempting to preserve the Wayfinding method. Modern Wayfinder Nainoa Thompson offers two observations that are relevant to sense-making and to project management.

First, finding a tiny speck of land in the middle of a vast ocean is a daunting task in which complex and incomplete information must be processed to determine direction. This is true not only for exploratory trips but also when traveling to a known island.

In words that could just as readily apply to navigating complex projects, Nainoa Thompson states: "The majority of navigation is observation and adjusting to the natural environment."[15]

Thompson's second point addresses the strategy for reaching a destination that is not seen until later in the project. Rather than spend inordinate attention to the details that are not yet known, he focuses on getting to the *vicinity* of the destination, in his case, a "box" several hundred miles across. "The first part of the journey to Tahiti is not trying to get to Tahiti, but to make sure that you hit this box."[16]

For those of us trying to make sense of complex projects, Thompson's words offer much wisdom. We will unravel the mystery during the course of the journey—if we understand our purpose well and pay attention to the environment. When attempting to make sense, our most important job is to make sure we hit the box. ▪

ENDNOTES

1 Christopher Vogler, *The Writer's Journey,* Second Edition (Studio City, CA: Michael Wiese Productions), 1998, p. 239.

2 Mark Stein, "The Critical Period of Disasters: Insights from Sense-Making and Psychoanalytic Theory," *Human Relations,* Vol. 57, No. 10, 2004, pp. 1243–1261.

3 Ibid.

4 "How Business Can Be Good," Jeffrey L. Seglin, *Sojouners,* January/February 2000.

5 "Our Credo," www.johnsonandjohnson.com. Accessed October 2006.

6 David J. Snowden, "Multi-Ontology Sense Making: A New Simplicity in Decision Making," *Management Today Yearbook 2005*, Vol. 20.

7 Ibid.

8 A. J. Shenhar, "One Size Does Not Fit All Projects: Exploring Classical Contingency Domains," *Management Science,* Vol. 47, No. 3, 2001, pp. 394–414.

9 Nigel Wadeson, "Projects as Search Processes," *International Journal of Project Management,* Vol. 23, No. 6, 2005, pp. 421–427.

10 Ibid.

11 Christian Jensen, Staffan Johansson, and Mikael Lofstrom, "Project Relationships—A Model for Analyzing Interactional Uncertainty," *International Journal of Project Management,* Vol. 24, No. 1, 2006, pp. 4–12.

12 Thomas A. Stewart and Nancy Einhart, "How to Think with Your Gut," *Business 2.0,* November 1, 2002.

13 Adam Bosworth's weblog, "ISOSC04 Talk," http://www.adambosworth. net/archives/000031.html. Accessed August 2006.

14 B. Michael Aucoin, *From Engineer to Manager: Mastering the Transition* (Boston: Artech House, 2002), pp. 117–125.

15 Nainoa Thompson, "Non-Instrument Navigation," http://www.pbs.org/ wayfinders/wayfinding2.html. Accessed March 2007.

16 Ibid.

CHAPTER 13

■ A Trip to the Laboratory: Experimenting and Adapting

My mind is my laboratory.

ALBERT EINSTEIN ■

When I introduced the statistics module in a university engineering course I was teaching, I remarked to the class that if I was ever stranded on a deserted island with only one book, I would want that book to be a statistics text.

Lest you think I am an incurable geek, let me explain: it is really a matter of survival.

Statistics is the one subject from which just about all other knowledge can be derived. Well, at least knowledge that would be relevant to someone who needed to survive.

For example, say that I get hungry and need to kill wild boar on the island. Unfortunately, the boars always escape before I can catch them. I come up with a plan to use a catapult-like device to hurl a large stone at them from a distance. By using statistics, I can run a few experiments and derive a relationship for the flight of a projectile. In little time, I can predictably hit what will soon be dinner.

In our project organizations, dinner results from a project job well done. With a complex project, the job well done results in part from the strategy to experiment wisely, learn from the experiment, and adapt accordingly. We use statistics, either explicitly or intuitively, to make sense of what we observe and then to make use of these observations reliably on the project.

■ A Trip to the Laboratory

Let's consider for a moment the function of a laboratory, perhaps a corporate laboratory or even one at a university. What is the underlying foundation, the *raison d'etre*, of the lab?

An obvious answer might be to gain knowledge. But knowledge can be found in other ways too, such as in the library. While other sources can be very valuable, sometimes they are not available or not appropriate. Perhaps we have an issue that is novel, or one that is very specific to our situation.

We eventually come to the conclusion that we can attain the knowledge we seek only through *doing*. The laboratory is a place for learning founded in action. Even when the knowledge can be discovered in other ways, many times the quickest and most economical path to an answer is through experimentation.

With any trip to the laboratory, what is discovered may previously have been an "unknown unknown." This result actually *increases* the uncertainty of the project. It is therefore important to preserve flexibility in determining the direction of the project, as well as decisions about its termination.[1]

■ When to Experiment

Suppose you are in the planning stage of a project. Like many project managers, you may be having trouble estimating task durations and costs. You may even have difficulty describing some tasks clearly.

In case you're wondering, this is a clear indication that it is time to get into the lab and do some experimentation. Many projects first start getting in trouble in the planning stage. When warning signs appear, heed them!

■ An Experimental Attitude

The approach we need to adopt to deal with complex projects depends to a significant extent on attitudes, or worldviews. This is definitely true for attitudes about experimentation.

For organizations where the corporate culture is built on the need for predictability, the concept of accepting or embracing experimentation can be quite uncomfortable. If the environment is predictable, then we can count on a known future, within reason. If the environment is uncertain, then a worldview that insists on predictability is a recipe for frustration.

What, then, is an appropriate approach for navigating an uncertain world? Clearly, a worldview that embraces adaptability is needed.

Adaptability can take the form of a *reactive* strategy or a *proactive* strategy. With a reactive strategy, we change based on how the world changes around us. With a proactive strategy, we probe the environment to determine its behavior, and we make plans accordingly.

But that's not the end of the story. If we understand the complexities of the project environment, every move changes the environment. Behavior that was previously understood may no longer exist. It's Heisenberg's uncertainty principle and observer effect in real life. We must continue to probe, observe, and adapt.

Importantly, this adaptive worldview is not opposed to planning. Planning has great value, but problems arise when teams execute plans blindly or fail to pay attention to the environment.

An adaptive worldview values extensive planning, particularly the aspect of planning that involves modeling scenarios and responses. In short, an adaptive worldview values both planning and experimentation.

Learn to Learn

Think again about the conventional project worldview, and pick a point in the middle of a project. We execute the project plan; in other words, we execute what we *should* do according to what we believed prior to the start of the project.

In the complex worldview, we execute according to what we have learned since we made the plan. We accommodate the learning that has taken place—we *adapt*.

Of course, the adaptation cannot go on indefinitely or without limits. Remember that we have established boundaries for the project; for example, schedule may form one boundary. We cannot proceed with an adaptation if it causes us to violate those boundaries.

Plan to Experiment

On a complex project, there is no escaping the need to experiment. Whether we are developing a fledgling technology, a new process, or a new team, it is not possible to know with certainty ahead of time which choices will be best. The information we need to make those choices can come only during execution of the project.

In the complex world, much is unknown; learning will take place on the project. No doubt we have some educated guesses about how things will transpire, but we cannot nail down the details with confidence.

This glaring reality is hard to admit in organizations that expect predictability. The customer, the sponsor, and management in these companies insist on a firm schedule and budget, and will hold the project manager's feet to the fire.

Such a worldview is not only inappropriate, but in the end it is costly, both in time and money. Trying to force a complex project into a conventional mold requires a lot of energy on the part of the team, not the least of which is the energy needed to keep up the appearance that the "conventional" project is proceeding just as planned.

What essentially takes place is that two projects are conducted. The formal, external project has its own set of books and appearances, and the informal project bends the rules and keeps the "real" books.

The truth is that with a sense-making approach, we can put boundaries on the effort, seed experimental investigations, and rather quickly close in on understanding the unknowns. We must do what seems paradoxical: plan to experiment.

We once again need the approach that we used so well in childhood projects. The appropriate model is no more sophisticated than this:

Try stuff, and see what works.

But we don't just try stuff at random; there is a method to our experimentation. We can intelligently choose what experiments to conduct, and as we learn, we adapt appropriately.

■ Efficient Experimentation

One of the critical tasks for the project manager at the start of a complex project is to devise tactics to reduce the uncertainty in a cost effective-manner. What is needed is smart experimentation. Researcher Nigel Wadeson has observed that this smart experimentation process is really an exercise in economics.[2]

Suppose someone is in the market to buy a product and has several possible options. First, the buyer will seek information that is useful in selecting a product. While the price of each option is important to the decision, the buyer must also consider the costs of continuing the search throughout the process.

What we are after is the optimum search path, or at least a good search path, since we may not know ahead of time what is optimum.

This perspective is useful for the project manager to consider in planning the experimentation strategy.

A variety of tools are available to assist in such efforts, such as computer simulation and rapid prototyping. Once again, statistics offers concepts that can help.

■ Thanks, Mr. Pareto

In the early 1900s, an Italian economist named Vilifredo Pareto observed that 20 percent of the people in Italy held 80 percent of the wealth. Adopting this principle and calling it the Pareto principle, the quality guru Joseph Juran many years later observed this 80/20 effect in a variety of areas, differentiating the "vital few" from the "trivial many." In a supermarket, for example, a small percentage of products generates the majority of sales. In any club, usually a few active members are responsible for the vast majority of what the group accomplishes. The Pareto principle serves as a valuable rule of thumb for any manager, including a project manager, seeking to focus attention on important matters.

Pareto's contribution to civilization was to identify what we humans do intuitively. To make sense of the busy world around us, we intuitively use this simple but powerful truth. Without a means to focus our attention, we would become hopelessly overloaded with information.

Using the Pareto principle, we can plan and execute projects in a complex world and have some confidence that we will get it mostly right. In the face of uncertainty, we can proceed with a reasonable level of experimentation and be confident that we will discover meaningful patterns that will guide our path forward. Pareto made it possible for us to design our experiments in a way that gives us meaningful results without requiring inordinate effort.

■ Solving the Right Problem

The project management profession has taken the Pareto principle to heart, in the form of identifying critical success factors on projects. This concept enables us to highlight the few issues that will make or break the project's success.

In the projects I manage, I try to make a point of focusing on the one or two, maybe three, critical issues that will largely determine how the project will be judged. In some cases, the issue is schedule, in others, cost; in yet others, addressing a technology question or market acceptance is critical.

Not only is this approach needed for sense-making, but these critical success factors should drive our strategy for experimentation. If we address the uncertainties in issues related to the critical success factors early in the project, we can then adjust strategies as appropriate.

■ Selling the Stakeholders

Many stakeholders are uncomfortable with the concept of starting a project using the strategy of deliberate experimentation before committing to the project. Something just doesn't sit right about waiting until after key questions are answered to nail down the rest of the project.

Here is a suggestion for managing the expectations of the stakeholders: appeal to their pecuniary interests. In other words, show them the money! (The money to be saved, that is.)

Tell them you can cite evidence documenting that the fastest, most cost-effective path to a successful project is through smart experimentation. Also tell them about more evidence of the immense cost of projects that are terminated after substantial investment. Smart experimentation is a great way to identify those project dogs very early, before significant dollars are spent.

The well-known approach of using stage gates is an excellent way to incorporate experimentation into the project. With this approach, the project is divided into phases and a formal decision gate is conducted at the end of each phase. This strategy enables the sponsor and stakeholders to evaluate progress and decide accordingly whether to continue the project or to terminate the effort.

Right-Brain Toolkit: Design of Experiments

In a simple world, we could perform simple experiments to reduce a project's uncertainty. In a complex project environment, we may have to run a lot of experiments to accurately characterize the playing field, particularly if we have little control over some variables and other variables interact significantly. Doing so can be very costly and time-consuming, however. As a project manager, if I want insight on the issues that have a major effect, I need help, and that help comes in the form of design of experiments (DOE).

DOE is a systematic, statistically valid way to plan and analyze experiments to identify those variables that produce the greatest effects. DOE is most valuable and cost-effective when many variables are involved, when some variables are difficult to control, and when variables interact with one another.

When it comes to sense-making, perhaps more than any other tool, DOE approximates the processing that occurs naturally and speedily in the right brain. In many respects, we do DOE intuitively. We naturally pay particular attention to parameters that seem to have the greatest effect. The right brain scans the unknown and uncertain environment looking for clues and patterns among the noise. DOE does the same in a mathematically valid way, and in so doing, augments the sense-making efforts of the right brain. DOE helps illuminate and make clear the patterns that the right brain seeks. DOE complements the Pareto principle in that it identifies significant influences and effects.

In addition to thanking Mr. Pareto, let us also thank Sir Ronald A. Fisher. Sir Fisher, a brilliant mathematician and geneticist at a small agricultural research station in England, was working to improve crop yields in the 1920s and 1930s. It was Sir Fisher who first conceived DOE and developed the concept.

Conventional thinking in statistical methods at the time held that only one factor could be varied at a time during an experiment. In the real world, such a strategy is often time-consuming and expensive when multiple factors must to be considered. Furthermore, the one-factor-at-a-time strategy completely misses any interactions among factors.

Consider experiments on baking a cake. Time and temperature are two factors that interact in baking—increasing temperature decreases baking time. In a conventional experiment, we would keep the temperature constant and vary time, then keep the time constant and vary temperature. Unless a large number of experiments was run, valuable findings could be missed entirely.

What Sir Fisher demonstrated mathematically and in practice was that with a logical and systematic design, we could vary all the relevant factors at the same time and quickly find the most meaningful results and interactions. Going back to our baking experiment, we could bake a cake at four different combinations of temperature and time and get a surprisingly good idea of the most significant influences on the cake. This approach saves a lot of time and a lot of money. Furthermore, with a follow-on technique called "response surface design," we can design experiments to find the combination of factors that produces the optimum results—the "sweet spot." This trick is not possible with conventional statistics.

We cannot overstate the power of such techniques for any project manager facing complex issues or uncertainty. While clearly applicable to the hard sciences, these techniques are perhaps even more valuable for the soft sciences, including, for example, market research.

Let's say you've just inherited a project to design a new high definition TV set. An important initial task in the project is to nail down the product features and characteristics that will be most appealing to the target market segment. Many factors must be considered, and the factors interact. With an appropriate DOE approach, test marketing can quickly and inexpensively show an optimum mix of cost and features.

One educator, George Box, has used a simple experiment to show the power and economy of DOE for a class of engineering students. With a simple set of experiments, the students can use DOE techniques to optimize the flight of a paper helicopter,[3] even with no background in aeronautical flight.

Figure 13-1 shows a sample set of data from these experiments.[4] Five combinations of three variables were selected for testing, requiring about six minutes to conduct the steps. If the variables had been evaluated one factor at a time, 125 steps would have been required instead of five, and they would have taken about two and one-half hours. Such tedium makes it tempting to cut back on steps, which could cause the experimenter to miss the optimization point that is clearly visible with the DOE approach. Even with only a few trials, substantial insights can be gained on the most significant influences. Detailed tests can then be run to fine-tune the analysis.

It is rare to hear gushing praise for a statistical method. But listen to Bill Kappele, who worked at Hewlett-Packard and Lexmark as a chemist. "Design of experiments ... has done more for my career ... than anything else I have learned. It is the most powerful tool for experimenters that I have ever seen."[5]

■ The Experimental Organization

Some organizations value rationality, or the belief that it is better to develop or learn by reasoning. Other organizations value empiricism, or the belief that it is better to develop or learn by doing and observing what happens.

These preferences are not "either/or." Of course, both approaches are valid and valuable depending on the context. And that is the heart of the matter: the context.

In an uncertain environment when answers are needed in a hurry (in other words, the contemporary project), the empirical approach trumps rationality.

A company that is widely recognized for implementing a corporate culture of experimentation is 3M. At 3M, employees are encouraged to devote up to 15 percent of their time to research or experiment

■ **Figure 13-1. Sample Data from Design of Experiments for Paper Helicopter**

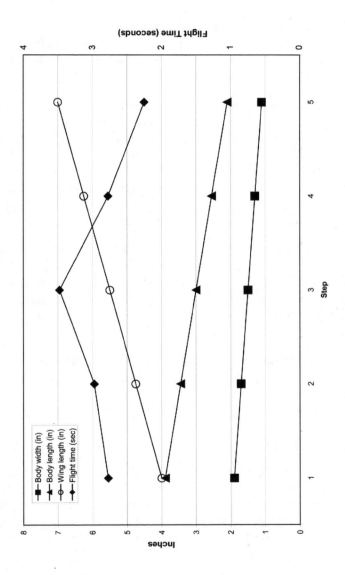

on any topic of interest to them. This professional "play time" has resulted in many profitable products for 3M over the years.

As we mentioned earlier, projects are the vehicles many companies use to implement and bring about corporate strategy. Unfortunately, management strategy is one of those soft skills that eludes definitive understanding or characterization.

Returning to our statistics theme, for many hard sciences, we can run experiments where we can control variables effectively. But for some hard sciences and for pretty much all the soft sciences, the variables are tough to control or even completely characterize. An astronomer cannot run controlled experiments on the birth of a star, nor can a market researcher completely characterize the buying behavior of drivers. In such cases, we can perform only quasi-experimentation to test theories and determine relationships.

This is also the case in organizational strategy, and for much of project management in an uncertain environment. As UCLA professor Olav Sorensen has written, strategy is itself quasi-experimentation.[6] In other words, in strategy, as in much of management, we must make inferences from limited information and learn by trial and error.

With an attitude that values and embraces experimentation and adaptation, we can learn to make sense of the complex and uncertain project environment.

■ Just Do It

Many in the project management community believe that too little planning is done on projects. I would second that position when it comes to predictable, familiar projects. On the other hand, an alternative and equally valid school of thought believes that on uncertain and complex projects, perhaps the best approach is to get moving and do something.

We can do too much planning or too little. Effectively moving toward an objective requires a combination of action, evaluation, reflection, and the appropriate strategy based on context. As always, it is important to keep our brains engaged and not depend on a recipe. Project organizations should make a conscious and deliberate effort to choose the management style that is appropriate to the needs of the project[7] and to experiment as appropriate on the complex project.

Well, enough statistics. It's time to forge new ground ... to create. ■

■ ENDNOTES

1 Nigel Wadeson, "Projects as Search Processes," *International Journal of Project Management,* Vol. 23, 2005, pp. 421–427.

2 Ibid.

3 George Box, "Teaching Engineers Experimental Design with a Paper Helicopter," *Quality Engineering,* Vol. 4, No. 3, 1992, pp. 453–459.

4 "Stat-Teaser: Playing with Paper Helicopters," www.statease.com, September 2004. Accessed October 2006.

5 Bill Kappele, "A Personal Story of DOE," http://www.strategy4doe.com/Newsletters/BackIssues/Vol2/February1999.htm. Accessed August 2006.

6 Olav Sorensen, "Strategy as Quasi-Experimentation," *Strategic Organization,* Vol. 1, No. 3, 2003, pp. 337–343.

7 Aaron J. Shenhar, "One Size Does Not Fit All Projects: Exploring Classical Contingency Domains," *Management Science,* Vol. 47, No. 3, pp. 394–414.

CHAPTER 14

■ Painting without Numbers: Creating the New Reality

■
■
■

Where all think alike, no one thinks very much.

WALTER LIPPMAN ■

When I was a kid, I received a paint-by-numbers kit for a birthday present, and soon completed one of the paintings. Thanks to the makers of these kits, anyone can paint a decent rendering of any number of subjects.

The conventional project is much like the paint-by-numbers approach to art. It provides excellent results if you can follow directions and keep within the lines. But what about the canvas with missing lines? What about the blank canvas?

At some point, we must figure out where to place the lines, or we may choose to approach the painting freehand. We may end up with considerably different paintings depending on the choices we make. Depending on the project, we may have to invent much—or all—of the picture.

When we face the blank or incomplete canvas, we draw upon the creative process. While this process can occasionally be haphazard, most of the time it is hard work for the brain, specifically the right brain. The effort to identify and place those lines or brush strokes is what makes an incomplete picture whole. We want the resulting picture to make sense. The sense the picture makes may be familiar, but it often represents something new—a new way of looking at reality.

■ Projects Are Creations

A project is an act of creation, whether it simply repeats a product that has been made before or boldly attempts something novel. It is part of the unique human experience to create. How we apply the creative process is an important consideration for project management.

In a significant way, the complex project calls upon our creativity, especially at the fuzzy front end of such projects. One of the ways that we make sense of the complex project is to *create* sense.

But creativity is not a random crapshoot. It is a sophisticated, computationally intensive effort of the right brain to form new patterns where patterns are incomplete.

The process of creating involves both originality and appropriateness. An original thought is nice, but if it doesn't fit anywhere, it is simply noise. An original thought that solves a nagging problem or resolves uncertainty—and is therefore an *appropriate* original thought—is a thought that has value.

Contemporary projects demand creativity, not only to make innovative products but also to solve complex social relationships and to work around challenging boundary limits. For example, the rise of the virtual project team has significantly complicated the work of project teams. A high level of creativity is often necessary to meet aggressive schedules.

In short, every contemporary project must draw upon the creative capabilities of its team members.

■ Creativity and Innovation

In corporate press releases and annual reports, companies often claim that they value creativity and innovation. But what exactly do they mean?

When an executive manager says she values creativity, she is most likely saying that she values the ability and motivation of staff to solve problems in the context of their responsibilities. She values staff behavior that results in efficient, productive, and profitable breakthroughs or that resolves conflicts with stakeholders. She does not value staff efforts to find wicked ways to eliminate the bureaucracy, apply accounting practices "creatively," or unilaterally incorporate a contemporary painting into a customer report.

In other words, managers want you to be creative, but not too creative.

This can be confusing: how can you be creative and simultaneously put the brakes on creativity? It is important to recognize and respect the interface between the creative idea and the environment. Creativity is valued when the ideas produced are considered appropriate for the environment.

Often, the distinction is made between creativity—an individual's novel ideas—and innovation—the process by which an organization applies new ideas in its products, services, and operations. The organization will have processes for screening ideas and will allow only those considered appropriate and valuable to proceed.

Innovation is the interaction of the environment with creative ideas and the adaptation or implementation of ideas deemed to have merit. The environment accepts or rejects ideas; in turn, ideas change the environment. When innovation produces something worthwhile, creativity and the environment have worked together to bring forth something of value. The first right-brain principle, the compelling purpose, is key to creativity and innovation.

This interface with the environment benefits the overall process. The environment provides a framework of rules and patterns. New ideas really begin to take shape when they are accepted and implemented in the organization.

Figure 14-1 is a representation of the "innovation funnel." The innovation funnel represents the concept that most creative ideas do

▪ **Figure 14-1. Innovation Funnel**

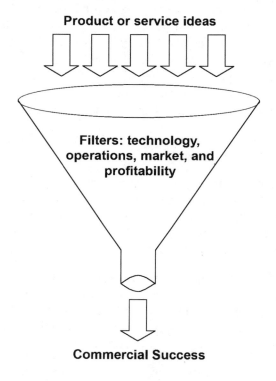

Product or service ideas

Filters: technology, operations, market, and profitability

Commercial Success

not lead to successful products. In fact, research shows that it takes 3,000 new ideas to result in only one successful product.

In reality, this is the partnership between the right- and left-brain styles. The right brain conceives ideas, and the left brain implements.

■ Who Is Creative?

Creativity is not owned solely by artists, musicians, and literary professionals. Everyone has the ability to create, but perhaps in varying degrees. Creativity is sorely needed in every profession, particularly in any role that requires problem-solving skills.

Any engineer, architect, construction manager, IT professional, manager, or other professional relies on creativity to solve problems that are unfamiliar or complex. Although science is not particularly known as a creative profession, the major scientific advances have been the result of the creativity of individuals.[1]

"Creativity is not just for artists. It's for businesspeople looking for a new way to close the sale; it's for engineers trying to solve a problem; it's for parents who want their children to see the world in more than one way."[2]

■ Patterns of Thought

We can consider the needs of a project from the perspective of two different kinds of thought processes: *convergent thinking* and *divergent thinking*.

Convergent thinking is the thought process that is directed toward the singular, correct solution to a problem; divergent thinking is the generation of multiple answers to a problem. Convergent thought is the left-brain application of rules; divergent thought is creativity in the right brain attempting novel approaches.

An example of convergent thought is 5+5=10. For this type of problem, one answer is appropriate and even necessary; we don't want people to invent all sorts of answers to simple arithmetic problems. Similarly, while driving, if I see a stop sign, I would do best to stop, not to explore other "creative" options.

Divergent thought is more appropriate for open-ended questions, for situations that demand novel approaches, or to resolve impasses. As a project manager, if the critical path for my project extends beyond what is acceptable to the sponsor, some creative solutions may be in order. If the staff can't stand the weekly project status meeting, it may be valuable to come up with some new ways to conduct the meeting.

Convergent thinking is the left-brain application of rules and logic. Divergent thinking is the right-brain exploration of new options, connections, and relationships. Both types of thinking are valuable and critical to individuals and organizations. The key is to apply each type appropriately.

It is important to understand that while divergent thinking will create some useful ideas, it will also necessarily generate concepts that are not useful, perhaps even some that are downright ridiculous. As D.K. Simonton has indicated, creativity is a Darwinian process,[3] much as biological systems are: many creative concepts will not survive, in large part because they do not fit with the environment. Many people have difficulty with this screening process and are afraid to have their ideas rejected. With organizations, the difficulty is even more pronounced.

▪ Creativity in an Organization

Most organizations have a certain inertia and are slow to change. We often like a little change, but resist radical change.

In other words, people and human organizations are very much like Newton's first law of motion: an object in motion will tend to stay in motion in the same direction unless acted upon by an external force. Human and organizational inertia tend to inhibit significant change.

The reasons for inertia involve fundamental human behavior, as well as the fact that most of us live in the left-brain world. Our daily patterns are usually well-established, comfortable, and predictable. Customers may get upset if you make dramatic changes in the product they have come to like. Likewise, people come to rely on established organizational processes—"better the devil you know." Of course, some of the people in an organization have come to benefit from the status quo.

Organizational rules and customs get established for a reason, and creative challenges to them are resisted. However, with a compelling reason, even deeply ingrained ruts can be overcome.

Because many organizations value rationality in their operations, they tend to ignore or discount the potential benefits of creative approaches. Thus, organizational culture plays a significant role in creativity in an organization. In her book, *Companies Are People Too*, Sandra Fekete notes that just as individuals have personality preferences, organizations also exhibit personality styles. Companies that value and encourage creativity are more "Intuitive" and "Perceiving" than those that do not.[4]

When they challenge the conventional rules and question them in a way that causes a community or organization to critically examine its values, potentially worthwhile ideas can seem threatening or heretical. When Galileo postulated that the earth was not the center of the universe, his notion completely upset the worldview held by many and prompted a profound examination of cultural values.

■ Birthright or Skill?

Are some people more creative than others, or is creativity a skill that can be learned?

The answer to the first part of the question is likely "yes"; the brain structure of some people promotes creative thought. As evidence of these findings, consider the case of Albert Einstein. In addition to all that his brain gifted to humanity while he was alive, he willed his brain to be studied after his death.

While Einstein is rightfully recognized as a genius, his parents may have had their doubts when he was a toddler. At the age of three, they took him to a pediatrician because he could not yet talk; he had developmental dyslexia. His left brain was delayed in development, and some have postulated that his right brain compensated by developing above-average functionality. Examination of Einstein's brain revealed a high degree of connectivity, which enabled advanced spatial processing. "It was Einstein's view that his own creativity was heavily dependent on spatial reasoning."[5] The delayed development of his left brain may have made Einstein's genius possible.

The creative process is often stimulated by considering new perspectives or new relationships between familiar concepts. Einstein reported that the theory of relativity came to him while riding on a train. He observed a passing train and noticed that his perception of the speed of the other train was unusual; he soon deduced that what he perceived was influenced by the fact that as an observer he was moving. He then understood that what he perceived was the difference in the speeds of the two trains. This simple metaphor, passing trains, sparked one of the greatest discoveries in physics.

For those of us with average, non-Einstein brains, creativity is a skill that can be developed with practice. Exercising this skill starts with a willingness to see the environment, as Einstein did, from a new perspective—to reevaluate rules and assumptions.

■ Breaking the Rules

While both hemispheres in the brain are always active, the left brain typically controls thinking and the right brain defers. This structure enables us to function capably in the world, but it can get in the way of creative thought, especially when we are trying to improve our creative skills.

The roadblock occurs because the left brain is trying to execute rules and patterns regarding the situation at hand, rather than explore potential new patterns. In essence, the left brain says, "This is the pattern, there is no other," and continues to control the game. To get past this roadblock we need to bypass the left brain or to trick it.

In the first case, we deliberately talk to the right brain. Where the left brain processes words, we start using pictures. Where the left brain executes the familiar, we deliberately invoke the unfamiliar.

In the second case, we temporarily suspend known rules (or assumptions). Because no pattern is recognized for the temporary situation, the left brain turns the matter over to the right brain.

A number of techniques can be used to stimulate creative thought. These techniques serve to quiet the left brain temporarily, allowing the right brain to explore new avenues and uncover new perspectives.

Which Rules Do We Break?

In the movie, *A Few Good Men*, Tom Cruise plays a Navy lawyer, Lieutenant Kaffee, who defends two Marines accused of the murder of a fellow Marine at Guantanamo Bay. They had inflicted a form of hazing known as a "Code Red" as punishment for him threatening to blow the whistle on a fellow Marine. In a dramatic courtroom scene, Kaffee takes on the tough-as-nails commanding officer, Colonel Jessup, played by Jack Nicholson. In the climax, Jessup admits that he ordered the Code Red. The two Marines are acquitted of the murder charges, but they are found guilty of conduct unbecoming an officer and given dishonorable discharges because they should have disobeyed the order.

This movie illuminates an important tension in creativity: which rules should we follow and which rules should we break?

The question is certainly valid for issues such as the physical features of a product, but it can reach heightened significance for social and organizational rules. Often, the decision is not clear-cut. Obedience to rules is important, yet it is morally preferable to disobey orders or rules that are harmful. Certainly, the safety and welfare of people is a valid reason to break the rules, but what about more mundane reasons? How do you navigate this grey area when existing rules can threaten progress on a compelling project?

This is one of the reasons why maturity in personal development and moral reasoning are important elements in the success of the complex and aggressive project. Rules must often be challenged and broken for the project to meet its objectives.

It is important to use the core principles of the organization to guide behavior when considering whether to break the rules. Core principles that are beneficial and are articulated well should be given priority over rules and customs that hinder project accomplishment.

■ Right-Brain Toolkit: New Rules

The creative process depends on both divergent and convergent thought. Divergent thought is needed to prompt new concepts, and convergent thought is needed to test ideas for their usefulness—to implement imagination appropriately.

While tapping imagination is easy for a child, adults often have to prime the pump a bit to quiet the left brain and stimulate different perspectives. A four-step process can stimulate creativity:

1. Priming
2. Exploring
3. Building
4. Evaluating.

This four-step process can lead to the creation of a new pattern, new rules, or a new "reality." The priming step gets the process going, the exploring step enables the consideration of new characteristics, the building step creates new patterns, and the evaluating step selects patterns that are useful and rejects those that are ineffective. As noted, this is necessarily a Darwinian process—trying new things and keeping those that work.

▪▪▪ PRIMING

Let's start with how to quiet that bossy left brain. One approach is to use pictures. In their book, *Unleashing the Right Side of the Brain: The LARC Creativity Program*, Robert H. Williams and John Stockmyer[6] suggest that the first step in creative thought is to draw a picture of your subject. The picture is used solely to quiet the left brain temporarily and talk to the right brain, not to make a pretty or useful image.

A second priming approach is a change in perspective. In her popular book, *Drawing on the Right Side of the Brain*, Betty Edwards uses drawing to stimulate creative thought.[7] In her years of teaching, she noticed that students could draw images more accurately if the perspective of the subject was changed. For example, drawings of the image of a face were often distorted when the subject was in the typical facial position. But a fledgling artist could draw quite accurately when the subject's face was turned upside down. This simple trick permitted the right side of the brain to take over the process because it turned a familiar image into one that was unfamiliar.

A third approach to priming is "inversion," or deliberately suspending known rules. This approach works well with assumptions, including those beliefs that have been held for so long that they are considered to be beyond challenge. We have already covered some examples of priming by using the "po" operator in Chapter 6.

Suppose that our standard policy is for employees to work only between the hours of 8:00 a.m. and 5:00 p.m. What if we now say that this practice is abolished? What if we forbid anyone to work this schedule? In the next step we can explore what the organization might look like without this policy.

■■■ EXPLORING

A key activity in the development of a creative concept is to expand upon the new perspective identified in the priming step. In fact, we would like to direct considerable attention to the many ways that we can articulate or describe the concept. In creating a new reality, we want to explore thoroughly what that reality might be. The exploring step involves asking and answering many questions about the characteristics of our idea.

Another way of approaching this step is to consider that the new reality *already exists*, and our task is only to discover it. Rather than being novel, perhaps what we seek to discover has merely been hidden from sight or hasn't been considered seriously before.

Suppose we want to be creative about uses of a baseball bat. We might develop a list of characteristics such as the one in Table 14-1.

In Chapter 6, we also discussed the tool of mind-mapping diagrams. Such a visual tool is an excellent way to explore the characteristics and issues associated with our subject.

▪ Table 14-1. Sample of the Exploring Process: Characteristics of a Wooden Baseball Bat

Characteristics
Made of wood
Shape is long and tapered cylinder
About 3 feet long and 2–3 inches in diameter
Weighs about 2–3 pounds
Comes in different colors, usually natural or black
Usually has text stamped on it
Has monetary value (that may increase)
May have sentimental value (specific bats)
Structure is solid

▪▪▪ BUILDING

Now the fun really starts. We look through all the characteristics we developed during the exploring step and start looking for interesting new relationships or patterns. Many of these will be ridiculous, but some could be winners.

From the characteristics of Table 14-1, we might suggest the following uses for a baseball bat:

- Pointing device (a batter calling where a home run will be hit)
- A unit of currency (that camera cost me ten bats)
- A meaningful memento (I treasure the bat my son used in Little League)
- Rolling pin (to roll out dough)
- A source of heat when placed in a fire.

Where we typically think of a baseball bat only as a piece of sports equipment, we have now developed a range of ideas that convey entirely different uses and meanings. The objective in this stage of the exercise is to come up with creative ideas without analysis or criticism; that will take place in the next step.

Going back to *A Few Good Men,* over the course of the movie, several scenes show Kaffee holding a baseball bat. He nervously prepares for the trial and the confrontation with Jessup. Stretching for a creative way to probe Jessup, Kaffee searches for the object that prompts his creativity: "I need my bat. I think better with my bat. Where's my bat?"

In all the potential uses we may have envisioned for a baseball bat, here's one that may never have occurred to us: it is Kaffee's crutch to stimulate creative thought!

▪▪▪ EVALUATING

We finally come to the place where our potential new ideas meet the environment. Which of our ideas will really work? Which won't? If we have done our work well, we will likely hit upon some provocative concepts that may be breakthrough ideas. Some experimentation may be necessary to prove or disprove some of the concepts.

Evaluating creative ideas must be done in the context of the need. It may seem that no one in their right mind would think of tossing their autographed Cal Ripken, Jr., baseball bat into a fire. Yet, if I am lost in the desert on a cold night and that bat is the only fuel around, well, sorry, Cal.

▪ Professional Play

Warren Bennis has spent much of his career examining leadership. Some of his work has involved analyzing "great groups," project teams that accomplished astounding results. One of his observations is that such groups engage in "professional play." While the work is ultimately serious, it is nonetheless also playful because it involves the passionate application of imagination. Professionals in an environment that allows them to be creative and work on a compelling purpose often talk about their creative work as professional play.

The creativity and collaboration exhibited in groups are built to a significant extent on professional play. Professional play applies knowledge and tools in innovative and perhaps mischievous ways. The content of the play is absolutely serious but the process is amusing and playful. In other words, the purpose is important but the means to achieve it are informal and casual. Professional play is primarily about discovery.

The process of discovery often takes us off the map, into uncharted territory. It is not a process that can be specifically orchestrated with a cookie cutter approach. The trip is made possible by what Roger Von Oech calls "creative destruction,"[8] the demolition of the limitations of existing systems. "Many Great Groups are fueled by an invigorating, completely unrealistic view of what they can accomplish. Not knowing what they can't do puts everything in the realm of the possible."[9]

This is the essence of creativity: when there are no limits, nothing is impossible.

We have painted a picture in this chapter using some existing lines and creating some new ones for creative approaches to the complexities and uncertainties of contemporary projects. Creativity and professional play reach fruition in an environment of trust, which brings us to the next principle of right-brain project management. ▪

▪ ENDNOTES

1 D. K. Simonton, *Origins of Genius: Darwinian Perspectives on Creativity* (New York: Oxford University Press, 1999).

2 Twyla Tharp, *The Creative Habit* (New York: Simon & Schuster, 2003), p. 7.

3 D. K. Simonton, *Origins of Genius: Darwinian Perspectives on Creativity* (New York: Oxford University Press, 1999).

4 Sandra Fekete, *Companies Are People, Too* (Hoboken, NJ: John Wiley & Sons, 2003).

5 Fred Balzac, "Exploring the Brain's Role in Creativity," *NeuroPsychiatry*, Vol. 7, No. 5, May 2006.

6 Robert H. Williams and John Stockmyer, *Unleashing the Right Side of the Brain: The LARC Creativity Program* (Lexington, MA: Stephen Greene Press, 1987).

7 Betty Edwards, *Drawing on the Right Side of the Brain* (New York: St. Martin's Press, 1979).

8 Roger Von Oech, *A Whack on the Side of the Head: How You Can Be More Creative* (New York: Warner Books, 1998).

9 Patricia Ward Biederman and Warren G. Bennis, *Organizing Genius: The Secrets of Creative Collaboration* (Reading, MA: Addison-Wesley, 1997), pp. 15–16.

CHAPTER 15

■ Doing Business with a Handshake: Exercising and Fulfilling Trust

■
■
■

Few things help an individual more than to place responsibility upon him, and to let him know that you trust him.

BOOKER T. WASHINGTON ■

Have you ever done business "with a handshake"? Instead of using a written contract, the parties sealed an agreement by shaking hands?

A handshake is a powerful image of trust. The physical contact of two humans is a metaphor for the commitment to honor an agreement as well as the belief that the other will do likewise. It is ultimately a sign of faith in the relationship that it is more powerful and meaningful than a document.

But it is more than that. Where trust is strong, each person knows that both will go the extra mile for the other, or for the cause. In a world that produces lengthy legal agreements, quickly jumps to litigation, and seeks loopholes and excuses, the concept of trust may seem anachronistic, something that is no longer possible.

Complex projects sorely need trust. More to the point, in the contemporary project environment, if we want to navigate an aggressive project schedule and accomplish major breakthroughs, project team members need the ability to make agreements and decisions quickly without bureaucratic red tape. Speed, agility, and creativity can be achieved only through trust.

How important is trust?

In the Skunk Works®, the two parties, a large corporation and the U.S. government, did not execute a contract until four months after work started. Had Lockheed insisted on a signed agreement before starting work, Germany might have developed the jet fighter first. Lack of trust could have tipped the war in Germany's favor.

Working environments characterized by a low level of trust are typically described as stressful, threatening, divisive, unproductive, and tense. High-trust environments are typically described as fun, supportive, motivating, productive, and comfortable.[1]

Which type of environment is more conducive to project success?

Unfortunately, because a project team is a temporary organization, individuals often do not have the opportunity to develop a track record of trust with one another. It is therefore important in the early stages of the project to focus on and facilitate the development of trust.

While not discounting appropriate skepticism, humans are built to trust one another when the environment is right. Do we dare do business on a handshake? On a complex and aggressive project where we are seeking to achieve the improbable, do we dare not?

■ A Tale of Two Worlds

Consider two opposite worlds.

The first world is cutthroat; people cynically take advantage of others. Information is withheld or deliberately altered; trust is minimal or nonexistent. I have to proceed through the world doing everything for myself. If I weren't already, I would soon become paranoid in such a world.

In the other world, trust is abundant. I can operate freely and I can implicitly depend on many others. I can believe in what they are saying and be confident that they have the best interest of the relationship at heart.

Our organizations, our society, and our civilization are possible because a substantial level of trust is built into daily life. We believe that the bank will keep the money we deposited safe. We believe that the mail will arrive every day. We believe that the driver on the cross street will observe the stop sign.

When a high level of trust is present, people can invest themselves in their work and know that there is not a hidden agenda in play. Workers are able to make decisions according to their authority and be confident that they will not be second-guessed. When trust is present, daily work becomes much more productive because emotional energy is directed toward accomplishment rather than trying to figure out what is "safe" to do.

■ The Payoff of Trust

On a project, a high level of trust has a significant bottom-line payoff.

In their book, *Driving Fear Out of the Workplace*, Kathleen Ryan and Daniel Oestreich identify ways in which a low level of trust hurts productivity:

- Workers do only what is expected and avoid extra effort.
- People make more mistakes and invest added effort in hiding them.
- Teams become dysfunctional, working on the wrong priorities with poor decision-making and problem-solving methods.
- The project suffers from little or no creativity, motivation, and risk-taking.[2]

In other words, a low level of trust hurts project teams in all the areas that are needed for success in complex, contemporary projects.

Complex and aggressive projects demand a high level of motivation and creative problem-solving. Because they often involve new teams, these projects also require the establishment of patterns of behavior and relationships for effective project work.

In graduate school, I was involved in testing on a 500,000 volt electric power transmission line in northern Minnesota. The final test of the project involved shorting one line to ground—a night-time test that promised some spectacular fireworks. It was a once-in-a-career kind of test.

The afternoon of the test, a custom computer board in our measurement equipment failed. The only one way to get the equipment ready in time was for me to fly to Minneapolis, meet a computer tech at the airport who would give me a replacement board, and fly back.

A conventional project environment has difficulty with unorthodox solutions to pressing problems. The bureaucracy wants competitive bids and documentation. The bureaucracy sees my last-minute, round-trip courier airfare as an unjustifiable expense that cannot be approved.

But when there is a compelling purpose, bureaucratic rules must become subordinate to a singular rule: do whatever it takes to make the project succeed. It becomes necessary to trust that team members are acting for the good of the project and not just taking advantage of the system. Because our group had established a relationship of trust, the bureaucracy approved my creative courier work. I spent the afternoon flying round-trip from Hibbing, Minnesota, to Minneapolis, got the board, and we got our data.

Many of us have worked on projects that demanded timely, creative solutions for the project to succeed. These demands of contemporary projects are thwarted by cumbersome rules, cynicism, and distrust. Clearly, trust is a key ingredient for accomplishing the phenomenal project.

■ Components of Trust

To explore how trust can contribute to project success, let us begin by considering the components of trust for the scenario of project work. When I think of trusting someone else on a project, I think of four aspects:

- *Integrity*. I believe the other person will be honest, forth-right, and follow commitments. In other words, I believe I will not be manipulated.
- *Benevolence*. I believe the other person wishes good for the relationship and for me.
- *Capability*. I believe the other person has the abilities to do what I expect.
- *Alignment*. If I trust the other person with a task, after we discuss it, I expect her to understand, agree, and value the objective as I do. Our values are aligned and our under-standing of how to implement those values is clear.

This interpretation of the concept of trust is purposely some-what broad. Specifically, we are concerned with working together on a project. In such a situation, trust involves a significant degree of *dependence* on one another for accomplishment of the project objec-tives. In some situations, the elements of capability and alignment may not be relevant, but for project work, they are very important components of trust.

◼ Developing Trust

People entering into any relationship do not automatically trust one another, and for good reason. It is healthy to be somewhat wary and self-protective when we do not know others' intentions for the relationship.

The process of developing trust is an exercise in risk-taking for the parties involved. The process can be modeled as a spiral that proceeds upward if trust grows or downward if trust diminishes. I develop a perception of the trustworthiness of the other person, and act accordingly.

An element that is critical to trust but is often overlooked is how we address breaches to trust. Humans, being imperfect, are prone to letting others down, even if inadvertently. If the breach is repaired well, however, trust can actually grow through the experience.

For example, a customer can actually grow in loyalty to a business after a bad experience if the business makes a genuine effort to repair the breach. This is particularly true if the customer perceives that the company has "gone the extra mile" to make things right.

■ Self-Trust

As we discussed in Chapter 2, one of the ways that we become more skilled at projects is through personal development. This truth is certainly at work in the area of trust that we will call "self-trust," or confidence.

If I have appropriate confidence—appropriate self-trust—I believe I can handle situations that may arise, even if they are challenging. I trust in my ability to adapt, cope, and do well. This confidence allows me to trust others to a greater extent. Even if they let me down, I can recover from their failure.

"Well-adjusted people are comfortable with themselves and see the world as a generally benign place. Their high levels of confidence often make them quick to trust, because they believe that nothing bad will happen to them."[3]

This confidence does not mean that I naively ignore my instincts about others, nor do I ignore their history. But this confidence allows me to collaborate more openly and believe that the outcome will be positive.

■ Power and Hierarchy

A discussion of trust cannot ignore the fact that organizations and project teams have hierarchical structures where some individuals hold greater power than others. We are not advocating, nor does trust require, an approach where everyone is on equal footing.

In an environment of trust, collaboration, and shared goals, the differences in authority become complementary rather than divisive.

■ Alignment of Goals

To promote trust, the most fundamental elements an organization can help establish are common core goals and values. When individuals in a group have a common agenda and a common set of attitudes, a climate of trust will develop naturally. When members begin to have divergent objectives, it is easier to fall into an "us" versus "them" mindset. Such a mindset naturally involves questioning the motives of others; in other words, distrust.

We have already addressed this subject with respect to finding a compelling purpose for a project and establishing a set of lasting core values for the organization. Let us also revisit the concept of spiritual survival.

We noted earlier that one of the elements of spiritual survival is "membership," or belonging to a group that affirms a person and his values. This element of membership is often used to motivate sports teams before games. It is also a significant component of the loyalty of many to the Apple Macintosh. That customer community shares a strong bond to values that are perceived to be in contrast to the values represented by PCs and Microsoft Windows.

How can a project leader promote common values among team members on a project? This can be done in large part by recognizing that human endeavors have a certain universality to them.

Find the universal story that fits, but remember that it is "our" story rather than "my" story. As Peter Drucker said:

The leaders who work most effectively, it seems to me, never say "I." And that's not because they have trained themselves not to say "I." They don't think "I." They think "we"; they think "team." They understand their job to be to make the team function. They accept responsibility and don't sidestep it, but "we" gets the credit .... This is what creates trust, what enables you to get the task done.[4]

Projects are not only about delivering products. Look deeper, and a story of mythical proportions unfolds. What movie best describes our project? Is it *The Gladiator* or *Napoleon Dynamite?* Both have heroes who overcome adversity and have a strong set of core values.

Teams that develop strong core values and that progress through important emotional events together often develop into clans where trust is abundant. This is a good development for a group, but be aware that a clan does not become separated from the core values of the rest of the organization and fight against that organization.

■ Respect

A high level of trust goes hand-in-hand with respect for the other members of the team. Respect can be defined simply as wishing well for the other person.

Let us return to our introduction of emotional intelligence and emotional development from Chapters 2 and 3. Maturity in moral reasoning brings us to a higher level of emotional intelligence; in this context, morality implies respect.

Take any group of individuals, put them in an office together, and they can be *with* one another. With respect and trust, the group becomes *for* one another.[5] This is an important point of trust. When we have no personal relationship with someone, it is natural to apply morally impersonal decisions to them. When our relationship is personal, we will care for their interests and our decisions will be morally personal—and therefore respectful.

■ Conflict

The subject of conflict comes up in any discussion of human relationships. No two people in the world will agree on everything, so it is naive to think that an environment of trust means that we will always agree with and be pleasant to one another.

Conflict is an inevitable part of human relationships, as much as saying "hello" and "goodbye." It is what we do with conflict that determines whether that conflict is healthy and leads to better solutions, or if it is unhealthy and destroys a relationship.

The individuals on a team come to an issue with different perspectives. The resulting conflict of ideas can lead to better solutions if trust and respect are givens. Conflict becomes unhealthy when it becomes about a person, when it is subversive, or when it becomes about me winning and the other person losing.

Trust is not the same as harmony, although the two are related. In a trusting relationship, the inevitable conflict can be expressed in a constructive way and then resolved. This is a paradoxical characteristic of conflict and trust: the two are integral parts of one another when they exist in an environment of respect in which value is placed on maintaining the relationship.

This paradoxical character highlights the difference between superficial trust and genuine trust. It is certainly more pleasant to work in an amiable rather than a cutthroat environment. When everyone is playing nice all the time, however, they are not always being honest. It's actually more productive to have a workplace where people trust one another enough to disagree and tell the truth in a respectful way.

■ Trust: Relationship Repair

How can we proceed if someone violates our trust and lets us down? It is no doubt true that trust remains superficial until it is tested. Trust can be rebuilt if the parties talk about the breach openly and work to repair the damage to the relationship.

It is inevitable that someone will let you down at some point. From time to time, all of us make morally imprudent decisions. Relationships can be tested or even broken.

One response to a breach of trust is to impose rules and withhold trust. Another approach is to view the breach as temporary and work to repair the relationship. In many cases, the breach is indicative of a structural problem in the relationship that may be difficult to resolve. In these cases, it is foolish to blindly trust someone who has demonstrated a history of not honoring that trust. On the other hand, in many cases repairing the relationship makes for a stronger relationship over the long run. Forgiveness is a necessary ingredient of teams that incorporate trust on their projects.

■ Trust on Projects

Consider conventional project management. Among its other purposes, the project plan is a social contract among the parties. We all agree to do certain things in a certain way on a certain schedule. The social contract consists of dozens, perhaps hundreds, of social subagreements.

The formality of the project plan can reflect the level of trust on a project. In an environment of distrust, we had best put everything in writing and spell it out in detail so that the agreements can be enforced. In an environment of trust, we can be less formal in the agreements.

For example, documentation on a project can serve three purposes: as a tool to assist in communication and understanding, as a method to memorialize what has been done, and finally, as accountability on an agreement. On projects where the level of trust is high, we may have less of a need for documentation to provide accountability; accountability is part of the trust. (Documentation remains essential, however, for the other two purposes.)

We can improve on efficiency when we do not need to reduce accountability to paper. Doing business on a handshake can significantly increase productivity—in a highly trusting environment.

■ Compelling Purpose

In addition to its other benefits, a compelling purpose for the project also provides an abundant emotional reserve for team members to trust one another.

On typical projects, we usually develop a comfortable zone of trust with other team members. We have learned not to expect more of them, and they likewise do not expect more of us.

What if a project comes along with a compelling need? What if it is a matter of life or death?

On other projects, we could tolerate delays or even complete failure to meet objectives. On the compelling project, the objectives are so important that we are driven to meet them. In such a situation, the project simply will not succeed without trust. Since project success is more important than the potential for damaged or broken trust, we choose to trust.

This is one of the key lessons from the case studies of the Skunk Works® and the Red, White, and Blue Out. When else would the U.S. government commit to a major project without inches-thick paperwork and approvals? Under other circumstances, it would have been laughable for a college student to ask a vendor to ship thousands of T-shirts on only a promise to pay later.

If the government bureaucrat withholds approval of the jet fighter development, there may soon be no government to run. If the T-shirt vendor laughs, says "no," or takes the time to check credit, the rare opportunity to make a stadium-size human palette of colors will forever pass. It is only because the bureaucrat and the vendor trust enough to say "yes" that the projects can proceed.

The establishment of trust early in a project often pays substantial dividends later. I once worked for a small engineering firm that planned a product development project with General Electric. Negotiations were complicated and drawn out, and the GE product team feared losing a market window. We agreed to start the project without an executed contract. It is one thing for a gigantic conglomerate like GE to proceed without a contract, but doing so can threaten the viability of a small company that will have to incur expenses without certainty of being paid. Nevertheless, the trust we built early on helped significantly later in the project when we had to substantially revise upward a mistaken bid for the second phase of the contract.

When there is a compelling purpose, trust turns what is otherwise laughable and risky into something natural and motivating. The bond of trust created becomes a rich part of the legend of the project.

◼ Breaking the Rules

When trust is low, an organization typically relies on an abundance of rules to guide and enforce required behaviors. With rules, authority and decision-making are usually centralized. These factors contribute substantially to inefficiencies.

When trust is high, detailed rules are not needed; fewer high-level guidelines generally suffice. This right-brain approach provides guidance while permitting team members to create patterns of interaction that work effectively.

◼ Distributed Leadership

Complex projects on an aggressive schedule need the emotional commitment and creative problem-solving abilities of the entire team. But they also need decisions to be made in a timely fashion.

Layers of bureaucracy and committees can grind the decision-making process to a crawl. On the other hand, it is not appropriate to allow anyone to make a decision at whim.

The concept of distributed leadership can also be called *appropriate decision-making*. It is the recognition that many decisions can be made without the involvement of the project manager or major stakeholders. It is also the recognition that some decisions *must* involve those parties. Decision-making, and therefore leadership, is distributed, and it is promoted where it can be carried out most effectively and most efficiently. This approach requires a high level of trust.

The concept of distributed leadership fits with the Theory Z style of management and with the identification of a compelling purpose for the project. When individuals know what is most important, and when they are trusted to work toward that purpose, they are free to apply themselves fully and creatively. When individuals are uncertain about project objectives, if objectives don't seem important, or if their decision-making is not trusted, they will hold back and work halfheartedly.

To a certain extent, distributed leadership means that teams become self-organizing. This approach represents a significant departure from conventional project techniques, which emphasize the organizational skills of the project manager.

Self-organization does not imply a lack of leadership. Rather, an informal organization and its leadership are allowed to develop naturally. This is generally a very efficient and effective way for people to tackle a project.

With a self-organizing approach, leadership focuses on the application of a limited number of *meta-rules*, or a framework that guides detail. "A project is an open, mobile, changing system. The organization of the project must therefore be adaptive and flexible, and allow for evolution."[6]

This approach recognizes that there is no recipe or cookie cutter that applies to complex projects. It gives project managers and their teams the latitude to apply meta-rules in the manner that is most efficient to meet their unique needs. Self-organization trusts project teams with autonomy.

In a company that has previously applied conventional project management techniques, it can be challenging to implement a new methodology based on meta-rules and self-organization. Significant effort will likely be required in effecting such a substantial cultural shift. "The problem is to replace an organization built around fixed rules with an organization built around a set of rules that are in continual movement."[7]

The self-organizing approach is not appropriate for all circumstances. As we have seen, for many projects, conventional techniques are the right fit.

Again, it is important to be attentive to the project's environment and to be selective about a self-organizing strategy. Where it is appropriate, it may be most effective to establish individual project teams outside the parent organization. This approach was used successfully in the Skunk Works®.

Entrepreneurial Projects

Carl Pritchard

In my presentations and courses, I promote the concept of "inventiveness" in project work. Project management is not just about Gantt charts and critical paths. It is about being excited and being creative; there are strong ties between projects and entrepreneurial behavior.

For example, we can take the perspective that the work breakdown structure (WBS) is a mundane set of tasks, or even an oppressive regime to be satisfied. What if we turn the tables and view each WBS package as an entrepreneurial activity? This perspective opens up dramatic possibilities for motivation.

This attitude is consistent with Ouchi's Theory Z style of management. A WBS package is structured to give control for detailed decisions to the person responsible for the task, not the project manager. The work is structured with clearly defined boundaries: as long as the task deliverables stay within these boundaries, the task leader has the freedom to choose details. The work package is the level of control, and the project manager turns over control to the team member.

Too many project managers micromanage their projects, but sooner or later they have to learn to let go. Not only is this attitude entrepreneurial, it is also consistent with the *PMBOK Guide*®! This approach ignites a lot of energy and ownership in the person responsible for the work package.

When we talk about turning over control for a work package, we must also address the subject of risk. I think the best approach is to identify a nominal or acceptable level of risk for the work package. In other words, the project manager should set a limit of risk for the package.

Say that a work package includes procurement of equipment from a vendor. One element of risk may be the late delivery of the equipment from the preferred source. The project manager may allow the owner of the work package the latitude to seek alternative sources to meet the delivery schedule even if those sources are more costly. In such a case, the level of risk is driven by schedule, with some discretion for cost.

It is important to be clear about the distinction between what is truly uncertain and the anxiety that accompanies a hard decision we want to avoid. Harold Kerzner uses the example of the famous quote "Damn the torpedoes, full speed ahead" by Admiral David Farragut in the Battle of Mobile Bay in the Civil War. It is commonly believed that this quote illustrates a reckless and risky attitude, when in reality it was a calculated decision to minimize risk. At the time of the Civil War, a torpedo was a stationary mine. While sailing into waters where mines may lurk is fraught with risk and uncertainty, during the battle it would have been more risky to retreat or to proceed cautiously.

A balance can be struck between left- and right-brain styles in project management, and many of the left-brain tools offer opportunities for right-brain activities. For example, the earned value technique (EVT) is very left-brain oriented, and most project managers can't stand it. However, if you can tolerate it, EVT can serve as the springboard to stimulate right-brain communication. It can even promote better relationships and alliances with the people in the accounting department, providing all sorts of right-brain benefits. This effect is much like the function of scorekeeping in sports. The scoreboard is an integral part of the game, and it doesn't detract from the passion of the game.

The subject of entrepreneurial project management is an important one for our time. In my extensive work in the project management community, I see the potential for those in the profession to be viewed as administrators only and not as leaders. It is perhaps understandable how this has happened. The *PMBOK Guide®* and conventional project management concepts can be interpreted merely as administrative tools. Such a perspective misses the point, however. Project management is not administrative overhead; it is a value-added function.

Above all, a project manager must be a leader, and the project must be viewed as a dynamic engine of innovation. With these perspectives, projects can be great sources of entrepreneurial energy for an organization.

Carl Pritchard, PMP, is the principal and founder of Pritchard Management Associates. He is a recognized lecturer, author, researcher, and instructor. Considered a leading authority on risk management, he presents on a variety of management topics. Carl has worked with many leading international organizations, as well as private clients and the Project Management Institute. He is the author of several texts, including The Project Communications Toolkit *and* Risk Management Concepts and Guidance.

■ Communication

Problems with communication are often cited as prime reasons for failure to meet project objectives. If this is the case, any improvements in communication will promote project success. Improved trust encourages open communication and sharing of information.

Where the level of trust is low, people are reluctant to share information, to be proactive with communication, and to take risks in communication. These reservations dampen efficiency and creativity on a project, with unfortunate effects on the bottom line.

In short, as Steven M. R. Covey has said, trust promotes speed on projects because trust promotes confidence.[8]

◼ Right-Brain Toolkit: Elements of Trust

Project plans usually provide explicit objectives for cost, time, features, and quality, but generally stop short of incorporating specific work processes and relationships. One way to promote trust in a project team is to specifically plan for it. "Such 'soft' goals can be that participants will treat each other with respect, communicate promptly and openly, solve problems quickly, and in general try to help all project actors reach their goals."[9]

How can project teams accomplish these worthy goals?

A great place to start is by deliberately addressing these goals as part of the project plan and taking steps to discuss group norms openly. Based in part on characteristics identified by Kathleen Ryan and Daniel Oestreich in their book *Driving Fear Out of the Workplace*,[10] the following outline of norms can be serve as a starting point in promoting an atmosphere of trust on a project:

- Give credit for good work that is done and avoid blame when things go wrong.
- Take responsibility for the success of the project and resist the urge to make excuses.
- Share information openly.
- Collaborate on important issues.
- Speak in terms of "we" and not "us and them."
- Focus on common purpose and avoid getting sidetracked by differences in details; always keep the compelling purpose in mind.
- Respect each other's position and role.
- Take steps early in the project to establish trust. On a demanding project, situations that demand unorthodox solutions will no doubt arise. If trust is already established, the team can avoid roadblocks and breeze through such issues.

- Voice concerns, criticisms, and conflicts openly.
- Speak positively about the project and avoid cynicism, even when discussing problem areas.

Once a project manager incorporates these or other group norms in the planning and kickoff of a project, it is critical that she model and apply such behaviors in the execution of the project. Teams will look to the project manager for cues on accepted and valued behaviors. As good as it is to "talk the talk," it is more important to "walk the walk."

■ Distrust Is Risky

Trust on a project can also be considered from the perspective of uncertainty management or risk management.

Distrust among project team members adds uncertainty to the project. For example, in communications with stakeholders, I may feel uncertain about their intentions or whether they are being forthright. I may even question whether they have an interest in the overall good of the project or are more intent on protecting their positions. Some of these uncertainties are natural at the start of any working relationship, but if they persist, they will hinder the team's ability to make sense of the project.

Distrust is also a risk management issue because it threatens the achievement of project objectives. Although distrust is a condition and not a discrete event, it can be modeled on a project as a series of discrete events that diminish trust. For example, at today's project review meeting, the sponsor publicly denied a prior commitment to additional project funding. Separate from the funding issue, the project has just become more risky because the team has learned not to believe in commitments made by the sponsor.

The individual recognized as the father of the quality movement, W. Edwards Deming, said it succinctly: "Drive out fear."[11]

■ Voluntary Trust

Earlier, we mentioned Peter Drucker's observation that knowledge workers are ultimately volunteers. His perspective illuminates the topic of trust: these "volunteer" workers are naturally attracted to workplaces where they are trusted:

> *People want work environments where they are valued as individuals, where they can learn and contribute, where they feel they can be most useful and will be treated as adults. They want to feel good about themselves and have the chance to be themselves by openly bringing their unique strengths, skills and intelligence to their work. They want to be proud of what they do, where they work, and who they work for.*[12]

It is trust that provides people with this type of work environment. ■

■ ENDNOTES

1 Robert F. Hurley, "The Decision to Trust," *Harvard Business Review,* September 2006, pp. 55–62.

2 Kathleen D. Ryan and Daniel K. Oestreich, *Driving Fear Out of the Workplace* (San Francisco: Jossey-Bass, 1998), p. 45.

3 Robert F. Hurley, "The Decision to Trust," *Harvard Business Review,* September 2006, pp. 55–62.

4 Peter F. Drucker, *Managing the Non-Profit Organization* (New York: HarperCollins, 1990), pp. 18–19.

5 Charles R. Wright, Michael R, Manning, Bruce Farmer, and Brad Gilbreath, "Resourceful Sensemaking in Product Development Teams," *Organization Studies,* Vol. 21, No. 4, 2000, pp. 807–825.

6 F. Jolivet and C. Navarre, "Large-Scale Projects, Self-Organizing and Meta-Rules: Towards New Forms of Management," *International Journal of Project Management,* Vol. 14, No. 5, 1996, pp. 265–271.

7 Ibid.

8 Stephen M. R. Covey, *The Speed of Trust* (New York: Free Press, 2006), p. 5.

9 Anna Kadefors, "Trust in Project Relationships—Inside the Black Box," *International Journal of Project Management,* Vol. 22, No. 3, 2004, pp. 175–182.

10 Kathleen D. Ryan and Daniel K. Oestreich, *Driving Fear Out of the Workplace* (San Francisco: Jossey-Bass, 1998).

11 W. Edwards Deming, *Out of the Crisis* (Cambridge, MA: Massachusetts Institute of Technology, Center for Advanced Engineering Study, 1986), p. 59.

12 Kathleen D. Ryan and Daniel K. Oestreich, *Driving Fear Out of the Workplace* (San Francisco: Jossey-Bass, 1998), p. 45.

CHAPTER 16

■ All That Jazz: Hitting the Sweet Spot

The difference between composition and improvisation is that in composition you have all the time you want to decide what to say in fifteen seconds, while in improvisation you have fifteen seconds.

STEVE LACY (JAZZ SAXOPHONIST) ■

There is perhaps no better metaphor for the management of contemporary projects than jazz music. With its interplay of form and experimentation, jazz corresponds well to the partnership and functions of the left brain and the right brain on projects.

When I was a fledgling teenage musician, I was awestruck while listening to musicians playing solos during songs. As a self-taught guitarist with no understanding of musical theory, it appeared to me that soloists must have spent hours experimenting with note patterns until they hit on a sequence that worked.

Years later, at my first jazz guitar lesson, the instructor handed me a sheet with a series of scales to practice. He said that once I had practiced scales for a week, I would be ready to solo. Seeing my look of incredulity, he explained, "A solo is simply notes played from a set scale." I was flabbergasted, but the following week performed my first solo (albeit a pretty rough one).

I had learned a fundamental element of music theory. I didn't realize until much later that I had also learned a profound truth about innovation and improvisation on projects.

Creativity and experimentation have meaning or value only when they are expressed within a form or context. In other words, you can break the rules only if there are rules to break; you can think outside the box only if there is already a box, that is, a frame of reference.

So it is on projects. When a situation demands a creative solution, it also demands some link to what is familiar. Depending on the situation, the need, and the sought-after results, the deviations from the norm can be slight or significant.

We have already seen that the degree of uncertainty on a project is a significant factor in the level of experimentation needed. Projects with more uncertainty demand more experimentation and potentially greater deviations from what is known and familiar.

Yet there must still be considerable integrity to the process to enable the overall objectives to be accomplished. Without integrity, the project could degenerate into a free-for-all.

For contemporary projects, a paradoxical balance must be established between rules and experimentation. How can we find that balance, that sweet spot?

■ Degrees of Freedom

Jazz is the combination and interplay of a structured framework with creative improvisation. Most of what is called jazz consists of a musical theme interspersed with improvised solos:

> *A defining quality of creative improvisation is precisely the generation of the unpredictable, the unusual, the unforeseen, within the pre-existing structures of the song form navigating the edge between innovation and tradition .... In jazz improvisation, a commonly shared goal is to create within a musical and social context, requiring both control and spontaneity, constraints and possibilities, innovation and tradition, leading and supporting.*[1]

How far can we venture from the structured framework on our projects?

In jazz, there are four levels of departure from the written score of a song, ranging from a style closest to the written score to a style that is only loosely based on the score:

- Interpretation
- Embellishment
- Variation
- Improvisation.

It is entirely coincidental that projects can also be classified into four categories of uncertainty and complexity. Again, projects work best when the management style is adapted to the level of uncertainty and complexity, with increasing freedom allowed for projects with the highest levels of complexity.

For the purposes of this chapter, we will talk generically about the process of creative variation on a theme as "improvisation."

The Project Is the Song

For a complex project, rote execution of a plan is likely to fail. In the jazz performance, the project is the song. A rote performance of written music may be pleasing, but it is not jazz—and it is not what jazz audiences expect. With jazz, the expectation *is* deviation from the expected. Whether the jazz works or not depends on how pleasing the deviation sounds in the context of the overall framework of the song. In other words, the deviations or the experiments still must conform to rules.

If all this sounds a bit circular and confusing, you're on the right track. This is the paradox of improvisation.

Consider a product development project that involves adapting an existing technology to a new product line with a new market segment. The development team has a set of "rules" that have worked for the existing product and market, but these rules are likely to change for the new line and market. Experiments must be conducted, but within the context of larger themes. For example, customers like good service and a good value for their money. Experiments that violate these givens, or rules, are destined to fail.

Likewise, if a serious jazz musical group is playing a soft, bluesy ballad, and along comes a soloist who experiments with a raucous rendition of "Mary Had a Little Lamb" on kazoo, the audience is likely to respond with boos and catcalls. On the other hand, if this performance is part of a comedic music festival, the audience may laugh and hoot in approval.

It all depends on the context; it all depends on the theme; it all depends on the framework.

This is why conventional project management techniques cannot work when applied via a one-size-fits-all methodology. But rather than discard these valuable, tried-and-true techniques, let's give them room to breathe.

◼ Improvising the Project

Improvisation, whether in jazz, comedy, or theatre, is the spontaneous creation of a portion of the performance within a framework or a set-up. Watching an improv performance is exciting because the performers are literally making up their lines on the spot.

On a project, we don't necessarily expect or want team members to perform in real time, although this often happens in crisis situations or on hyper-aggressive projects. On any complex project, because the team and individual performance required is without precedent, some improvisation is always involved.

For a musical performance, a song can be composed ahead of time and then performed precisely as composed. This is analogous to a conventional project with conventional management: plan the project, then execute the plan.

With improvisation, although much composition occurs before the performance, composition also takes place during the performance. Such is also the situation for the complex, uncertain project.

For project improvisation to work, there must be a bridge between the theme and the variation. Within the structure of existing rules, the team is given the authority to experiment, or improvise. This is the "sweet spot" of interplay between right- and left-brain approaches.

As shown in studies by Collins and Porras, companies that consistently perform well do so because they steadfastly preserve core values while allowing everything else about them to change. This is the place where improvisation works, and works well.

The Theory Z approach to management is consistent with the jazz metaphor. Workers operate within a structure that is consistent with project objectives. They are given the latitude and authority to use creative approaches to meet objectives as long as those approaches are consistent with the structure and the meta-rules, and they don't violate agreed-upon boundaries.

■ Complexity = R&D

The complex project can most accurately be considered in the context of research and development. What makes an R&D project successful?

One study of 62 R&D projects found both formality and discretion on successful projects. Formality was defined as structure and rules, and discretion was defined as spontaneity and the breaking of rules.[2]

It is important to emphasize that what is needed is *both*, not *either*. Formality and discretion must be present simultaneously on R&D projects and complex projects for success. "[T]oday's employees are required to be creative, yet also conform to rules and standards, and work efficiently to meet time and budget constraints."[3]

In a jazz performance, we witness the application of both rules and spontaneity. Often, the performers lay the framework and then offer improvisational solos or phrases while the accompanists play the structure.

In like manner, the project can be executed with rules and structure as well as creative improvisation where appropriate or needed. Both the left brain and the right brain are working. Formality is satisfied by the general framework that defines processes and milestones, or what needs to be done. Discretion is satisfied by allowing the project team to decide *how* it should be done.[4]

■ The Framework and the Sweet Spot

Both the jazz performance and the complex project are paradoxical in practice. Improvisation is both structure and freedom. It is often perceived as the edge of chaos, and indeed it sometimes goes there. But the edge of chaos is typically where the complex project lives and where it must go to succeed.

Let us return to the subject of sense-making for a moment. One of the ingredients of sense-making is identifying boundaries. These boundaries are not only the objectives and deliverables of the project, but just as importantly, the boundaries of the *process* for executing the project. The boundaries are the framework for the product of the project and the framework for the social interactions through which we will together make the product real. The social framework is every bit as important as the content framework.

We can contrast the performance of an orchestra to that of the jazz group. The social framework for the orchestra is the requirement that each musician play the written score exactly and defer to the conductor for any cues.

While the social framework for the jazz group is considerably more relaxed, very important conventions must still be followed and limits imposed. The score is written, but variations are allowed. The solos are improvised, but they fit within musical scales that are pleasing to the ear. The solos follow an order, with artists taking turns in both leadership and supporting roles, taking cues from one another.

How is it possible for musicians to manage these dynamic processes and produce an inventive and integrated musical outcome? The answer lies in two sets of structural conventions contained in the jazz profession: musical structures and social practices. These structures serve to constrain the turbulence of the jazz process by specifying particular ways of inventing and coordinating musical ideas .... Paradoxically, these structures enable collective musical innovation by constraining the range of musical and behavioral choices available to the players.[5]

With improvisation, we permit and promote creative experiments, but we specify and agree upon the *ways* in which these will be allowed and coordinated. We also specify the limits of experimentation.

This is how we are able to operate near the edge of chaos while being confident that we will not topple over the edge. It is how we make sense of the complex project. When a jazz performance has a great sound, when it hits the "sweet spot," we are hearing the synergistic balance between structure and variation.

The Improvisational Attitude

Doug DeCarlo

Project managers often ask me what they must do to achieve success in the volatile environments facing projects today. My immediate answer is to change their mental model of a project.

Most people think that the progression of a project must look like a straight line or follow the waterfall model. What I see on today's projects looks more like a looping, squiggly line that travels all over the place, in large part because of what is unknown early in the project. With a different mental model comes a different approach to managing the project. We manage "unknowns" differently than we manage "knowns."

When we must work in a complex and high-velocity environment, it is important to keep the approach simple, particularly when it comes to the organizing principles and procedures. As Dee Hock, Founder and CEO Emeritus of VISA International, said, "Simple, clear purpose and principles give rise to complex, intelligent behavior. Complex rules and regulations give rise to simple, stupid behaviors."

In this new environment, experience is more worthwhile than classroom training. Mastery of the new project environment is 10 percent education and 90 percent perspiration. Start with real projects and what I call "just-in-time" project management—training on the fly. As needs arise, mentor and coach the teams so that they can adapt to what they encounter. It is better to create successful experiences early rather than attempt to create a detailed project plan.

David Schnarch, author of the book, *Passionate Marriage* (1998), offers a great approach to applying this new mental model: "It is easier to act your way into a new way of thinking than to think your way into a new way of acting."

Conventional project management focuses on the mechanics of projects. eXtreme projects succeed through management of the dynamics. The dynamics of a project, if not managed well, will defeat mechanics every time. It is rare to find a project that fails because a new technology did not work; it is all too common that project failure resulted from failure to manage the project dynamics.

We must unleash the motivation of project teams. When a project involves a high level of risk or uncertainty, team members commonly feel a high level of anxiety. They need a shared set of values that will guide and support their efforts through the complexities of the project. One of my favorite approaches is the Agile Project Leadership Network (www.apln.org). APLN is a community of project managers who work with the realities of complex, high-velocity projects. The group has formed a "Declaration of Interdependence" that provides a good model of the values that will successfully guide agile project management. Even the use of "interdependence" in this statement of values reflects the group's recognition of the need for teams, sponsors, and customers to work closely together to achieve project success.

People may not feel motivated to work on a "project," but a "cause" is something to get fired up about. Tom Peters suggests that we find the "WOW! factor" in our projects, something that is exciting, revolutionary, or culture-changing. For example, in the early days of Apple Computer, Steve Jobs offered associates the opportunity to "put a dent in the universe." Now that's a project that will get people excited.

I am a percussionist, and I have often used jazz musical performances in workshops to illustrate the dynamics of eXtreme projects. Sometimes the seeming informality of the jazz performance masks how much discipline the genre involves. People enjoy jazz and the improvisation that defines jazz, but they enjoy it because they expect improvisation to take place.

It can be the same way for projects: we can adapt our thinking, expect improvisation, and enjoy the experience. To help us do this, eXtreme project management and other forms of agile project management have their own set of tools, practices, and techniques, many of which are intuitive and easy to apply. But there is also room for project managers to adapt conventional project management tools such as the work breakdown structure.

Here's another way to look at this connection. In ultra avant garde jazz, the music sounds very chaotic because there is little or no structure. Most people find such a performance discordant and unpleasant. Similarly, if a project is completely chaotic, it will be a bad experience for all. The combination of structure and improvisation works well for the jazz performance and also for the eXtreme project.

In changing our attitudes about project models, it is worthwhile to understand that attitudes come from belief systems. When we resist investigating our beliefs, we run the risk of being controlled by "ghosts" or hidden beliefs. For example, if we use a project model that incorporates the belief, "Clients should not change requirements during a project," the ghost belief may be, "Change is not good." With this ghost lurking, the relationship between the project manager and the client can become adversarial.

If we change the project model to deliver the result sought by the client (not necessarily the planned result), we can now embrace alternative beliefs: "Clients should change requirements during a project" and "Change is good."

If change is good for a project, then perhaps change is also good for our attitudes about project management. But rather than stray into chaos, we will improvise on the structure and the tools that are valuable and successful.

This is the challenge of all challenges on projects: to change our way of thinking on how to manage projects. When we do so, we can truly enjoy and succeed at the experience.

Doug DeCarlo *is a consultant, facilitator, trainer, columnist, and keynote speaker in project management. He is the author of* eXtreme Project Management: Using Leadership, Principles and Tools to Deliver Value in the Face of Volatility. *Through The Doug DeCarlo Group, he works with clients who undertake projects in demanding environments of high speed, high ambiguity, and high stress to lead them to project success.*

■ Hit the Zone

When we become experienced and skilled at an activity, the activity becomes practically intuitive or second nature. We enter a "zone" that is effortless, much like the experience of riding a bike or driving a car.

This state is well-known to professionals and performers in a variety of disciplines—athletes, actors, musicians, speakers, computer operators. Even laborers can get into a rhythm of action where work becomes smooth. Many professionals speak of getting into the zone, a Zen-like state where one is on autopilot; the body and the mind just know what to do. This is not an unconscious state. On the contrary, it is often described as a state of heightened consciousness.

Some athletes report that their best performance occurs in this state of "playing without thinking." Interestingly, studies have shown that when athletes are working at what they think is 90 percent effort, they typically put forth their best performances. Perhaps this is because, when told to give 100 percent or even 110 percent, they become so preoccupied with success that they make mistakes or feel so pressured that they put in a sub-par performance.

While much of what is done in the zone is the result of a lot of practice and is familiar, it is not only "automatic" or "robotic" types of tasks that can be performed. Paradoxically, this is the state where improvisation comes most easily and naturally.

For project teams to improvise, it is worthwhile to seek the zone. Here are the ingredients for getting to the zone for project improvisation:

- *Lots of practice.* A certain level of competence and skill must come naturally to be in the zone. You don't need to be a world expert, but you do need to invest appropriate practice to achieve the level of competence needed for the task. You must be skilled enough to perform well naturally.
- *Confidence.* Improvisation works best when the mind is active but relaxed, when it is not afraid. Improvisation involves experimentation, and the experiments do not always work. A person cannot be in the zone if he fears failure or is performing in an environment of distrust.
- *A sense of "professional play."* As we noted in Chapter 14, professional play means approaching the task with a sense of curiosity, experimentation, and optimism that is "playful." Professional play is also serious work, though, because it represents the frontier of significant innovation and breakthroughs.

The jazz performance done well is an example of professional play and getting into the zone. It is the essence of improvisation.

■ Right-Brain Toolkit: Professional Play

Improvisation and professional play are the paradoxical overlay of form and freedom. For the jazz musician, the song and the social contract with the group impose the requisite order within which freedom is exercised:

> *Jazz, more than any other music genre, seems to have an inherent contradiction between the discipline required to play the notes, versus the imaginative style for which the genre is known. Jazz is a delicate balancing of head versus heart, left brain versus right, known versus unknown, planning versus improvisation—and the parallels to leadership are strong.*[6]

Organizations can model the structure of the song through mission, values, project objectives, and prototypes. A compelling purpose provides the transcendent framework that guides team members in their creative experiments on the complex project:

> *Organizational slogans such as Avis's "We try harder" are catchy phrases awaiting embellishment, encouraging individual members to elaborate on their version of the melodic path that fits within the tacit constraints. Organizational stories and myths, such as the Nordstrom's employee who paid a waiting customer's parking ticket, persist as markers to remind and seed other employees to embellish on the melody, initiating unusual actions to satisfy customers.*[7]

In essence, when we talk about compelling purpose, values, mission, and the like, we are really talking about the social glue that keeps a team of people working together on a common endeavor that has meaning, in a manner that is enjoyable. It is the operating style of the tight jazz group and also of the achieving project team on the complex project.

Remember that improvisation on a project is a *social* innovation. The conventional project plan describes the interactions that will make the project. When we improvise on the right-brain project, we must create the ways that we interact, but we must do so within a broader framework of values and purpose.

This interplay is one of the prime reasons why the right-brain project can proceed with agility and power. We can improvise confidently, creatively, and comfortably because we are free to soar yet are still grounded within a framework of values. Those values guide us to the sweet spot. ▪

▪ ENDNOTES

1 Alfonso Montuori, "The Complexity of Improvisation and the Improvisation of Complexity: Social Science, Art and Creativity," *Human Relations,* Vol. 56, No. 2, 2003, pp. 237–255.

2 Eitan Naveh, "Formality and Discretion in Successful R&D Projects," *Journal of Operations Management,* Vol. 25, No. 1, January 2007, pp. 110–125.

3 Ibid.

4 Ibid.

5 David T. Bastien and Todd J. Hostager, "Jazz as a Process of Organizational Innovation," *Organizational Improvisation,* edited by Ken N. Karmoche, Miguel Pina e Cunha, and João Viera da Cunha (London: Routledge, 2002).

6 Katie Daniel, "Improvising Leadership: Finding Comfort in Ambiguity," *Leadership Compass* (Alberta, Canada: Banff Centre, Summer 2006), p. 29.

7 Frank J. Barrett, "Creativity and Improvisation in Jazz and Organizations," *Organizational Improvisation,* edited by Ken N. Karmoche, Miguel Pina e Cunha, and João Viera da Cunha (London: Routledge, 2002).

CHAPTER 17

■ Telling the Story: Leaving a Legacy

We create stories and stories create us.

CHINUA ACHEBE ■

O ne day a successful businessman has an experience that few of us ever will: he has the unusual opportunity to truly see how others see him. Upon receiving this insight, he is stunned—and forever changed.

You may have heard the story. Alfred Nobel reads his own obituary in the morning paper one day in 1888. Other than the news of his death, the obituary is a factual description of his life and accomplishments.

Nobel invented dynamite and was the president of a large company that manufactured munitions. The erroneous obituary expressed a sort of relief over Nobel's death: "The merchant of death is dead .... Dr. Alfred Nobel, who became rich by finding ways to kill more people faster than ever before, died yesterday."[1]

What he reads is true, but it leaves Nobel troubled. This is not how he wants to be remembered.

The event is so momentous in his life that he commits to an entirely different path. He decides to use his considerable wealth gained from war to promote peace and human achievement. Nobel establishes and funds an organization to recognize and reward significant efforts for world peace and the advancement of knowledge. This organization presents the annual awards for the Nobel Prize for Peace, as well as awards in the sciences and literature.

Perhaps Nobel received a gift that few of us will ever receive: the ability to see our legacy objectively while there is still an opportunity to change it.

We won't get too philosophical here and delve into the deep subjects of where you want to go in your life or how you would like to be remembered after you're gone. But the question is relevant to project management.

■ The Project Legacy

What do you want the legacy of your project to be?

This is a worthwhile question to ponder while planning or executing a project. Every project leaves a legacy of some kind, whether it is a prideful smile or a bitter scowl.

Earlier, we presented the principle that the underlying objective of any project is to put smiles on the faces and pride in the hearts of all who are involved. We want the project to elicit positive emotions in all those touched by it, and we want these positive emotions to linger long after the project is closed. This is the ultimate critical success factor for a project. This is the legacy we aspire to leave when we complete a project.

■ Objective and Subjective Success

Much of conventional project management focuses on objective measures of how a project is managed. These objective measures include earned value, adherence to schedule, and the accomplishment of documented objectives. These are necessary analyses, but they tell only one part of the story.

The other measure of success is subjective, perhaps based in part on objective analysis, perhaps not. Some projects are managed well and meet all their objectives, yet are somehow perceived as unsuccessful. On the other hand, the Sydney Opera House, which took 15 years to build and was 14 times over budget, is widely appreciated as an engineering and architectural masterpiece.[2] People have forgotten, if they ever knew, the dreadful "objective" project performance.

If a project is defined by scope, schedule, and resources, then it is ultimately scope that dominates the perception of project success. But it is not just objective measures of the delivered scope that matter; it is also the subjective perception of the delivered scope.

It is useful here to differentiate rational or factual memory from emotional memory. These two types of memory reside in different parts of the brain, and they make different contributions to decision-making. They also make different contributions to our perceptions of a subject or experience. Positive emotions associated with a subject or experience create positive perceptions, and negative emotions create negative perceptions. Emotional memory can readily dominate factual or rational memory; in fact, we often attempt to recast facts according to what our emotions say.

■ Looking at the Long Run

The project management community is coming to the realization that as important as it is to achieve project objectives, doing so is not enough to ensure that others view the project as a success. For example, the holistic perspective considers the value of a product over its entire life cycle rather than only at its handoff at the end of the project.[3]

The perception of a product long after it is introduced is one component of a project's legacy. If a product is highly regarded, it is natural that the project that brought forth the product will likewise be seen as a success, even though schedule and budget may have been missed.

In other words, as Doug DeCarlo notes, it is most important that the team finish the project with the *right* product, not necessarily the *planned* product.[4] It is more likely that the project will be viewed as a success if the project produces the right product.

This effort gets complicated when the "right" product is not known at the start and may seem to be a moving target. For this reason, on a complex project, it is critical that the team be allowed the discretion to "get it right."

To a large extent, the perceptions of the resulting product form the legacy of the project outside the project organization. Customers do not see the inner workings of the project organization; they see only the results of the effort. An external sponsor is more familiar with the progression of the project, but unless performance on reaching project objectives is poor, the sponsor's perception of the legacy is also dominated by the product.

■ Traveling through Time and Space

Legacy is really a set of lasting emotional memories. I still have strong memories of projects I worked on 25 years ago—proud thoughts of projects that were significant accomplishments and feelings of cynicism for projects that were dysfunctional throughout.

If we could travel into the future—in effect that is what Nobel was able to do—we could see firsthand the legacy of our project. Depending on what we saw, we could plan our project to ensure the desired legacy. In other words, we are building the connection between the legacy that people will perceive in the future and our vision in the present. When done well, vision and legacy are one and the same (or close to it). Toward this end, it is critical that we step outside ourselves and what we want to accomplish, and think carefully about how others will likely perceive our efforts.

Legacy is a timeless concept. How our team feels about the project right now and about how the project will turn out will have a significant influence on how stakeholders will view the project long after it is over. We have a vision of the legacy, we plan for it, we act on it, and if we do our work well, others enjoy its benefits.

To get a handle on the legacy and thus do well at crafting a vision, we need to travel through both time and place. We need to visit the future and see our work through the eyes of others.

■ Bridge of Perception

Traveling through time is the easy part. Getting out of yourself and into another's head, well, that's another matter altogether. Yet that is what we need to do to internalize the experiential and emotional insights that form a legacy and that can then be translated into a vision.

What do we know about the people who will use the product of our project?

When preparing for a movie, actors study for the role they will play. A conscientious performer may travel far and study for months to portray a role accurately. The performer gets "into character" to see the world through the eyes of the person he or she is playing, to perceive the world as the character does. This requires a change in perception, and it takes work.

How do we learn to see and feel differently?

Put yourself in the position of your customer, or the user of your product. How do you want to feel when you use it? What do you want the overall experience to be like? What if there is a problem with your product, and you have to call for support; what do you want that experience to be like? What are your experiences when you see the product, hold it, touch it? What do you want those feelings to be like?

This exercise is a good start in understanding the project legacy and crafting the project vision. What this exercise does is build an *emotional* bridge that transcends time and place, and thus enables us to change our perception to experience and feel what our customers and others will. Ultimately, emotions will determine how well your project performs, so we had best understand and plan for them.

The movie, *What Women Want*, portrays the difference between a superficial understanding of the customer's experience and a deeper perception of a customer's life.

Nick Marshall, played by Mel Gibson, works for an advertising agency. To reach women with ads better (and thus sell more stuff), his new boss, a woman, assigns the team to use a series of women's products. Wearing pantyhose and using bikini wax gives Nick no real insights. It is only through a freak accident that Nick starts to hear in his own mind what nearby women are thinking. He finally finds the emotional bridge when he sees the unfortunate results of how he has previously treated women. He sees his legacy, and he is able to change it.

To develop the right product, we must perceive in the present what the project will achieve months or even years into the future. To aid our perception, it is helpful to feel the emotions that we would like to be associated with the project.

This task is not as daunting as it seems. It is as simple as working with the intuitive and natural parts of people wanting to do something meaningful with projects.

It is as simple as telling a story. People like stories, and they particularly like stories with a happy ending. To twist a well-known phrase ... every project tells a story.

■ Preparing the Vision

Stories can offer meaning in several ways: they can convey values and behaviors, and they can describe identity and character. The classic and timeless stories often show individuals and groups move through the midst of challenges and change to a place of heightened awareness. With the new awareness comes both internal and external esteem.

In Chapter 18, we will look at stories from a different perspective. For now, let us consider a story to be a prediction of the future. Let us consider the vision story.

This is the kind of story that is made for a project. It is also the kind of story that leads us back to Abraham Maslow and the concept of spiritual survival.

Recall that most of us in the workplace are operating with needs in the higher levels of Maslow's hierarchy—needs for esteem and recognition, for self-actualization, knowledge, and aesthetics. We also feel passion about certain elements of spiritual survival that are meaningful to us. These needs are fulfilled (though never completely) through project accomplishments and the positive emotional memories of a beneficial legacy—that is, through a project with a good story line and a happy ending.

Creating the story and living out the story provide the motivation and emotional energy to make the legacy come true.

■ Vision as Future Story

If we are starting a project, and if the project legacy is the story told after the project is over, what can we do now to create the story that we will want to be told? We start with the desired future story and work backward.

The goal of storytelling, at least in the context of a project, is to evoke certain behaviors; it should also illuminate present choices. We want the story to convey a shared vision and inspire the values and motivation needed to reach the vision.

Storytelling accesses the right brain and its emotions in a powerful way. If we are working on a familiar project, we may have little need for a vision and perhaps little need for motivational help; the left brain can work effectively by applying known rules and patterns. On the other hand, a complex project demands that individuals and teams stretch their limits. This process is best accomplished by momentarily turning off the left brain and its rules, patterns, and limits. By suspending the rules and talking to the right brain, the story can help us see and believe in what is possible through new patterns.

A story uses metaphor as a tool to break through habitual mindsets, common frames of reference, and belief systems. It enables us to produce a virtual experience and to personalize it.[5] We can begin to create new patterns through the right brain.

While stories can be used for different purposes, we will concentrate on using a story to build a project vision. Again, the driving force for this effort is to make the concept of project legacy more tangible and to explore how we can promote positive emotions about the project.

Four elements are involved in developing the story to form a vision:[6]

- *Knowledge.* For a team, a story must start from a common base of information or knowledge. Elements of the story may need to establish groundwork that forms a common level of information.
- *Experience.* Stories work when a group of people has common experiences to draw upon. In essence, a story will call upon the patterns of those experiences and the associated emotions to direct changes and future efforts.
- *Boldness.* The intent of the vision is to break through previously established limits and rules. It takes a certain boldness to envision and believe in a new frame of reference.
- *Passion.* Finally, a story should promote a sense of passion about the new vision. Without passion (or compelling purpose) it can be challenging to navigate and overcome the inevitable obstacles to achieving the vision.

These elements combine into the vision story. A helpful tool for crafting the vision story is to make a virtual trip into the future to experience the vision in reality and in action. In this visit to the future, we record the experience in considerable detail, including the perceptions and emotions that are associated with the vision.

The typical vision statement developed by companies and teams is short, sometimes a paragraph or a sentence. A vision story is considerably longer; it is analogous to a detailed specification, but is narrative and emphasizes the *total experience* of the project, the *results* of using the product, and the *emotional legacy* of the interaction with the customer. The story uses adjectives, metaphors, and emotions about the team and its customers.

Here are a few questions to consider in crafting the vision story:

- What images or feelings are created in the story?
- What key messages are conveyed through the story?
- What does the story say about our core values, philosophy, and identity?
- To deliver the experience of the story, what will we need to include for the total system we are offering over its lifetime: what features, what support?

The story of Alfred Nobel is one such example of a great story line. He saw his legacy and felt distress, and then used that distress to craft an entirely different legacy.

Writing a vision story takes work. It is not just simply a clever motivational tool constructed by the marketing department to get the team to work. It is the embodiment of who we are, who we want to be, and what we want to do, and it must be genuine. The vision story is the conscious and deliberate statement of our legacy—and the commitment to making it happen.

■ The Hidden Project

A helpful way to approach the vision story is to explore the "hidden project." For every project that is readily visible and has scope, schedule, and resources, there is a hidden project that is built on the emotional legacy. The hidden project either builds or tears down relationships. The product of the hidden project is a set of emotional memories, which can be either positive or negative.

I recall hearing a story about an organization that operated a small group of Burger King restaurants. A fast food franchisee is the type of business that can readily be driven by external rules and financial considerations. But the owner of this business saw what was hidden to most.

He emphasized to all employees a set of core values that made his franchise into a standout success in the Burger King chain. The core values were built on a simple philosophy: customers lead busy, stressful lives. The restaurants in this business are intended to be respites from the toils of daily life. The experience of eating in the restaurants is designed to be calm, supportive, and uplifting. Customers go there to eat because they leave feeling emotionally nourished.

It seems challenging, even counterintuitive, for a fast food restaurant to be a place of calm and comfort. But the owner had a vision for the legacy of the business, a legacy that tells a wonderful story.

The obvious project for this business was to deliver a hamburger and fries. The hidden project, the *real* project, was to be an emotional oasis in a crazy world.

If we want to excel at the complex contemporary project, we need tools to address its formidable challenges. Even mundane projects, such as delivering a burger and fries, can use a strong dose of looking at the hidden project.

Businesses and employees who recognize the importance of exemplary customer service already get this. Even if their product or service is ordinary, they find a way to make the *experience* an extraordinary one. They see the hidden project clearly. They recognize that a customer will more likely have a positive impression of the visible project if the hidden project is handled well.

When we pay attention to the hidden project and allow it to proceed, we unleash abundant, positive emotional energy—energy that makes the visible project a more likely success story.

What is the hidden, but real project behind your apparent project? What will be the legacy of your project?

If there is one guiding principle, even one guiding word that will help make the hidden project more clearly visible, perhaps that word is "human." In our fast-paced, technologically advanced marketplace, what conveys meaning and promotes a beneficial legacy is that which is most human. We should endeavor with our projects and products to create experiences that are positive and durable,[7] in other words, human.

The Curtain Rises

If a project tells a story, then the telling of the story is a performance. To tell a good story, and to tell it well, think of the project as a performance.

In their book, *The Experience Economy*, B. Joseph Pine II and James H. Gilmore argue that as we expand the service economy, companies differentiate according to the experiences they offer to customers.[8] They liken the transaction between provider and customer to a performance. In this light, the project itself and the product of the project are both opportunities to perform.

Consider for a moment that your project is a play at the theatre, and your customer is a critic in the audience. After the performance is over, she will write a review analyzing your work according to what she experiences during the play. In this context, it is important to focus on the overall impressions the critic will take with her when she leaves the theatre.

How are those impressions formed?

While conventional project management focuses on the content of the play itself (with good reason), let us also recognize that the delivery of the play is every bit as important to the critic. It is the *experience*—the legacy of the performance—that ultimately determines the critic's review.

A significant strand of leadership thought sees the work of an organization as performance theatre. The sociologist Erving Goffman recognized this connection in 1959, when he analyzed commonplace social interactions from the perspective of performances.[9]

If conventional project management focuses on *what* is done, it is time to also consider *how* it will be done. This is the fundamental point of acting with intention:

> *Merely completing an activity is not enough; some underlying motivation must invigorate the performance so that it ultimately affects the buyer of the final offering. Everyone can, for example, detect the difference between a receptionist who merely takes names and calls for parties and one who graciously greets each visitor and performs otherwise identical tasks with intentional style and color. The encounter in the lobby, however brief, affects the guest and sets a particular tone for the entire meeting that follows—and on occasion, perhaps even alters the outcome.*[10]

As Goffman expands on this metaphor, he notes four ways that individuals can approach the *character* of their work:

- *Oblivious.* The worker is unaware of the performance aspect of the work.
- *Apathetic.* The worker recognizes that the work is a performance but cares little about the outcome.
- *Manipulative.* The worker focuses on manipulating the experience of the customer in a cynical way, creating a false experience.
- *Sincere.* The worker is aware of the role and the performance, and believes in the role and in the impressions derived from the role.

For a little fun, think of any well-known and recognized performance role and apply these categories to it. Can you imagine Clint Eastwood as an oblivious or apathetic Dirty Harry, casually or timidly delivering, "Go ahead, make my day"?

For manipulation, consider that the career of singing duo Milli Vanilli was finished when they were famously caught lip syncing. While many artists lip sync their live concerts, what set Milli Vanilli apart was that they were lip syncing other, anonymous artists on their albums. The duo gave a good visual performance but neither could sing, so their recordings were entirely the work of others. The pair was stripped of their Grammy award—and their legacy lives on.

From where the critic sits, a performance that is vacant, uninspired, or manipulative will be panned, regardless of the content of the play. It is those performances that are done well, and done with sincerity and genuineness, that leave lasting, positive impressions on the critics.

The project experience for the customer will be improved and enhanced if the project team members recognize that their project is a performance and they are playing roles as characters in the performance. If team members fully embrace this relationship with the customer and play their roles well, they clearly are aware of and believe in the legacy they are creating.

■ Right-Brain Toolkit: Something Special

If a team hopes to eventually leave a worthwhile project legacy, their work starts with developing the vision of the story they want to tell. Developing that vision starts with the decision to do something special.

The 1990 movie, *Pretty Woman*, is an improbable story of redemption. Edward Lewis, played by Richard Gere, is a phenomenally rich and successful businessman with the personality of a killer shark. His style is predatory: he acquires a business and then sells off the pieces of the company to maximize his return on investment.

Lost while driving, he picks up Vivian Ward, a street prostitute, played by Julia Roberts. She becomes his contractual companion for a week—a week during which they "rescue" each other from the dark influences of their respective lives. She is redeemed by growing in self-respect; he is redeemed by becoming more human.

A key story line in the movie involves Edward's acquisition of a business run by James Morse, played by Ralph Bellamy. Morse has worked for years to build his company into a successful one, and is wary of the acquisition. Edward initiates a takeover of Morse's business, and for good measure, pulls some congressional strings to hurt the company and force a lower purchase price for the acquisition.

Before the deal is closed, though, Vivian has gotten to Edward's conscience. He decides to redirect his business life—to build a better business *with* Morse rather than dismantling Morse's life efforts.

Edward turns to Morse and says, "I think we can do something very special with your company." This line represents the core of what it means to create a vision for the project legacy.

It is certainly possible to manage a project with conventional techniques and achieve suitable, even outstanding results. When a team endeavors to do something *special*, though, they necessarily bring the right brain into the game.

The "special" element is what creates the lasting positive emotional memories, in other words, the legacy. "Special" may be a way to turn a familiar project into a unique customer experience, it may be a technological breakthrough, or it may be a record turnaround time. *Any* project can become special in some way, if the team so decides.

The project awaits. Let's do something special together. ▪

....
■ ENDNOTES

1 "Alfred Nobel," http://en.wikipedia.org/wiki/Alfred_Nobel. Accessed October 2006.

2 Kam Jugdev and Ralf Moller, "A Retrospective Look at Our Evolving Understanding of Project Success," *Project Management Journal,* December 2005, pp. 19–34.

3 Ibid.

4 Doug DeCarlo, *eXtreme Project Management* (San Francisco: Jossey-Bass, 2004).

5 Ira M. Levin, "Vision Revisited—Telling the Story of the Future," *Journal of Applied Behavioral Science,* Vol. 36, No. 1, March 2000, pp. 91–107.

6 Ibid.

7 Jonathan Chapman, *Emotionally Durable Design: Objects, Experiences, Empathy* (London: Earthscan, 2005).

8 B. Joseph Pine II and James H. Gilmore, *The Experience Economy* (Boston: Harvard Business School Press, 1999).

9 Erving Goffman, *The Presentation of Self in Everyday Life* (New York: Anchor Books, 1959).

10 B. Joseph Pine II and James H. Gilmore, *The Experience Economy* (Boston: Harvard Business School Press, 1999), p. 116.

CHAPTER 18

■ The Hero in Us All:
The Moral of the Story

■
■
■

God created people because he likes a good story.

ELIE WIESEL ■

I didn't learn to swim until I was 34 years old. I took a few lessons as a kid but got sick and missed the last half of the class. No one pressed the issue after that, and I grew to be afraid of the water. In college, one of my best friends drowned, and that only solidified my fear. As an adult, I avoided swimming and boating.

As an avid runner in my twenties and thirties, I developed knee trouble. The doctor told me to stop running and take up some other form of exercise; he highly recommended swimming.

While learning to swim is a common childhood experience for many people, for me it had become something larger. It was not a skill, it was a nemesis; it was a fear that needed to be overcome.

At the age of 34, I enrolled in an adult learn-to-swim class. To my amazement, I found other adults who were also H_2O-challenged. Like everyone else who has ever learned to swim, I inhaled water and glubbed and blubbed, and finally graduated.

In the following days and weeks, I felt pride, but I felt something more. Something had been released inside; my Lex Luthor had been defeated. Other challenges in my daily life seemed less daunting. I started sweeping away problems like they were so many autumn leaves on the sidewalk. Perhaps even more surprisingly, my project work became more successful and rewarding.

I started to swim often; I started to swim a lot. Soon I could swim a kilometer, then a mile. I signed up for a program to swim

100 miles over a school year, and completed every mile—every last one of 7,000 laps in the pool.

Sure, I learned a basic skill, one that is easily learned by many five-year olds. But something much more profound had happened. A message was imprinted in my brain, an image that I have relied upon ever since:

If I can learn to swim, I can do _____.

Learning to swim became an important metaphor for me to draw upon for strength to face far greater challenges of work and of life.

In all humility, the simple skill of learning to swim built character in me.

Becoming Better at Projects

To become better at managing or executing projects, we could take a left-brain approach or a right-brain approach. The left-brain approach might include taking a conventional course toward earning a PMP® certification.

The right-brain approach could include developing skills in the seven principles we have discussed in this book. The right-brain approach could also include something a bit different and unexpected.

I learned to swim and became a better project manager.

We can become better at projects by becoming better people, by maturing in character. We can become better at projects by maturing in emotional intelligence and moral reasoning.

Developing Maturity

Let us briefly recall two subjects from Chapter 2, the stages of maturity and the elements of emotional intelligence. Table

18-1 provides a description of Loevinger's four highest stages of ego development, and Table 18-2 provides a summary of the five elements of emotional intelligence.

Important components of personal development include the ability to tolerate ambiguity, as well as the development of moral-

- **Table 18-1. Loevinger's Highest Stages of Ego Development**

Stage	Characteristics
Conscientious	Has goals, ideals, and sense of responsibility; sees self apart from group and internalizes rules; sees self from other point of view; sees motives of others; guilt is from hurting another, not breaking rules
Individualistic	Can become distant from role identities; greater tolerance of self and others; recognizes that relationships bring dependency; psychological cause and effect; awareness of inner conflict
Autonomous	Tolerates ambiguity; concern for emotional interdependence; self-fulfillment; integrates ideas and identities
Integrated	Transcends conflicts; self-actualizing

- **Table 18-2. Goleman's Five Elements of Emotional Intelligence**

Knowing one's emotions	The ability to identify one's emotions; to understand links among emotions, thought, and actions
Managing emotions	The capacity to manage one's emotions; to control emotions or to shift undesirable emotions to more effective ones
Motivating oneself	The ability to enter into emotional states by choice; to summon emotions toward the attainment of goals
Recognizing emotions in others	The capability to empathize; to read, and be sensitive to, other people's emotions
Handling relationships	The ability to sustain satisfactory and beneficial relationships; to lead and influence the emotions of others

ity and decision-making skills. Maturing in emotional intelligence improves a person's ability to work with others.

Research and experience correlate project success with maturation in ego development and emotional intelligence. But how do we go about growing in these areas?

The easy answer (well, easy to say but difficult to do) is to experience life and to respond well to it. We develop in character to a significant degree when we encounter events and experiences that test us and give us the opportunity to grow.

■ The Moral of the Story

Contemporary projects need a high level of trust, and the foundation of trust is a sense of benevolent morality, or moral intelligence, among the team members. Our moral decisions demonstrate more consideration for others on the team when the team members feel a personal connection with each other. While "everyday" morality is largely automatic and quick, the process of moral reasoning is more deliberate. Individuals exercise moral reasoning in considering decisions, but groups must also process moral reasoning. Thus, it is important for leaders to have maturity in moral reasoning and to be able to help their groups mature in it.

Lawrence Kohlberg has offered a model of moral development in people. This model and its underlying theory hold that the basis for ethical behavior is moral reasoning, which matures through six developmental stages (see Table 18-3).[1] Under Kohlberg's theory, a person progresses sequentially through these stages. When facing a moral dilemma that is not resolved with the reasoning available at the previous stage, he or she seeks the next higher stage.

The typical stage of moral reasoning for adolescents and adults is the conventional level, consisting of stages 3 and 4. In these stages, morality is judged and moral reasoning is carried out according to societal views and expectations. In the post-conventional level, the

▪ **Table 18-3. Kohlberg's Levels of Maturity of Moral Reasoning**

Level	Stage	Description
1 Pre-conventional	1	Obedience and punishment orientation
	2	Self-interest orientation (what's in it for me)
2 Conventional	3	Interpersonal accord and conformity (good boy/good girl attitude)
	4	Maintenance of authority and social order (law and order morality)
3 Post-conventional (autonomous or principled)	5	Social contract orientation, awareness of relativism of personal values
	6	Universal ethical principles, conscience guided by principle (e.g., Golden Rule)

individual perspective can take precedence over what society considers right and wrong, and ethics becomes more situational than absolute.

In stage 6, the highest stage, a person exhibits behavior *because it is right*, not because society or a law says it is right. Few people consistently use stage 6 moral reasoning.

In *Pretty Woman* the change in Edward included a development in morality. He was able to see Morse as a human being to be respected rather than as a unit of monetary value.

This development in morality corresponds to the maturation from Taylor to MacGregor and Ouchi, and from scientific management to Theory Z. It is the recognition that human beings are not cogs in the machine—that we can do better projects together when we share a belief in and respect for the value and dignity of people.

Upon reflection, the link between morality and project success is clear and profound. Human beings are the ones who execute projects and whose emotions are inextricably tied to project success. A moral compass that builds people will also make it possible for us to carry out better projects together.

■ Character Is the Story

Navigating the complex project is often hard work. It is challenging both intellectually and emotionally. These challenges come as tests to our limits, and these tests often stir internal conflict. We may feel that our values, perceptions, and beliefs are subject to trial. Successfully navigating these waters takes a certain degree of personal poise and self-assurance, perhaps even a degree of courage.

Sigmund Freud captured this view when he said, "I am not really a man of science, I am not an observer, I am not an experimenter, I am not even a thinker. I am nothing but an adventurer—a conquistador—with all the boldness and the tenacity of that type of being."[2]

This conversation about personal development can be framed as the building of character. It is really about the discovery and growth of the hero in us all. A great way to study the development of character is through a story.

In the movies and in literature, character development comes about through conflict that occurs in the performance or in the story. As noted by Lagos Egri in *The Art of Dramatic Writing*, "A character stands revealed through conflict; conflict begins with a decision .... No man ever lived who could remain the same through a series of conflicts ... of necessity he must change, and alter his attitude toward life."[3]

Conflict tests us; it causes us to reflect on our values, our *moral reasoning*. Through a conflict, we have the opportunity to mature, but the decision to do so is entirely voluntary. Regardless of external conflict, it is internal conflict that spurs the development of character. In other words, character development starts with trouble!

The classic structure of a dramatic story has three components:

1. Point of departure
2. Conflict
3. Point of destination.

Of course, external and visible elements contribute to the point of departure for the story. However, the true story—where conflict, decisions, and character development play out—is internal.

In the story, we see the character get in trouble and face options for how to address the trouble. The choices the character makes reveal and build maturity or integrity. The character struggles with the conflict, then makes a decision that causes him or her to grow in maturity.

Character development is a fundamental construct of storytelling, whether in a novel, a movie, or even cartoons. Viewed in this way, the story is a change process. The character is different at the end than at the start, hopefully different in a better way.

In the story, the external challenge makes apparent the internal flaws or missing pieces of the character. Through conflict and through paradox, the character chooses growth that corrects the flaws and fills in the missing pieces.

The classic story line typically follows what is called a character arc (see Table 18-4 and Figure 18-1).[4] The journey around the character arc is a progression of stages and experiences through which the individual's growth is revealed.

We see character development in the great stories that humans have told over the ages. These are the stories of humans making good decisions and poor ones. They are stories that stretch from Greek mythology all the way through *The Terminator.* They are stories of spiritual survival.

While spiritual survival can take many forms, its underlying theme is universal. Great writers over the centuries have understood this, and so it is possible for Shakespeare's "To be or not to be" to convey a similar concept to a theatre patron in Elizabethan England and to a middle manager in the anonymous hierarchy of a major corporation. As Lewis Carroll said through the character of The Duchess in *Alice's Adventures in Wonderland,* "Everything's got a moral if you can only find it."

▪ **Table 18-4. Steps in the Character Arc**

1	Limited awareness of a challenge, problem, or flaw
2	Increased awareness of a challenge, problem, or flaw
3	Reluctance to change
4	Overcoming reluctance
5	Committing to change
6	Initial experimentation with change
7	Preparing for significant change
8	Attempting significant change
9	Consequences of the attempt (improvements and setbacks)
10	Rededication to change
11	Final attempt at significant change
12	Final mastery of the challenge, problem, or flaw

Many of the universal human stories were handed down as myths centuries ago, but because the myths are timeless, they operate just as well in our modern technological world as they did in Ancient Greece. The Greeks had their heroes and their stories of good versus evil. We have the same in *Star Wars* and *The Matrix*. Character development is evident even in comedies, from *The Three Stooges* to *Seinfeld*.

Perhaps the most universal story is the hero story. In its dramatic versions, it involves great quests and dramatic victories. But there are more mundane versions of the hero story, and they deal just as much with internal conquests as external ones. These are stories from everyday life where we choose better paths.

Mastery of the complex, contemporary project is just as much the choice to overcome self-limiting perspectives as it is the solution of challenging project content and process issues.

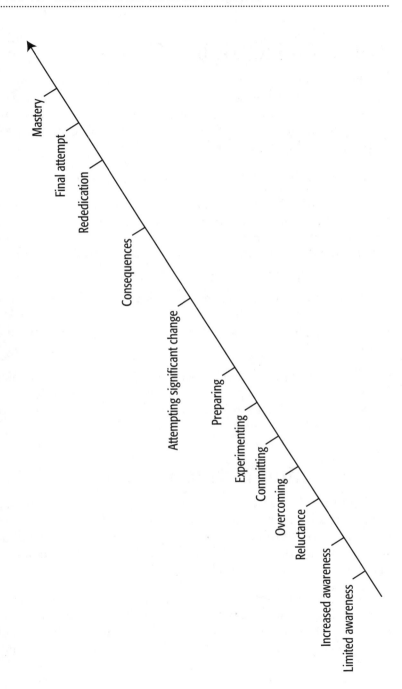

Figure 18-1. Character Arc: Journey to Overcome a Challenge, Problem, or Flaw

■ The Project Builds Character

If we choose to see the project as Frederick Taylor might have, then a project team consists of workers who efficiently follow a script and crank out what the script tells them to do. They may be motivated enough, but they are not emotionally invested in the project. At the end of the project, they are no different than at the start.

Here is an alternative way to view the project.

In a manner similar to the story, we can see that the journey through the project, especially the complex, contemporary project, encounters conflicts and paradoxes. This journey presents opportunities for decisions and for growth through the development of character and maturity.

What if we see a project as more than lines of code, the assembly of silicon chips, or the printing of a document? What if we see what is hidden in the project, the external and internal challenges to be overcome?

What if the project has a plot that describes a story of spiritual survival? This kind of project presents the opportunity for us to grow, to mature, and to develop. It engages the right brain in a powerful and profound way.

■ Becoming Better at Projects

Conventional wisdom holds that the way to get better at managing projects is to improve in project management skills—to become better at the skills of planning, estimating, making work breakdown structures, and the like. The recommendation is to become more mature, but in the context of domain skills.

We fully concur with the development of project management maturity, but do not want to stop there. What about the value of becoming more mature in the skills of life? Evidence shows a definitive link between our ability to manage projects successfully and our level of maturity in life—not in chronological age, but in our progression through the stages of personal and emotional maturity.

Mohandas Ghandi said, "As human beings, our greatness lies not so much in being able to remake the world ... as in being able to remake ourselves."

Improving at managing projects is as much about character development as it is about skill. While the character development needed encompasses many dimensions of personal and moral maturity, it is just as much a skill in adapting to the changing landscape of the project workplace.[5]

The complex project is the story; it may even be a heroic story. It is the story of taming the uncertain and ambiguous into something useful and predictable. It is the exploration of the Wild West, the landing on the moon, the discovery of penicillin.

It is unlikely that any of us will have the opportunity to slay a dragon. The technology has not yet been developed for someone to have a light saber fight with Darth Vader. Our characters and journeys involve more mundane issues like deliverables and difficult clients.

But the internal issues are universal. They involve themes such as the courage to overcome fear, the choice of right over wrong, and the decision to trust.

The complex project environment offers many opportunities for development and maturity. We just need to look for them.

■ It's Child's Play

All this talk about conflict, maturity, character development, and morality may sound a bit heavy, inaccessible, and not worth the trouble. On the contrary, and in keeping with the paradoxical nature of the topic, it is just as much the work of children as it is of adults.

We can cite dramatic examples of stories from *Romeo and Juliet* and *The Odyssey*, but we can just as easily use examples from many children's stories and movies. Themes of character development, moral choices, and spiritual survival in *Beauty and the Beast*, *The Lion King*, and *The Mighty Ducks* are just as relevant to the project manager.

The story and storytelling have meaning throughout life from childhood all the way through adulthood. They apply on the playground, in the home, and in the workplace.

In the movie, *School of Rock*, Jack Black plays Dewey Finn, a rock musician who suffers for his craft. Needing money, he sets his sights on winning the cash prize at a battle of the bands. But there is one problem: his band members fire him because he is so musically maniacal. To pay the rent, he masquerades as a substitute teacher at a stuffy private school and goes through the motions. That is, until he hears the 10-year-olds play in the classical music class. The crazy idea comes to him to turn these little Mozarts into a rock band and win the prize.

We could stop right there and highlight two relevant right-brain project management points. Initially, Dewey's interest in this job is to collect a paycheck, but he becomes consumed when he sees an outlet for his passion. We can also recognize this clever act of project bricolage: with no band to take him, Dewey turns to the only musicians around. But let us look to a third project management component, the hidden project.

Whatever the visible work, the hidden project goes straight to the human element. The hidden project may have a variety of human themes: the thrill of teamwork, a rewarding growth in confidence, the pride of a new skill, or the achievement of greatness. It is often nothing less than a hero story about overcoming a formidable challenge. The hidden project may be different for each of the actors on the project, but it often involves personal development, emotional connection with others, and the human touch.

Many contemporary projects test us and stretch our limits, and in the process they can cause considerable self-doubt. These hidden project doubts threaten the accomplishment of the visible project. The reserved and geeky keyboard player Lawrence approaches

Dewey with his self-doubts about being in the band: "I'm not cool enough. People in bands are cool. I'm not cool." Lawrence believes this because no one ever talks to him.

When the emotionally intelligent project manager hears these words, he or she drops everything and attends to this task that has suddenly appeared on the critical path: the task to find the way through the self-doubt. Dewey tells Lawrence that after he performs in the band he will be one of the most popular kids in school. We see Lawrence smile.

The hidden project is classically right-brain and serendipitous, so it is the sort of thing that can't be planned in any detail. But it is *always* there. We need only to look out for it, make sense of it, and be ready to nurture it.

Dewey and the band do not achieve the planned project; another group wins the battle of the bands. But they do accomplish the *right* project. Despite Dewey's initial disdain for kids and teaching, he grows into a wise, albeit unorthodox, mentor. The more dramatic hidden projects involve the kids and their parents. The formerly stifled, straight-laced kids become respectable rockers, and their passion and self-confidence soar through their new, cool talents. The parents learn to loosen their domineering control and, with pride, let the kids blossom.

THE PROJECT CHALLENGE

Colin Funk

On many projects we reach the "project challenge," a particular issue unique to the project that requires an uncomfortable stretch or full immersion into the project. Successful progress or completion of the project requires something more of me, or requires that I invest myself in the project in a personal way. It is really a "tipping point"—a shift from a purely cognitive response to one that is often more on the emotional and intuitive scale.

In managing projects when I reach such a point, I definitely get a sense of cognitive dissonance. The space is pure paradox: it is at the same time both frightening and soul-enriching. It is a place that typically requires creative thought to navigate through a relatively uncomfortable space. While it can be tempting to back away and find a more comfortable or familiar path, I know that I must proceed through.

How do we get through the project challenge? I get through by becoming present to the challenge and by actively looking and waiting for the tipping point.

I find it very helpful to draw upon my experience in the theatre. As actors, we spend a great deal of our time in training, working on enhancing our ability to quickly transform into various character types. This takes considerable skill and practice, and is very much a whole-brain process. This state of invoking the imagination to become something other than yourself can be accessed in part through various mental exercises that help focus us on becoming the role, or in this case, becoming present to a challenge. This process allows us to break through prior limitations and restrictions and enter a new state with new possibilities. We can then truly see the problem challenge through another person's eyes. It is a very creative place to be and one that is rich with promise for solving problems.

As an example, in one recent project, our organization committed to expand the areas used for our classes in leadership development. As one might expect for a leadership course, it is very important that the environment contribute to the learning experience. Being situated in Banff National Park, we have a truly special environment and it is an integral element of our path of leadership development.

My particular project challenge was to obtain approval from executive management for the project. An executive in any organization gets many requests for new proposals, so there is always competition for projects. I wanted to differentiate my request and demonstrate our special vision for the leaders in our program, but I was uncertain how to do this. I could send a standard memo with an outline of my proposal, but I wanted to do something more. My project challenge was to describe the vision and benefits in a way that would engage the executives personally in the project.

After struggling for a bit, I decided to become present to the challenge and the tipping point. I went to the proposed new space and tried to experience it as it would ultimately be, to see and touch what the participants and presenters would soon see and touch. Even more, I wanted to experience the emotions that they would soon experience in this place. This was a bit of daydreaming, but it worked—I became part of the finished product.

As I did this, I passed through the tipping point and my own enthusiasm for the project grew dramatically. I could now convey my experience in words and pictures so that the executives would understand and appreciate the final product and grow in their own excitement for it.

By using more of a right-brain approach—visual images, being present, and experiencing the emotions of future participants—I could communicate the rich information that the decision-makers needed. I encountered the project challenge, navigated the tipping point, and used my right brain to succeed on a project.

Colin Funk is the Creative Programming Director for Leadership Development at the Banff Centre, located in Banff, Alberta, Canada. The Banff Centre offers courses in leadership development for individuals from all types of organizations, including many project managers.

■ Common Thread: Repairing the Disconnect

Our journey to follow many of the threads of contemporary project management has led us back to Descartes and the rise of rational, reductionist thought. Our objective has been to retrace and examine the steps that got us here. Descartes was not the first to place value on rational thought, but he did elevate it to an unprecedented level. Descartes' philosophy also introduced a disconnect: prevailing thought recognized the integration of the rational mind with the whole person, while Descartes saw the rational mind as a separate and controlling mechanism of the person. It is this disconnect that is in need of repair for success with the contemporary project.

In Chapter 3, we introduced Antonio Damasio, the physician who has studied the role of emotion in decision-making. Dr. Damasio wrote a book with the compelling title, *Descartes' Error: Emotion, Reason and the Human Brain.* While we have much to thank Descartes for, we now understand that his "error" was an imbalance or a disconnect.

Take the famous Descartes quote, "I think, therefore I am." As Damasio points out, this quote sums up Descartes' rationalist, reductionist philosophy. It holds that we can disconnect the rest of human experience from the left brain.[6] We have come to discover that in project work, we cannot separate the left brain from the right brain. Adaptation kicks in where planning leaves off, emotion fuels the drive to achieve objectives, and character is just as necessary as the Gantt chart. We cannot separate project work from who we are and what we experience as human beings. Pulling on the thread that leads to Descartes makes it clear that we need to understand and apply Kant.

What is wrong with project management as it is commonly practiced is not that it takes a left-brain approach. Rather, it is that project management relies on the left brain to the exclusion of the right brain. This is the disconnect.

What is needed on contemporary projects is an integration of left- and right-brain principles. Because the practice of contemporary project management relies so heavily on left-brain skills, we have focused on developing right-brain skills, but always with the understanding that an appropriate balance is optimal.

This concept in project management is similar to that of cross training in sports. Many athletes who train intensely for one sport or one activity have found that such training leaves them at a disadvantage and vulnerable to injury. A football player who only builds muscle bulk can often be easily knocked over because he has weak core muscles and poor balance. In recent years, emphasis has shifted to conditioning athletes in a variety of ways to ensure balance, flexibility, and resilience. When you see football players practicing yoga, you know that sports has already seen the disconnect in its domain and is taking steps to readjust.

To improve the management of contemporary projects, we must repair this disconnect between left- and right-brain styles, recognizing that in addition to a brain that can analyze and plan projects, we also have a brain that can create, feel, make sense, visualize, motivate, improvise, and communicate in alternative ways.

It is a paradox that we have separate right and left brains but they still form an integrated whole. We must embrace the paradox.

■ Embracing the Paradox

When we encounter paradox, we often experience conflict, both internal and external. The ability to tolerate and embrace paradox is one of the skills that is so important to personal maturity as well as to maturity as a project manager.

Paradox is persistent on the contemporary project. It is present in the interplay between the external, visible project and the hidden, internal project. It is there when we say that complex projects need both structure and improvisation. The most critical paradox we need to embrace is that the contemporary, complex project needs to be approached with both the right brain and the left brain.

To really engage and apply the right brain on a project, think of it this way: a project is as much about who we become as it is about what we do. Embracing this paradox is what moves us through the changes needed to master the complex project.

■ The Project Is the Story

Taylor would see project work as the activity of cogs working through a machine. Taylor has fallen out of favor because his treatment and his attitude toward humans was ... well, inhuman.

We now know that project work is an act of creation accomplished by thinking, feeling, creative, motivated, intuitive, emotional beings. It is:

- Discovering fire
- Solving a mystery
- Experimenting in the lab
- Painting without numbers
- Doing business with a handshake
- Performing in the jazz ensemble
- Leaving a legacy.

Through it all, we face challenges, and with them opportunities to stretch beyond boundaries and work with others to accomplish something special. Perhaps this is what most makes a project a right-brain endeavor. When we choose to break through our limits, we must summon emotional energy and we must create new patterns of thinking. On the contemporary project, we ourselves change as much as (or even more than) what we create through the project. It is no less than leadership of our selves. "Ultimately, the driving force of new leadership is the process of *destroying one's own mindset to build a completely new picture.*"[7]

The German philosopher Hegel said that contradiction is the power that moves things. When we encounter paradox on projects, when we enter the conflict and become part of the process of character development into maturity, we find the power to move the things that make projects what they are.

It all makes for a good story.

In the typical style of the paradox, we have reached the end of our journey together, but it is early in your journey of right-brain project management.

What we call the beginning is often the end.
And to make an end is to make a beginning.
The end is where we start from.
　　　　　　　　　—*T. S. Eliot, Four Quadrants, 1943*

Picture yourself as a jazz musician on stage during a performance. The ensemble has set up the structure of the song. It is now time for your solo; it is your turn to improvise.

The spotlight turns to you. Have at it! ▪

ENDNOTES

1 Lawrence Kohlberg, *Essays on Moral Development, Vol. 1: The Philosophy of Moral Development* (San Francisco: Harper & Row, 1981), pp. 17–19.

2 E. Jones, *Sigmund Freud, Life and Work* (London: Hogarth Press, 1955).

3 Lajos Egri, *The Art of Dramatic Writing* (Boston: The Writer, Inc., 1960), pp. 60–61.

4 Christopher Vogler, *The Writer's Journey,* Second Edition (Studio City, CA: Michael Wiese Productions, 1998), pp. 212–213.

5 Jason Hughes, "Bringing Emotion to Work: Emotional Intelligence, Employee Resistance and the Reinvention of Character," *Work, Employment and Society,* Vol. 19, No. 3, 2005, p. 620.

6 Antonio Damasio, *Descartes' Error* (New York: Putnam, 1994), pp. 248–252.

7 Bastiaan Heemsbergen, *The Leader's Brain* (Victoria, BC, Canada: Trafford Publishing, 2004), p. 64.

■ Index